GLAMOUR'S®
GOURMET ON THE RUN

GLAMOUR'S
GOURMET ON THE RUN

A Busy Woman's Guide to
30-Minute Meals
and Effortless Entertaining

By Jane Kirby
GLAMOUR Food Editor

Condé Nast Books
Villard Books
New York

ISBN 0-394-56417-0

Most of the recipes in this work were previously published in
Glamour *magazine.*

Manufactured in the United Stated of America
98765432   24689753   23456789

First Edition

*Grateful acknowledgment is made to the following
photographers for use of their photographs: Edgar DeEvia: front
jacket, back jacket: upper left photo, right photo, pages 10–92,
98, 99, 102, 103, 118, 119, 130, 131, 149, 154, 165, 168,
185, 186, 192, 195; David Frazier: pages 134, 135; Joshua
Greene: pages 110, 111, 112, 145; Bradley Olman: pages 122,
123, 126, 127, 201; Michael Skott: page 2; Bruce Wolf: back
jacket: lower left photo, pages 94, 95, 96, 97, 106, 107, 114,
115, 117*

Frontispiece:
Glacéed Oranges with Sugar Straw, page 142
Strawberry Nut Tart, page 202;
Chocolate Heart Cookies, page 206;
Blueberry-Peach Compote with Raspberry Sauce, page 142

PROJECT STAFF
FOR CONDÉ NAST BOOKS
Jill Cohen, Director
Phyllis Starr Wilson, Editorial Director
Ellen Maria Bruzelius, Project Manager
Kristine Smith, Project Assistant
Judith Tropea, Editorial Assistant
Diane Pesce, Composition Production Manager
Biagio Lubrano, Quality Control Manager

FOR GLAMOUR MAGAZINE
Ruth Whitney, Editor-in-Chief
Jane Kirby, Project Editor
Pamela Deyo, Assistant Project Editor
Michelle Braverman, Designer
George Hartman, Design Consultant

Produced in association with
MEDIA PROJECTS INCORPORATED

Carter Smith, President
Judy Knipe, Senior Editor
Charlotte McGuinn Freeman, Assistant Editor
Bernard Schleifer, Michael Shroyer, Design Consultants

*The author would like to thank the following people for
valuable services rendered for* Glamour's Gourmet on the Run:
Susan Costa Cohn, Pam Deyo and Elizabeth Kirby

The text of this book was set in Trade Gothic Light and
Antique Olive Bold by the Composition Department
of Condé Nast Publications, Inc. The four-color
separations were done by The Kordet Group and The Color
Company. The book was printed and bound by
R. R. Donnelley & Sons. Text paper is 80 pound Consoweb
Brilliant Gloss. Manufacturing supervision by the
Production Department of Random House, Inc.

Contents

Entertaining
Page 92

When you're in the mood for…
Page 134

Introduction

Hurried cooks with sophisticated palates have been clamoring for this cookbook for years, because the need it fills is as real as every woman's wish to put together a delicious, elegant meal in a minimum of time. Even today, with the majority of women working outside the home (as well as in it) it's not easy to find menus and recipes that acknowledge a busy life, yet sacrifice not a soupçon of style or taste.

That is the achievement of this cookbook: unfussy stylish meals planned for the woman whose time is limited, but whose enthusiasm for dining well is not—whether she expects to eat alone, with a partner or with a group of friends.

The Gourmet On The Run section has been compiled from one of *Glamour*'s most popular monthly features. This book includes 60 Gourmet On The Run menus—each one planned to be ready for the table in thirty minutes or less. They range from romantic brunches to sophisticated pasta suppers to splendid exotic dinners. And they are easily achievable even for the woman (or man, for that matter) who worked late on the job. There are timing suggestions to help you keep preparations to a minimum, and clear how-to photographs to make complicated steps swift and simple.

The entertaining section comes next, and whether you entertain a lot or a little, you want to do it well. There are wonderful suggestions here for late-night suppers and scrumptious brunches, for cocktail dinner buffets, open houses and tempting dessert parties, all neatly divided into warm-weather celebrations and cool-weather celebrations.

And the entertaining comes easy. For each of these parties is organized and designed to keep the jitters down and the celebration up. The time-saving strategies provide a relaxed, foolproof plan of action. From drinks to desserts, you'll find uniquely special ideas to entertain friends.

On a more personal level, there are times when we all crave a special taste—the comfort of a savory soup on a raw day, for example, or the cool refreshment of a crunchy salad in midsummer, or a sinfully rich chocolatey dessert—anytime! They are all here, too, recipes designed to satisfy those special food cravings when nothing else will really do it but exactly what you're in the mood for.

Finally, perhaps the most useful tool in this book is the series of charts, charts which organize and clarify the options and combinations that produce unique salads and vegetable dishes, charts that give step by step directions to the newest, freshest ways to marinate and barbecue, charts that guide a beginner to the triumph of a quick loaf of bread fresh from the oven or a more seasoned cook through a wealth of variations on the basic chicken breast.

At its best, this cookbook should be a learning experience, as the reader finally makes its GLAMOURous and confident approach to food her own.

Ruth Whitney
Editor-in-Chief

Great ingredients, easy recipes and just minutes to a memorable meal

Gourmet on the run: 30-minute meals

Armed with these sophisticated menus that are table-ready in thirty minutes or less, you can handle almost any time crunch. Without resorting to loads of prepared or packaged foods, you can complete these menus—practically soup to nuts—in record time. They are the very best from *Glamour*'s monthly Gourmet on the Run section—tried, tested and true. If you keep staples stocked, you can easily invite a guest or two at the last minute with perhaps just a quick trip to the market. Or when you arrive home late for the little dinner party you've planned, you don't have to be frazzled! Turn to Gourmet on the Run, and you'll glide through the meal, knowing just what to do when, following the timing suggestions for peeling, chopping, sautéing, and garnishing. On-page photographs illustrate unusual ingredients and easy preparation tricks. Once you get the hang of Gourmet on the Run, you'll realize that even when eating alone there's no need to chow down half a can of tuna and a couple of carrot sticks. You'll learn to jazz up run-of-the-mill breakfasts, lunches and dinners, giving them little out-of-the-ordinary touches so that you can serve anything from beans to pasta to seafood with style—and do it fast, fast, fast.

weekend eye-opener

BLUEBERRY SCONES

SOFT-COOKED EGGS

WAKE-UP JUICE

Before you head out for the day, treat yourself and a friend to this easy, high-energy breakfast. You can have it on the table in just 20 minutes. Use fresh or frozen blueberries in this English favorite—scones. They're a slightly sweet first cousin to the muffin, but there's less fuss because there are no muffin pans to grease or wash. Soft-cooked eggs are a snap. In a saucepan, cover the eggs with cold water and slowly bring to a full boil. Cover pan tightly, remove from heat and let stand several minutes, depending on how well-done you like your eggs (1 minute for soft; 15 minutes for hard-cooked). Perch the eggs in their cups and lather butter onto the scones, hot from the oven, or serve them with their traditional accompaniment—jam and cream whipped just to the point of stiffness. To sip along with the meal, a chilled glassful of spritzy Wake-Up Juice. Freeze the scones you don't eat, then heat them.

BLUEBERRY SCONES

3 c. buttermilk baking mix
1 c. fresh or frozen blueberries
2 T. sugar
¼ c. milk
2 eggs, beaten
FOR GLAZE:
1 egg, well beaten
2 T. sugar

Heat oven to 400°F. In medium bowl combine the baking mix, blueberries and 2 tablespoons sugar. Pour milk into measuring cup. Add the eggs to the milk and beat with a fork until well mixed. Stir liquid into baking mix until moistened. (Dough will be crumbly.) Turn the dough onto a lightly floured work surface and pat into a 9-inch round, about ½-inch thick. Brush the dough with the beaten egg, then sprinkle with 2 tablespoons sugar. Cut the round into twelve wedges. Place on ungreased cookie sheet and bake for 10 to 12 minutes until golden. Serve scones immediately with butter or jam and cream. Makes 12 scones.

WAKE-UP JUICE

½ c. orange juice
¼ c. apricot juice or nectar
Sparkling water

In a tall glass, combine orange and apricot juices. Before serving, add a splash of sparkling water. Makes 1 serving.

HOW TO MAKE PERFECT SCONES:

Handle the dough minimally and quickly. Overmixing and overshaping can toughen it. If the dough seems a bit sticky when cutting, dip the knife in flour, then cut.

romantic brunch

GINGERED FRUIT SALAD

MINI BAGELS

CREAM CHEESE

SMOKED SALMON

HORSERADISH SAUCE

ENDIVE ONION PINWHEELS

CHAMPAGNE

This simple, splendid brunch is perfect for a special occasion for just the two of you. Make the Endive Pinwheels first, (see photos). Then, whisk equal amounts of unsweetened whipped cream and prepared horseradish to pair with wonderful smoked salmon. Toss together a tasty combination of fruit. Try some kiwi fruit, grapes, green apples and pink grapefruit sparked with ginger-lime dressing. Arrange everything on a pretty tray—don't forget the champagne—and crawl back into bed.

GINGERED FRUIT SALAD

1 small Granny Smith apple
1 kiwi fruit, peeled and sliced
1 c. seedless grapes, halved
½ pink grapefruit, cut into sections
¼ c. honey
1 T. minced preserved ginger
1 T. syrup from preserved ginger
1 T. fresh lime juice

Quarter and seed apple; cut into bite-size chunks. Combine apple with kiwi fruit, grapes and grapefruit. In small bowl, combine honey with remaining ingredients. Pour over fruit and toss. Makes 2 servings.

ENDIVE ONION PINWHEELS

1 Belgian endive
½ 4-oz. package onion-flavored cheese spread

Carefully remove about eight outer endive leaves, placing them in a row in front of you in the order in which they are removed. You will have the heart of the endive left; set aside. Starting with the last leaf removed, carefully spread a thin layer of cheese on the inside of the leaf and press the leaf back onto the heart of the endive; the cheese will hold it in place. Repeat with remaining leaves until the endive is reassembled. With sharp knife, cut each endive into ½-inch slices. Makes about 8 pinwheels.

PINWHEELS: HOW TO

Endive is a pricey vegetable, so serve it when you need a little splurge. Its slightly bitter flavor pairs well with the creamy, pungent cheese filling. To make ahead, assemble, but do not cut into slices until ready to serve.

leisurely breakfast

TOMATO JUICE

BOURBON FRENCH TOAST

BACON

FRESH FRUIT WITH POMEGRANATE TOPPING

COFFEE

When Sunday morning finally rolls around, take advantage of every glorious minute of it with this great breakfast for two. It's the kind of meal to savour with a thick copy of the Sunday paper. Start with glasses of icy cold tomato juice. Next, try thick luscious slices of French toast spiked with bourbon. Serve it with regular or Canadian bacon—it only takes a few minutes to sauté. (The microwave makes cooking bacon a breeze.) To end the meal, enjoy bowlfuls of juicy and succulent fresh fruit. Make it with the market's freshest selections. These are topped with pomegranate seeds. The jewel-like fruit is a real exotic treat and adds not only brilliant color but an interesting crunch too (see photos). Then, get cozy and enjoy more coffee, more of the paper and more of Sunday.

BOURBON FRENCH TOAST

TOAST:
3 eggs
½ c. milk
1 T. bourbon
Grated rind from 1 orange
⅛ tsp. ground cinnamon
Dash grated nutmeg
4 slices (1-inch) thick, challah
** or French bread**
Butter or margarine
SYRUP:
⅓ c. maple syrup
1 T. bourbon
1 T. butter or margarine

In shallow bowl or pie plate with wire whisk, combine eggs, milk, bourbon, orange rind, cinnamon and nutmeg. Beat until well mixed. Dip bread slices into eggs mixture, turning to coat both sides. In large skillet or griddle over medium heat, melt enough butter to coat the surface lightly. Add bread and cook until well golden on both sides, adding more butter or margarine as needed. In small saucepan over medium-low heat, combine syrup, bourbon and butter. Heat until butter is melted. Serve syrup over toast with bacon. Makes 2 servings.

FRESH FRUIT CUP

1 medium apple, cored and
** cut into chunks**
1 medium pear, cored and
** cut into chunks**
½ c. red seedless grapes
3 to 4 T. honey
1 T. fresh lemon
** or lime juice**
¼ c. pomegranate seeds

In a medium bowl, combine all ingredients except pomegranate seeds. Toss until well coated. Just before serving, sprinkle some pomegranate seeds over each serving. Makes 2 servings.

GET THE MOST FROM A POMEGRANATE

Start from the stem end of the fruit and, using a small knife, score the skin into quarters. Then, simply pull the sections apart to expose the succulent seeds. Pluck them out leaving the bitter white membrane behind. The entire seed is edible.

soul-satisfying meal

EGGS BENEDICT

SAUTÉED ARTICHOKE HEARTS, ASPARAGUS SPEARS AND CHERRY TOMATOES

BLOODY MARINERS

Eggs Benedict—that ultimate brunch—also makes a great fast supper. Delicious Canadian bacon topped with poached eggs and smothered in hollandaise. Not everyday fare—it's high in calories—but it's perfect for a super-special Sunday brunch or supper. To make the complete brunch: Start with Bloody Mariners. Use your favorite Bloody Mary recipe but substitute tomato-clam juice for tomato. Next, poach the eggs. Reheat them just before serving. (See how-tos and photos). A nice accompaniment is artichoke hearts and asparagus spears. Use frozen, but cook only half the time the label recommends, then quickly sauté in about 1 tablespoon of hot oil. Toss in a half pint of halved fresh cherry tomatoes and sprinkle with a good pinch of dried thyme. Meanwhile, heat the English muffins. Canadian bacon just needs a quick toss in a pan to heat through. Reheat the eggs; keep everything warm in the oven. Finally, make the hollandaise. It's best to make it at the last minute—you can't keep it warm over heat; it will curdle.

EGGS BENEDICT

4 English muffins, split
8 slices Canadian bacon
8 poached eggs
Hollandaise Sauce (recipe follows)

Toast English muffins. In a small skillet cook bacon until heated through. Place two muffin halves on a plate; top each with a slice of bacon, then a poached egg. Spoon about ⅓ cup of Hollandaise Sauce over each two-egg serving. Makes 4 servings.

HOLLANDAISE SAUCE

6 egg yolks
¼ c. fresh lemon juice
1 c. butter or margarine, softened
¼ tsp. salt

In double-boiler top over hot, *not* boiling, water, combine egg yolks and lemon juice. With wire whisk, beat in 3 tablespoons butter until completely melted. Beat in remaining butter, 2 tablespoons at a time, stirring constantly with whisk until smooth and thick. Blend in salt. Makes 1⅓ cups or enough for four two-egg servings.

HOW TO POACH AN EGG WITHOUT A POACHER

Two facts to remember when poaching eggs: Be sure they're fresh—it's almost impossible to keep the whites together in the water if they aren't. Keep the water simmering. If it boils, the whites will scatter. If the heat is too low, they won't cook fast enough. If you're not a pro yet, do one or two at a time. (1) Heat 4 inches of water to boiling in a saucepan. Add 2 T. vinegar; (2) Reduce heat to low to maintain a gentle simmer; (3) Break one egg into a cup. Carefully pour into water; (4) Use a slotted spoon to coax the white gently around the yolk. Cook for about 3½ minutes; (5) Remove egg with slotted spoon; while still on the spoon, drain on paper towel. If you're serving a crowd, drop eggs as they're done into a bowl of cold water. When ready to serve, drop each into simmering water for a minute to reheat.

warm-weather supper

ZUCCHINI FRITTATA

DILLED TOMATO SALAD

WHOLE-WHEAT PITA BREAD

NECTARINE-BLUEBERRY COMPOTE

WHITE WINE SPRITZERS

To get you out of the kitchen in record time, here's a quick and easy version of an Italian omelet, known as a frittata. It's good hot or at room temperature, and you can pack it up as picnic fare, or serve it hot for a super-fast Saturday lunch. Either way, you'll have finished cooking in 30 minutes or less. Start by making the salad—cut the tomatoes into wedges and marinate in dilled lemon dressing. Next, drop the nectarines into boiling water for a few seconds to make them easier to peel. Cut fruit into slices and toss with blueberries and honey for a gently-sweet dessert. Finally, move on to the cheese-laced frittata, chock-full of zucchini and parsley, for a fresh, healthy flavor. Put out whole-wheat pita bread to serve with the meal. And, for cool sipping, make wine spritzers. For one drink, combine 3 oz. of white wine with ice cubes and a wedge of lime; add enough club soda to fill a glass.

ZUCCHINI FRITTATA

8 eggs
½ tsp. salt
Freshly ground black pepper
¼ c. grated Parmesan cheese
2 medium zucchini, thinly sliced
2 T. chopped parsley
2 T. chopped fresh basil
or 1 tsp. dried
1 T. olive or vegetable oil

In medium bowl with wire whisk, beat eggs with salt and pepper. Stir in cheese, zucchini, parsley and basil. Heat broiler. In 10-inch skillet over medium-high heat, heat oil. Reduce heat to low, add eggs and cook undisturbed over low heat about 10 minutes. Carefully lift edge to check the bottom—it should be golden brown. Place skillet under broiler for 30 seconds until top is golden. (If your skillet handle is not broiler-safe, wrap with foil before broiling.) Serve hot or at room temperature. Makes 4 servings.

DILLED TOMATO SALAD

3 T. olive oil
2 T. fresh lemon juice
1 garlic clove, minced
½ tsp. salt
4 scallions, cut into 2-inch slivers
2 T. chopped fresh dill
or 1 tsp. dried
3 tomatoes, cut into wedges

In small bowl combine oil, lemon juice, garlic and salt. Toss in scallions, dill and tomatoes. Makes 4 servings.

NECTARINE-BLUEBERRY COMPOTE

4 nectarines
½ pint blueberries
3 T. honey

Peel nectarines. Cut in half, remove pits, cut into wedges. In large bowl toss with blueberries and honey. Makes 4 servings.

QUICK WAY TO PEEL NECTARINES

Drop nectarines into boiling water for 10 seconds. Remove nectarines with slotted spoon. When cool enough to handle, use a small knife, remove skins— they should slip off easily.

meal for drop-in guests

PICTURE-PERFECT OMELETS

TOMATO-SCALLION VINAIGRETTE

SHOESTRING POTATOES

BISCUITS

FRESH FRUIT AND WALNUTS

SPARKLING WATER

Here's a simple, very savory supper—just for you and maybe a friend who's dropped by—a perfect meal after a long, hectic day. If you have eggs in the house, you can put together this meal anytime—no last-minute runs to the market. The plan: Bake frozen shoestring French fries according to label directions. Next, make biscuits from the recipe on the buttermilk baking-mix package. Then, prepare the Tomato Salad. Now, for the omelet. It takes just a few minutes from beginning to end, so have your filling ingredients ready. (See suggestions.) For dessert, put out fruit and a bowl of walnuts along with a nutcracker.

PICTURE-PERFECT OMELETS

2 eggs
2 T. water
Dash of salt

Beat together eggs, water and salt. Over medium-high heat, heat an 8-inch nonstick skillet with sloping sides. You'll know it's hot enough when a few drops of water dance across the surface. Pour in eggs. Tilting pan slightly, slip a spatula under the eggs, lifting cooked portion to let uncooked eggs flow underneath. When eggs are just set, but still creamy, place fillings across the center. Loosen the omelet from the pan and fold about ⅓ over filling. Grasping the handle in one hand, rest lip of the pan on a dinner plate. Tip the pan and plate toward each other. Quickly turn the pan upside down and the omelet will fall onto the plate.

TOMATO-SCALLION VINAIGRETTE

1 large ripe tomato
1 scallion
2 T. olive oil
Splash red wine vinegar
Freshly ground black pepper
Lettuce leaves

Cut tomato into wedges. With a sharp knife, diagonally slice scallion (white part only). Sprinkle with olive oil, vinegar and lots of pepper. Serve on lettuce leaves.

SOME FAVORITE FILLINGS

● *Grated Gruyère and crisp bacon*
● *Diced Brie and strips of baked ham*
● *Steamed spinach and mushroom slices*
● *Artichoke hearts, cut into strips, and chopped tomatoes*
● *Red caviar and sour cream*
● *Cubes of avocado and shrimp*
● *Cream cheese and watercress*
● *Chopped tomato, sliced mushrooms and scallions, and grated Cheddar cheese*

Moroccan dinner

SPICY VEGETABLE COUSCOUS

WHOLE-WHEAT PITA BREAD

TANGERINES

ALMOND COOKIES

MOROCCAN MINT TEA

elegant brunch

CORNMEAL PANCAKES WITH CHÈVRE AND RED PEPPER SAUCE

FRUIT COMPOTE

SPARKLING WINE

Have a few friends over for an informal brunch—this eye-catching menu won't keep you in the kitchen for long, and the results are spectacularly delicious. A tangy Red Pepper Sauce is the perfect foil for delicate Cornmeal Pancakes that are flecked with fresh coriander and served with warmed goat cheese. Make the pancake batter. While it stands, begin the Red Pepper Sauce. While the pancakes are warming with the *chèvre*, prepare the dessert. Combine sliced peaches and some of your favorite berries. Serve the meal with a Blanc de Noir sparkling wine—it complements the flavors and colors of the food perfectly.

CORNMEAL PANCAKES WITH CHÈVRE AND RED PEPPER SAUCE

1 c. yellow cornmeal
½ tsp. baking soda
¼ tsp. salt
1 egg, lightly beaten
1 ¼ c. buttermilk
¼ c. chopped fresh coriander
**   (cilantro) or parsley**
1 T. vegetable oil
8 ½-inch slices goat cheese
1 8-oz. can corn, drained
Red Pepper Sauce (recipe follows)

In large bowl mix cornmeal, baking soda and salt. Add egg, buttermilk, coriander and oil; stir just until moistened. Let batter stand 5 minutes. Over high heat, heat a large, greased skillet until very hot. Spoon batter onto the hot pan, making 2-to 2½-inch pancakes. Cook 3 minutes; turn and cook another 2 minutes. Keep warm in a 200°F oven. When all the pancakes are made, arrange three pancakes in the center of each plate. Overlap two slices of *chèvre* (goat cheese) on the pancakes. Scatter corn over each serv-ing. Return the plates to the oven and heat for 5 minutes or until the cheese is warmed through. Spoon some Red Pepper Sauce around the pancakes. Garnish each serving with some of the reserved red pepper. Makes 4 servings.

RED PEPPER SAUCE

2 roasted red peppers,
**   fresh or jarred**
1 c. crème fraîche
**   or ¾ c. heavy cream**

Finely mince one and a half peppers. Place them in a small saucepan and cook over low heat for 5 minutes until heated through. Stir in the crème fraîche and simmer over low heat for 10 minutes. Cut the remaining half pepper into matchstick-thin pieces; set aside for garnish.

ABOUT CHÈVRE
(goat cheese)

(1) Pyramide—This cheese is piquant when fresh, strongly flavored when older.
(2) Montrachet—These logs may be plain or coated with ash. New to goat cheese? Try this one.
(3) Crottin de Chavignol— Small rounds that are tangy and soft when fresh, sharper and firmer as they age, but still savory.

California salad supper

SHERRIED CONSOMMÉ

LAMB AND MIXED GREEN SALAD WITH WARM JALAPEÑO VINAIGRETTE

CORN MADELEINES

STRAWBERRIES ROMANOFF

CHARDONNAY

Enjoy this exquisite salad for a light supper or lunch. Start the meal with a light soup like sherried consommé. The salad of mixed greens and lamb is a breeze to prepare whether you grill a lamb steak or use leftover roast lamb. The sweet-sour pungency of the warm Jalapeño Vinaigrette is a zesty counterpoint to the lamb and mint. Serve the salad with Corn Madeleines—the classiest use for cornbread mix. Just smooth cornbread batter into greased madeleine (or miniature cupcake) tins and bake for 8 to 10 minutes. For dessert, serve Strawberries Romanoff.

SHERRIED CONSOMMÉ

1 10¾-ounce can beef consommé
2 T. dry sherry
¼ c. sour cream
Fresh chives

In a small saucepan over high heat, heat consommé and sherry to boiling. Pour into four bowls. Top each with a tablespoon sour cream and a snip of chives. Makes 4 servings.

LAMB AND MIXED GREEN SALAD WITH WARM JALAPEÑO VINAIGRETTE

1 ¼ lb. lamb steak
    or 1 lb. leftover roast lamb
2 c. Boston lettuce
1 ½ c. arugula
1 ½ c. radicchio
1 ½ c. watercress
1 c. fresh mint leaves
DRESSING:
3 T. olive or vegetable oil
¼ c. finely chopped onion
½ jalapeño pepper,
    seeded and chopped
3 T. rice-wine vinegar
1 T. honey
Pinch salt

If using lamb steak, heat broiler. Broil lamb about 4 minutes on each side, until pink and juicy. Set aside. Divide all the greens evenly among 4 large plates. Slice the lamb into thin slices. Arrange lamb on lettuce on plates. Make the dressing: In a small saucepan over medium heat, heat the oil. Add the onion and jalapeño and cook until onion is wilted, about 5 minutes. Remove from heat and stir in the vinegar, honey and salt. Pour dressing over salads and serve immediately. Makes 4 servings.

STRAWBERRIES ROMANOFF

1 pint strawberries, halved
3 T. orange liqueur
2 T. sugar
½ c. heavy cream, whipped
1 c. vanilla ice cream, softened

In a small bowl combine strawberries, liqueur and sugar; set aside. In another bowl combine whipped cream and ice cream. Serve cream over sweetened berries. Makes 4 servings.

HOW TO MAKE
CORN MADELEINES

Spoon about 1 tablespoon
of batter into greased tin;
level off with spatula.

last-minute meal

SPICED CHICKEN SALAD WITH ORANGE AND AVOCADO

HOT BISCUITS

HONEY BUTTER

GRAPE-YOGURT SUNDAE

ICED TEA

If you think it's easier to skip out to a restaurant than to plan, shop and cook ahead, here's an easy, almost no-plan-ahead solution: a light, delicious, cold chicken salad. You have to cook the chicken the night before, but if that's still too much planning for you, you can pick up a cooked chicken at the market or deli on your way home. Cut the meat into nice big pieces so you feel like you're really eating something. Hold the mayo and toss it with dressing: This one's light, fresh and spicy. Spoon the salad onto glass plates, and refrigerate until you're ready to eat. Cut the orange and avocado, and arrange alongside just before serving. When you're ready to eat, bake some refrigerated biscuits according to label directions. They take about 20 minutes. And make Honey Butter to spread on the hot biscuits. Team grapes with yogurt and brown sugar for a cool dessert. And, of course, a large glass of iced tea.

SPICED CHICKEN SALAD WITH ORANGE AND AVOCADO

2 whole chicken breasts, cooked (about 3 c. meat)
½ medium red onion, thinly sliced
½ medium green pepper, thinly sliced
2 T. olive or vegetable oil
2 T. tarragon or cider vinegar
½ tsp. salt
¼ tsp. crushed red pepper flakes
1 orange
1 medium avocado

Remove and discard skin and bones from chicken. Cut into 2-inch pieces. Combine with remaining ingredients except avocado and orange. Just before serving, peel orange; cut away all white membrane. Cut out orange sections (see photo). Peel avocado and slice lengthwise. Divide salad among four plates, and arrange a few avocado slices and orange wedges alternately on each plate. Makes 4 servings.

HONEY BUTTER

½ c. butter or margarine, softened
¼ c. honey

In small bowl with a fork, or in food processor with knife blade attached, blend butter with honey until combined. Makes ¾ cup.

GRAPE-YOGURT SUNDAE

1 lb. green seedless grapes
1 8-oz. container plain yogurt
¼ c. dark brown sugar
2 T. brandy

Rinse grapes; drain. Divide grapes among four dessert dishes or wine goblets. Spoon the yogurt and the brown sugar over each. Chill. (Sugar will melt.) Just before serving, pour brandy over each portion. Makes 4 servings.

SECTION AN ORANGE

With small sharp knife cut away peel and white membrane from oranges. Then, cut out sections leaving dividing membrane behind.

fresh seafood salad

TOMATO-ORANGE SOUP

FRESH TUNA SALAD

PESTO TOASTS

PEACHES AMARETTO

Serve this salad and the words "tuna salad" will never mean the same thing again. Fresh tuna steak is used here; swordfish, cod or any other firm-fleshed fish will work well, too (or, substitute two cans of water-packed tuna). Instead of the usual mayonnaise blend a hearty balsamic vinegar and olive oil for the dressing. Balsamic vinegar is pungent, aged red vinegar. Look for it in the gourmet food section of your market. For the first course, make cream of tomato soup, but substitute unexpected orange juice for half the water or milk. Then, make the salad and get the Pesto Toasts ready for the broiler. For dessert, serve slices of peaches, topped with crumbled amaretto cookies and a splash of amaretto liqueur. Ah, what a fabulous way to enjoy an afternoon.

FRESH TUNA SALAD

**1 lb. fresh tuna or swordfish,
   cooked and chilled**
1 head Boston lettuce, cleaned
1 bunch arugula
½ c. alfalfa sprouts
½ c. crumbled blue cheese
1 7-oz. can corn, drained
3 T. balsamic or red wine vinegar
1 T. olive oil
1 tsp. Dijon mustard
¼ tsp. salt
⅛ tsp. freshly ground black pepper

Cut fish into 1-inch cubes. Wash, dry and tear lettuce and arugula into bite-sized pieces. Add to fish in large bowl. Add sprouts, cheese and corn. In a jar with tight-fitting lid, combine vinegar, oil, mustard, salt and pepper; shake to mix well. Pour over salad. Toss and serve immediately. Makes 4 servings.

PESTO TOASTS

1 loaf whole-wheat Italian bread
**½ c. fresh basil leaves, finely
   chopped**
¼ c. butter, softened

With serrated knife, slice bread lengthwise in half. In small bowl, combine basil with butter. Spread evenly over bread. Heat broiler. Broil 3 to 5 minutes. Makes 4 servings.

*WAYS TO MAKE
A GREAT SALAD*

● *For extra crispness, toss salad with dressing and place in freezer for 3 minutes before serving.*
● *Thoroughly dry all salad ingredients.*
● *Tear, don't cut, lettuce leaves.*
● *A must: freshly ground black pepper.*

supper from the grill

GRILLED MEDITERRANEAN BURGERS

TOMATO-CUCUMBER SALAD WITH FRESH MINT

ICED GRAPES

CHILLED BEAUJOLAIS

S it down with glasses of slightly chilled Beaujolais while you light the grill for this barbecue dinner—you'll have about 20 minutes until the coals are just the right temperature for the burgers. Making the lamb patties takes only a few minutes. Why not make a group activity out of it...invite them to stuff their own burgers (see photos) while you chunk up tomatoes and cucumbers for the salad. Toss together all the salad ingredients and let stand at room temperature. This salad is definitely better if it isn't too cold when served. Now, grill the lamb and rolls. For a simply beautiful dessert, place a few bunches of grapes in a glass bowl, and add a tray or two of ice cubes, then fill the bowl with cool water. Include a selection of green and red seedless varieties. Make the bowl of frosty grapes your centerpiece—someone might just nibble one or two during dinner.

GRILLED MEDITERRANEAN BURGERS

1 lb. ground lamb
4 oz. soft goat cheese,
    cut in 4 slices
2 tsp. chopped fresh parsley
1 tsp. dried thyme leaves
4 sandwich rolls, split
Lettuce leaves

Light coals for barbecue or heat broiler. Divide the lamb into 8 portions. Shape each into a thin patty about 3½ inches in diameter. Sandwich goat cheese and herbs between 2 patties. Grill or broil for 2 minutes on each side. Grill rolls for about 30 seconds or until golden. Serve burgers on rolls with lettuce. Makes 4 servings.

TOMATO-CUCUMBER SALAD WITH FRESH MINT

1 cucumber, peeled, seeded,
    quartered lengthwise
3 tomatoes
¼ c. sliced scallions
2 T. chopped fresh mint
    or 1½ tsp. dried
2 T. olive oil
Freshly ground black pepper

With a sharp knife, cut cucumbers and tomatoes into ¾-inch chunks. Toss together in a large bowl. Add scallions, fresh or dried mint and olive oil; toss to combine. Season to taste with freshly ground black pepper. Serve at room temperature. Makes 4 servings.

STUFFING A BURGER

● *Place goat cheese on patty. Flatten to cover patty, leaving a ½-inch margin all around.*
● *Sprinkle with parsley and thyme.*
● *Top with another patty. Press together so that cheese is completely enclosed.*

French grilled brunch

BLOODY MARIAS

GRILLED HAM AND BRIE ON RYE

SLICED PAPAYA WITH LIME CREAM

CAFÉ AU LAIT

When tight schedules or budgets mean dinner parties are out—serve brunch. It's a great way to entertain friends without giving up an entire precious evening. Start with Bloody Marias—the tequila variation on the Bloody Mary. Next, serve a grilled cheese sandwich with a difference. Accompany with stir-fried snow peas (use fresh or frozen) for crunch and color. Dessert is a smash: Papaya with lime cream. Instead of "just coffee," end your meal with Café au Lait. Here's how: Heat some milk just to the boiling point. Then pour it into big mugs with equal parts hot coffee.

BLOODY MARIAS

2 c. tomato juice
1 c. tequila
⅓ c. fresh lime juice
1 T. Worcestershire sauce
¼ to ½ tsp. Tabasco
Freshly ground black pepper

In a large pitcher, mix all ingredients; chill. Serve over ice with lime wedges as garnish. Makes 6 servings.

GRILLED HAM AND BRIE ON RYE

¼ c. Dijon mustard
1 T. prepared horseradish
12 slices rye bread
1 lb. thinly sliced ham
1 lb. ripe Brie, rind removed
2 eggs
¼ c. milk
3 T. butter or margarine

In small bowl combine mustard and horseradish; spread on six slices rye bread and top each with some ham. Spread Brie on remaining bread slices and make six sandwiches. In medium bowl or pie plate, beat eggs and milk with a fork. In large skillet or on grill, melt butter until hot. Dip each sandwich in egg, then grill in hot butter 3 to 4 minutes per side. Makes 6 servings.

SLICED PAPAYA WITH LIME CREAM

1 c. heavy or whipping cream
2 T. sugar
2 tsp. fresh lime juice
1 tsp. grated lime peel
2 papayas

With mixer at high speed beat heavy cream, gradually adding sugar until stiff peaks form. Fold in lime juice and lime peel. Slice papaya in half horizontally. Scoop out seeds, peel and slice into wedges. Arrange on dessert plates. Spoon on cream. Makes 6 servings.

EXOTIC PAPAYA

Choose fruit with some yellow on its skin. Cut in half, and scoop out seeds. Then *peel for easiest handling.*

simple picnic lunch

SLICED STEAK AND RED PEPPER SANDWICH WITH BLUE CHEESE AND BASIL MAYONNAISE

OIL-CURED OLIVES

FRESH FRUIT

ICED TEA

Here's a simple yet spectacular lunch to enjoy at home or on a picnic. No need to get complicated or exotic, just serve a simple, classy sandwich. Start by roasting sweet peppers; they have a lovely, smoky flavor. Then, thinly slice steak or roast beef (use leftovers or buy precooked roast beef from the deli). Arrange curly leaf lettuce, or pungent arugula, the meat, and strips of roasted peppers, on half of a French baguette (try whole-wheat if you can find it); spread with mayonnaise. Tuck in blue cheese, or substitute goat cheese or Cheddar and, if you like, snips of your favorite fresh herbs such as basil or rosemary. Put out a crock of oil-cured olives and a cruet of olive oil to sprinkle on the sandwich. Serve with iced tea sparked with slices of fresh lemon and sprigs of mint. For dessert, serve fresh ripe fruit such as sweet nectarines simple and unadorned or juicy melon with a wedge of lime.

SLICED STEAK AND RED PEPPER SANDWICH WITH BLUE CHEESE

Basil Mayonnaise (recipe follows)
2 loaves French bread, cut in half
    and split down the middle
4 large leaves curly leaf lettuce
8 oz. cooked steak
    or roast beef, thinly sliced
2 red peppers, roasted and
    thinly sliced,
    or jarred red peppers
½ c. blue cheese, crumbled
Freshly ground black pepper
Olive oil

Spread the Basil Mayonnaise on the French bread. Divide the lettuce, steak, peppers and blue cheese and arrange evenly on four slices of bread. Sprinkle with ground pepper. Top with remaining slices of bread. Serve with olive oil on the side. Makes 4 servings.

BASIL MAYONNAISE

1 egg
1 T. fresh lemon juice
¾ tsp. salt
¼ tsp. freshly ground black pepper
1½ c. olive oil
½ c. loosely packed basil leaves

In food processor with knife blade attached, combine egg, lemon juice, salt and pepper. Process until blended. Add oil in a slow, thin, steady stream, processing until mayonnaise thickens. Add basil and process until finely chopped. Makes 1¾ cups.

HOW TO
MAKE MAYONNAISE

Making your own mayonnaise from scratch may sound a little complicated, but it's truly a snap if you have a food processor. And once you taste the difference, store bought will never quite measure up. The secret to perfect mayonnaise is to drizzle the oil in very, very slowly.

soup supper

POTATO LEEK SOUP IN BREAD BOWLS

MIXED GREEN SALAD

WALNUT SUNDAE

WHOLE-WHEAT SHORTBREAD COOKIES

CITRUS MINERAL WATER

his is a meal of "comfort food." Instead of serving it in the usual style, this soup is served in a bowl made from a crusty loaf of peasant bread. Look for loaves in your bakery that are about 6 inches in diameter. When you've finished eating the soup tear the bread bowl into chunks and enjoy it with your salad, that way you won't miss a drop. The inside of the "bread bowl" will be flavored by the soup with garlic, cheese and olive oil—irresistible! The whole meal—soup to nuts (topping the ice cream)—can be ready in half an hour. Here's the game plan: As the soup simmers, prepare the bread bowls (see photos). Toss a salad of arugula, radicchio and some roasted peppers, either fresh or jarred ones (yellow peppers are used here, but green or red are fine too), and dress it lightly with oil and vinegar. Have citrus-flavored mineral water chilling and slices of fruit to drop in each glass. For a simple but delicious dessert, top chocolate ice cream with crumbled walnuts and a splash of Kahlua. Serve it with whole-wheat shortbread cookies.

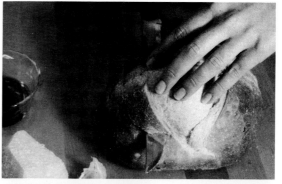

POTATO LEEK SOUP IN BREAD BOWLS

2 large potatoes, peeled and finely diced
2 large leeks, thinly sliced
4 c. chicken broth
½ tsp. salt
¼ tsp. freshly ground black pepper
¼ c. heavy or whipping cream
⅛ tsp. grated nutmeg
BREAD BOWLS:
4 round, unsliced loaves of bread
2 cloves garlic, crushed
4 tsp. olive oil
4 T. grated Parmesan cheese
Chopped parsley for garnish

In a large pot combine potatoes, leeks, chicken broth, salt and pepper. Over high heat, heat to boiling. Reduce heat to low, cover and simmer for 15 minutes. Meanwhile, make bread bowls (see photos). Place hollowed-out loaves and bread "lids" on a cookie sheet and bake in a 350°F oven for 15 minutes or until cheese melts. When the soup has simmered, use a sieve to strain soup into another pan. Place solids in blender or food processor with knife blade and process until smooth; return to soup in pan. Stir in heavy cream and nutmeg; heat through. Spoon hot soup into bread bowls and top with chopped parsley. Makes 4 servings.

HOW TO MAKE BREAD BOWLS

- *With small sharp knife, cut into loaf, leaving ¾-inch edge.*
- *Hollow out center, reserving leftover bread for croutons.*
- *Rub inside with garlic; brush with olive oil and sprinkle with cheese.*

chill-chasing meal

HOT-BUTTERED RUM
OYSTER STEW
CORN MUFFINS
BROCCOLI-WALNUT SALAD
APPLE PIE WITH MELTED CHEESE

Enjoy this warm, cozy supper on cold nights (it's great for lunch, too). Start with mugfuls of Hot-Buttered Rum—guaranteed to defrost even the coldest toes. While your guests are thawing, supper can be on its way. Here's how: Start with the salad. This creamy Oyster Stew is the fastest recipe ever. Clams are a good substitute if oysters are hard to find. To cut down on your kitchen time, buy corn muffins to serve with the stew and an apple pie for dessert from your supermarket or bakery. The muffins will need just a warming, but try this to dress up the pie: Sprinkle the top with grated Cheddar cheese. Pop it in a warm oven and cook until the cheese melts, bubbles and begins to soak through the crust.

OYSTER STEW

2 pints whole oysters with liquid
2 c. milk
1 c. heavy or whipping cream
2 T. butter or margarine
2 tsp. Worcestershire sauce
½ tsp. salt
¼ tsp. Tabasco
Chopped parsley for garnish
Freshly ground black pepper

Mince one fourth of the oysters in blender or food processor. In medium saucepan over low heat, combine with milk, cream, butter, Worcestershire, salt and Tabasco. Heat, stirring occasionally, to simmering but *not* boiling. Add remaining oysters and cook until edges curl and centers are firm. Sprinkle with parsley and pepper. Makes 6 servings.

HOT BUTTERED RUM

1-inch strip lemon peel
2 whole cloves
2 oz. dark rum
1 tsp. brown sugar
Cinnamon stick
Boiling water (about 6 oz.)
½ tsp. butter

Stud lemon peel with cloves. Place rum, sugar, cinnamon stick and peel in mug. Fill with boiling water; stir. Dot with butter. Makes 1 serving.

BROCCOLI-WALNUT SALAD

4 stalks broccoli
1 T. butter or margarine
⅓ c. coarsely chopped walnuts
1 head red leaf lettuce
⅓ c. crumbled blue cheese
Oil and vinegar dressing

With sharp knife cut buds from broccoli; reserve for another use. Slice stalks. Steam for 5 to 7 minutes or until just tender. Drain and run under cold water until cool. Heat butter in skillet. Add walnuts and sauté 2 to 3 minutes; drain. Clean lettuce and tear into bite-sized pieces. Add to salad bowl with broccoli and walnuts. Sprinkle with blue cheese. Add salad dressing; toss and serve. Makes 4 servings.

CUT BROCCOLI INTO COINS

Cut broccoli stalks into ¼-inch "coins." These oddly shaped discs are wonderfully whimsical in salad, or as a side dish.

soup and sandwiches

"CREAM" OF BROCCOLI SOUP

SUPER-SPECIAL GRILLED SANDWICHES

ICY FRUIT SORBET WITH ORANGE LIQUEUR

GINGERSNAPS

SPARKLING CIDER

This is a cozy supper—soup and sandwiches. Settle down for an evening of good food, friends and conversation. Before they arrive, you've made the soup. The sandwiches take just minutes. Grill them in a skillet or use a sandwich maker with a pretty pattern (see photos). Serve sparkling cider. For dessert, scoop icy fruit sorbet, drizzle with orange-flavored liqueur and serve with gingersnaps.

"CREAM" OF BROCCOLI SOUP

4 c. chicken broth
2 10-oz. pkgs. frozen broccoli
or 1 bunch fresh broccoli,
stems peeled
1 pear, peeled and chopped
1 medium onion, chopped
3 T. butter or margarine
Orange zest for garnish
Crème fraîche or plain yogurt

In large saucepan over medium heat, heat chicken broth. Add broccoli and cook 5 minutes. In skillet over medium heat, sauté pear and onion in hot butter until tender, about 5 minutes. Add to soup; heat through. Remove from heat and purée in a blender or food processor. Garnish with orange zest and a dollop of crème fraîche or yogurt. Makes 6 servings.

GROWN-UP SANDWICHES

The grilled sandwich grows up when you use one of these sandwich presses. The press used here works on top of the stove, but electric ones work fine. So the bread won't stick, use nonstick cooking spray (instead of butter or oil). Layer in the filling, close the press and heat on a burner about 1 ½ minutes per side, until golden brown.

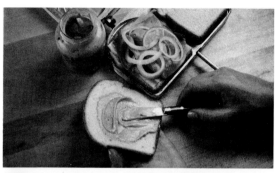

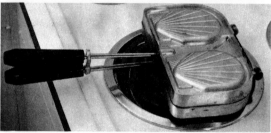

GREAT SANDWICH COMBOS

Any sandwich combo will work, especially if it has cheese that melts. Try:
● *Swiss cheese, ham, red onion rings and Dijon mustard*
● *Salmon salad (made like tuna salad), Muenster cheese and alfalfa sprouts*
● *Roast beef, horseradish and Cheddar cheese*
● *Sliced chicken, chutney, chopped peanuts and Swiss cheese*
● *Pizza sauce, shredded mozzarella and a sprinkle of oregano*
● *Sliced mushrooms, cooked bacon, avocado and blue cheese*

bistro supper

FILET MIGNON WITH WILD MUSHROOMS

STEAMED SNOW PEAS

FRIED SHOESTRING POTATOES

CHOCOLATE DECADENCE

CABERNET SAUVIGNON

Prepare this dinner for a very special person. It's a simple meal but truly a splurge. Buy the best filets you can find. (The secret to a beautifully browned steak is to dry the filets first and cook them in a hot-hot skillet.) Search out exotic mushrooms (see descriptions)—regulars will do fine, too. Instead of making the usual fries, run a sweet potato through the julienne blade of a food processor; rinse the strands in lots of water until no starch is left; dry them well on paper towels and flash-fry them in about 2 inches of very hot oil until just golden. If you don't have a food processor, prepare frozen shoestring potatoes as the label directs. For dessert: Chocolate Decadence!

FILET MIGNON WITH WILD MUSHROOMS

1 T. butter or margarine
1 T. olive or vegetable oil
½ lb. fresh mushrooms, sliced
2 4-oz. filets mignons,
**   each about 1 inch thick**
½ c. beef broth
¼ c. Madeira wine
1 T. fresh thyme or ¼ tsp. dried
**   leaves**
¼ tsp. salt
Freshly ground black pepper

In heavy skillet over medium heat, heat half the butter and half the oil. Add mushrooms and sauté quickly until lightly browned, about 5 minutes. With slotted spoon, remove and set aside. Add remaining butter and oil to skillet and heat over high heat. Pat filets dry on paper towels. Place filets in hot fat and brown well, about 3 to 4 minutes a side for medium-rare. Remove from skillet to platter and keep warm. Pour fat from skillet and add beef broth. Boil rapidly over high heat while scraping any brown bits from pan. Continue cooking broth until reduced to 2 tablespoons. Stir in Madeira, thyme, salt and pepper. Over high heat, heat to boiling. Add mushrooms and heat through. Serve mushrooms next to or on top of steaks. Makes 2 servings.

CHOCOLATE DECADENCE

½ c. amaretto cookie crumbs
2 scoops chocolate chocolate-chip
**   ice cream**
Fudge sauce
Almond-flavored liqueur

Spread cookie crumbs on a sheet of waxed paper. Roll scoops of ice cream in crumbs to coat. Place in freezer until ready to serve. Place each scoop in a serving dish. Warm fudge sauce, pour over ice cream and top each scoop with a splash of liqueur. Makes 2 servings.

TWO EXOTIC MUSHROOMS TO TRY

There are hundreds of varieties, but these are the ones you are most likely to see in the market. Chanterelles, left, range in color and size. They can be as small as the ones here or grow to 3 to 4 inches in diameter; the texture is firm and velvety. Shiitake (pronounced she tah kee), right, are much larger and are generally reddish brown to brownish black on top. Many people think they taste like lobster. Both mushrooms will last about a week, refrigerated. Place in a single layer on a barely damp cloth and fold to cover.

steak feast

STEAK AND SPINACH WITH MUSTARD SAUCE

WARM CORN-AVOCADO SALAD

FRENCH BREAD

GRAPEFRUIT WITH GINGER

PINOT NOIR

Here's a deliciously warming dinner for four. The steak is served on top of raw spinach leaves. The savory meat juices and piquant sauce will wilt the spinach, so there's no need to steam it first. For an unusual side dish, try a Warm Corn-Avocado Salad, full of slivers of Parmesan cheese and sweetly pungent red onion. To start, heat the corn and cut the vegetables and cheese (see photos). Next, cook the steaks, heat up French bread and then make the sauce. Just before serving, toss salad ingredients and arrange the steaks over the spinach, pouring some sauce over each. For dessert, serve grapefruit halves, sprinkled with chopped candied ginger. The wine choice—a pinot noir.

STEAK AND SPINACH WITH MUSTARD SAUCE

**4 steaks (club, sirloin or strip),
    about 1 inch thick
2 T. olive or vegetable oil
2 T. butter or margarine
2 scallions, minced
2 T. cognac or brandy
3 T. chopped parsley
1 tsp. prepared mustard
½ tsp. Worcestershire sauce
¼ c. beef broth
Fresh spinach leaves**

Trim steaks of excess fat. Pat steaks dry with paper towels. In heavy skillet over medium-high heat, heat oil and butter until very hot. Add steaks and sauté 3 to 4 minutes. Turn and cook 3 to 4 minutes more. (Small droplets of juice will appear on the surface of the steak when medi-um-rare.) Remove to hot platter; keep warm. Reduce heat; add scallions and sauté about 2 minutes. Add cognac, parsley, mustard and Worcestershire. Blend in beef broth and cook rapidly to reduce sauce by half. To serve: For each serving, arrange several spinach leaves on plate. Slice steak crosswise and place on spinach leaves. Pour some sauce over each. Makes 4 servings.

WARM CORN-AVOCADO SALAD

**2 c. whole-kernel corn
1 small red onion, cut in thin rings
1 avocado, cut into chunks
2 oz. Parmesan cheese,
    cut into very thin slivers**

In small saucepan, heat corn. Add onion. Just before serving, toss with avocado and Parmesan cheese. Makes 4 servings.

HOW TO OPEN AN AVOCADO

Here's an easy way to make a slippery avocado manageable. Cut around the fruit lengthwise. Twist in half. To remove the seed, whack a knife into it and twist. Then, carefully peel the skin from each half and cut or slice.

special café dinner

STEAK AU POIVRE
POMMES FRITES
BRAISED LEEKS
WATERCRESS-ORANGE SALAD
LEMON SHERBET WITH POMEGRANATES
CABERNET SAUVIGNON

When it's time for just the two of you, enjoy this romantic meal with each other. Start with the Steak au Poivre. What makes these pan-broiled steaks special is the cracked pepper pressed into the meat. Next, French fries—buy the shoestring variety and follow label directions. While the steaks are sizzling, make the salad of watercress, orange sections and blue cheese. Toss with a vinaigrette. Then make the leeks. Cabernet Sauvignon is the wine choice—uncork it while you're cooking so the flavor will develop or "breathe." Dessert's a snap. Scoop lemon sherbet into wine glasses and sprinkle with bright red pomegranate seeds. Look for a pomegranate about the size of a large orange, with a thin, leathery, red-purple skin.

STEAK AU POIVRE

**2 steaks (club, sirloin or strip)
    about 1 inch thick
1 T. cracked black peppercorns
1 T. olive or vegetable oil
4 T. butter or margarine
1 scallion, minced
⅓ c. canned beef broth
¼ c. brandy**

Pat steaks dry. Press cracked pepper into both sides of steaks. In heavy skillet, heat oil and 1 tablespoon butter until very hot. Add steaks and sauté 3 to 4 minutes, then turn and cook 3 to 4 minutes longer for medium-rare (small droplets of juice will appear on the surface of steak when medium-rare). Remove to hot platter; keep warm. Pour fat from skillet. Add 1 tablespoon butter and scallion; cook 1 minute. Pour in beef broth and boil rapidly while scraping any browned bits from bottom of skillet. Add brandy and cook 2 to 3 minutes more. Remove skillet from heat; stir in remaining 2 tablespoons butter, a little at a time. Pour over steaks. Makes 2 servings.

BRAISED LEEKS

**2 T. olive oil
4 medium leeks, trimmed and
    cleaned (see photos)
¼ tsp. dried thyme leaves
    or oregano
½ c. chicken broth
Freshly ground black pepper**

In large skillet over high heat, heat oil. Add leeks and brown, turning gently. Add thyme, chicken broth and a few grindings of pepper. Heat to boiling. Reduce heat to low; cover and simmer until tender, about 15 to 20 minutes. Makes 2 servings.

HOW TO HANDLE FRESH LEEKS

Leeks are a very dirty vegetable and require a thorough cleaning before cooking. Here's how: Start by trimming the leeks at the root end, then cut away the dark green leaves from the white stalk. With a small sharp knife, cut the leek, from end to end, halfway through to the center core. Then, under running water, flush out all the grit while pulling back the leaves. Shake to dry.

romantic dinner for two

LAMB CHOPS WITH BLUE CHEESE

HERB SAUTÉED POTATOES

SAUTÉED ZUCCHINI

FRENCH ROLLS

STRAWBERRIES WITH CREAM

BEAUJOLAIS

When you plan a special treat, there's nothing like perfectly cooked lamb—a rosy pink on the inside and deeply brown on the outside. It's a little on the extravagant side, so cut costs by serving it to just the two of you. Only 14 minutes under the broiler does it for chops. A little blue cheese makes a big flavor difference, too. Serve the chops with sautéed potatoes from the can—no peeling, no precooking, just heat them up (with a few additions, of course). An easy vegetable like zucchini needs only a quick toss in the pan. Heat-and-serve rolls and a fresh Beaujolais round out the meal. Chill the wine a bit. This is one red that will benefit. And what's a better dessert than fresh strawberries? Before you start the dinner, rinse a pint of the berries under cold running water; then remove the stems. Wrap them loosely in paper toweling. When you're ready for dessert, serve them with heavy cream if you opt for a calorie splurge, yogurt if you don't.

LAMB CHOPS WITH BLUE CHEESE

**2 loin lamb chops,
     each cut 1½ inch thick***
1 oz. blue cheese
2 tsp. Worcestershire sauce
*One chop should be enough for one
     person, but serve two for large appetites.*

Heat broiler. With small sharp knife, trim fat from chops. Use half of the blue cheese to stuff each chop. Press to close pocket. Place on broiler pan and sprinkle with Worcestershire, using ½ tsp. each side. Broil 7 minutes. Turn; sprinkle with remaining Worcestershire and cook 7 minutes or until pink. Makes 2 servings.

HERB SAUTÉED POTATOES

½ c. Italian-flavored bread crumbs
**1 16-oz. can whole potatoes,
     drained**
1 egg beaten with 1 T. water
3 T. butter or margarine

Place bread crumbs on sheet of waxed paper. One at a time, dip potatoes into egg, then roll in bread crumbs. Place on another sheet of waxed paper to dry. Over medium-high heat, in medium skillet, melt butter. When butter is very hot, add potatoes. Shake pan frequently to roll potatoes until browned evenly, about 5 minutes. Makes 2 servings.

SAUTÉED ZUCCHINI

2 small zucchini
2 T. butter or margarine
¼ tsp. salt
Freshly ground black pepper

Cut each zucchini crosswise into thirds; cut each into 8 wedges. Melt butter in skillet. When butter is hot, add zucchini, salt and pepper. Cook, stirring constantly, until tender-crisp, about 5 minutes. Makes 2 servings.

STUFF A CHOP

*With a small sharp knife,
make a deep slit in "fat side"
of each chop for a pocket.
Poke cheese inside.*

Mediterranean barbecue

LAMB BURGERS IN PITA BREAD

MINTY-GARLIC YOGURT SAUCE

TOMATO-CHEESE SALAD

BEER

PLUMS

Here's a great barbecue dinner you probably haven't tried. This recipe serves twelve and won't take any longer to prepare than a dinner for two. The first step is to light the coals. Use instant lighting charcoal to cut the time—it will be ready in only 20 minutes. While the briquettes are on their way, make the spicy, knock-your-socks-off yogurt dressing for the burgers. Refrigerate it to give the flavors time to mellow. Next, make an easy Tomato-Cheese Salad and let it stand at room temperature to marinate. The flavor is best if you don't serve the salad refrigerator cold. Last, mix all the burger ingredients; shape and grill. Use lamb and the unexpected flavors of cinnamon and clove to season. Serve the Lamb Burgers on pita bread instead of regular hamburger buns. Beer will taste great. For dessert, serve a bowl of juicy sweet plums. If you have the time, halve, pit and toss plums in honey and minced ginger.

LAMB BURGERS IN PITA BREAD

2 lbs. ground lamb
¼ c. plain yogurt
1 tsp. salt
½ tsp. ground cinnamon
¼ tsp. ground cloves
¼ tsp. freshly ground black pepper
12 small pita breads
Curly lettuce leaves

Combine lamb with remaining ingredients except lettuce and pita bread. Shape into 12 firm, round patties. Over hot coals, grill or broil 10 to 15 minutes, turn once, until desired doneness. Serve in pita bread with lettuce and sauce. Makes 12 servings.

MINTY-GARLIC YOGURT SAUCE

1 garlic clove
¾ c. plain yogurt
½ c. chopped scallions
3 T. finely chopped fresh mint
or 1 T. dried mint
2 small green chilies, seeded and
chopped (about 2 T.)
1 tsp. ground coriander

Mince garlic clove. Combine with remaining ingredients. Cover and refrigerate to blend flavors. Makes about 1 cup.

TOMATO-CHEESE SALAD

1 lb. feta cheese, drained
6 tomatoes
1 8-oz. can black pitted olives,
quartered
¼ c. olive oil
1 tsp. dried oregano
¼ tsp. freshly ground black pepper

Cut feta cheese and tomatoes into ¼-inch cubes. Combine with remaining ingredients. Cover and let stand at room temperature until serving time. Makes 12 servings.

*THE FASTEST WAY TO
PEEL GARLIC*

Use the broad side of a heavy large knife to crush a garlic clove. The paper easily peels off. Then, mincing is easy.

taste of spring

LAMB CHOPS WITH MUSTARD SAUCE

SAUTÉED SPRING VEGETABLES

NEW POTATOES

SPIRITED COFFEE

PINOT NOIR

Serve this marvelous dinner to three friends for a meal to remember. To start, steam peeled, small new potatoes for 15 minutes, then sauté them in butter to brown. Next, steam the vegetables to heighten color and sauté to add flavor. Use Brussels sprouts, radishes, baby carrots, snow peas, zucchini and mushrooms. Then, quickly brown the lamb chops and keep warm while you make a creamy Mustard Sauce. Serve dinner with a fruity pinot noir, slightly chilled. For dessert: Spirited Coffee. Add a splash of both cognac and a coffee-flavored liqueur to coffee. Top with whipped cream.

LAMB CHOPS WITH MUSTARD SAUCE

1 garlic clove, crushed
1 T. butter or margarine
2 T. olive or vegetable oil
12 rib lamb chops, about
    ¾ inch thick, trimmed
½ c. dry white wine
2 T. Dijon mustard
½ c. heavy or whipping cream
½ tsp. salt
Freshly ground black pepper

In large skillet over medium-high heat, brown garlic in hot butter and oil. Discard garlic. Increase heat to high and brown chops, a few at a time, about 3 minutes per side. Remove chops to a warm platter; keep warm. Pour wine into skillet and cook over high heat, scraping browned bits from the skillet. Blend in mustard, then cream, salt and pepper. Over high heat, boil sauce rapidly until slightly thickened; spoon over chops. Makes 4 servings.

SAUTÉED SPRING VEGETABLES

12 Brussels sprouts
12 radishes
8 baby carrots
12 snow peas
1 medium zucchini,
    cut into 2-inch by ½-inch pieces
8 large mushrooms, halved
2 T. butter or margarine
2 T. olive oil
½ tsp. salt
¼ tsp. dried thyme leaves
⅛ tsp. freshly ground black pepper

Steam Brussels sprouts, radishes and carrots 7 minutes, or until tender-crisp; rinse under cold water. Steam snow peas, zucchini and mushrooms 3 to 4 minutes until tender-crisp; rinse. In large skillet over medium heat, heat butter and oil. Add vegetables and sauté about 5 minutes until vegetables are tender. Sprinkle with salt, thyme and pepper. Makes 4 servings.

*PREPARING
BRUSSELS SPROUTS*

Always choose firm sprouts with tightly closed heads. Remove any damaged or yellowed outer leaves. Trim the base. With the tip of a small, sharp knife, cut an "x" about ¼ inch deep in the base of the sprout. This helps the sprouts cook evenly.

robust dinner

PORK CHOPS SPADARO

PECAN-ORANGE RICE

STEAMED BABY CARROTS

ITALIAN WHOLE-WHEAT BREAD

PEARS ANISE

SUGAR COOKIES

ROSÉ WINE

Serve this robust, festive dinner for six. The flavors and seasonings—orange, rosemary, vermouth and shallots—are strong-bodied, especially when combined with pork chops and nutted rice. To prepare this dinner in record time, start by boiling the water for the rice. Follow label instructions for perfect results. Then, brown the pork chops, add the shallots and the remaining ingredients and cook for 15 minutes or so. Meanwhile, scrape the carrots and steam 10 minutes or until tender. Use tender baby carrots, but sliced large ones are fine, too. Heat up a loaf of Italian whole-wheat bread. Then, toss the pecans and grated orange rind into the rice, and you're finished! Serve the meal with a dry chilled rosé, maybe an Anjou. For dessert: Thinly slice pears and sprinkle with Sambucca or anisette. Pass them with thin, crisp sugar cookies. Buy them from a bakery or make them from scratch at home.

PORK CHOPS SPADARO

**6 loin, rib or blade pork chops,
    about ½ inch thick
¼ tsp. salt
¼ tsp. freshly ground black pepper
2 shallots, finely chopped
½ c. dry vermouth
1 T. fresh rosemary or
    1 tsp. dried, crumbled**

Trim fat from pork chops. In large skillet over medium heat, rub fat over bottom of skillet to grease well. Discard fat. Add the pork chops and brown well on both sides. Sprinkle with salt and pepper. Add the shallots, vermouth and rosemary if using dried. Over high heat, heat to boiling, reduce heat to low, cover and simmer 10 to 15 minutes or until fork-tender. Remove the pork chops and skim any fat from pan juices. If using fresh rosemary, sprinkle it over chops now, then spoon pan juices over the pork chops. Makes 6 servings.

PECAN-ORANGE RICE

**1 c. long-grain rice
Chicken broth
1 16-oz. can pecans, chopped
Grated peel from 1 orange**

Cook rice according to package directions substituting chicken broth for water. Omit salt. When done, toss with chopped pecans and grated peel. Makes 6 servings.

A WORD ABOUT SHALLOTS

Shallots, kin to scallions and onions, are delicate and aromatic, with a sweet, slightly pungent flavor. Their papery skin can be brown, gray or rosy-colored. Buy those that are firm and full, without soft spots. Store in a cool, dry spot (preferably not the refrigerator) for up to ten days. To use in a recipe, just peel and slice or mince. They can be used cooked or raw (delicious in a salad!).

dinner from Alsace

PORK CHOPS LILLET

PARSLEY POTATOES

SAUTÉED CABBAGE

PUMPERNICKEL BREAD

RASPBERRY SORBET WITH CRÈME DE CASSIS

BEER

ndulge in this hearty supper for four. It's similar to a meal you might enjoy in Alsace—the region of France that borders on Germany. The pork chops have a fruity twist— a healthy splash of Lillet, a French vermouth flavored with bitter orange peel. Begin with them (see explanation of the different types of pork chops, before shopping). While they're simmering, put on the potatoes. Once in, they'll take about 15 minutes to cook. Move on to the cabbage. Next, finish the sauce for the pork chops and toss the potatoes with minced parsley. Put out a hefty loaf of pumpernickel bread and a crock of coarse grain mustard to serve with the pork. Beer is the perfect accompaniment to this meal. For dessert, punch up taste buds with scoops of sweet-tart raspberry sorbet, sprinkled with crème de cassis.

PORK CHOPS LILLET

4 pork chops, about ½ inch thick
¾ C. Lillet or dry vermouth
½ tsp. salt
Coarse grain mustard

Trim fat from chops and place fat in large skillet over medium-low heat; heat trimmed fat slowly until it leaves a thin film in skillet. With slotted spoon, remove and discard fat. Increase heat to medium-high; add the pork chops and cook until well browned on all sides. Add Lillet and salt. Cover and cook 15 minutes or until tender. Remove chops to platter; keep warm. Increase heat to high. Boil sauce rapidly until slightly thickened. Pour over chops. Serve with coarse grain mustard. Makes 4 servings.

SAUTÉED CABBAGE

3 T. butter or margarine
1 medium onion, thinly sliced
¼ head cabbage, shredded
1 T. sugar
½ tsp. caraway seeds
½ tsp. salt

In large skillet or saucepan over medium-high heat, melt butter. Add onion; sauté until tender, about 5 minutes. Add cabbage and sauté 2 minutes. Add sugar, caraway and salt. Reduce heat to low; cover and simmer, stirring occasionally, 10 to 15 minutes or until tender. Makes 4 servings.

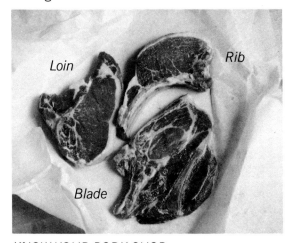

Loin   *Rib*   *Blade*

KNOW YOUR PORK CHOP

You've always heard that pork chops are fattening but the much-maligned pork chop is leaner than it used to be; it's around 13 percent fat and 70 calories per cooked ounce, which isn't that much more than chicken, which has about 50. You'll usually find three kinds of pork chops; blade, rib and loin. Rib and loin tend to be leaner and more expensive than blade. Count on four servings per pound for rib and loin and three for blade.

hearty harvest dinner

PORK CHOPS WITH SAUERKRAUT
SAUTÉED APPLES WITH CALVADOS
BLACK FOREST SUNDAE
FRENCH SPARKLING CIDER

Here's the easiest-ever dinner menu with enough panache to please six discriminating guests. It's a combination of the good tastes of apples, sauerkraut and pork. To get you out of the kitchen in 30 quick minutes, start with the pork chops. Sauté them; then simmer. Half-inch chops will take only 10 minutes to simmer or a few more for thicker ones. With the chops on their way, prepare the apples. Sliced and sautéed in butter and spices, they make a subtle, sweet counterpoint to pork. Flavor them with Calvados, a French apple brandy. Applejack or other apple-flavored brandy can be used, too. Serve a hefty loaf of whole wheat bread—no need for another starch at this meal. Dessert—the easiest. All store-bought. Start with sponge-cake rounds or pound cake. Drop a scoop of the richest chocolate ice cream you can find on top; drizzle with kirsch (cherry-flavored liqueur).

PORK CHOPS WITH SAUERKRAUT

1 T. vegetable oil
6 loin pork chops,
about ½ inch thick
½ tsp. caraway seeds
1 bay leaf
1 T. dark brown sugar
½ c. dry vermouth
2 lbs. sauerkraut,
rinsed and drained

In large skillet over medium heat, heat oil until hot. Fry pork chops quickly until browned. Drain off fat. Add caraway seeds, bay leaf, brown sugar and vermouth; heat to boiling. Reduce heat to low; cover and simmer 7 to 10 minutes. Add sauerkraut and heat through. Makes 6 servings.

SAUTÉED APPLES WITH CALVADOS

2 T. butter or margarine
3 apples, cut into 8 wedges and
seeded
½ c. Calvados (or apple brandy)
1 T. brown sugar
⅛ tsp. ground cloves

In medium skillet over medium heat, melt butter or margarine. Add apples and sauté until just tender, about 4 minutes. Stir in Calvados, sugar and cloves. Cook, stirring constantly but gently, over low heat for 3 minutes. Remove apples to serving dish. Increase heat to high and boil liquid until reduced by half. Pour the sauce over apples. Makes 6 servings.

TWO WAYS TO ENJOY APPLES BY THE GLASS

Here are two apple drinks to try:
● *French cider has more spritz than ours and has some alcohol in it.*
● *Calvados is a deep amber-colored brandy with a mellow apple taste. Serve as you would cognac or use it in cooking.*

meal with Italian flavor

PORK CUTLETS MERLOT

SAUTÉED FENNEL

STEAMED RADISHES

RIPE PEARS WITH GORGONZOLA CHEESE

SPARKLING CIDER

meal of familiar foods

PORK TENDERLOIN IN ROSEMARY SAUCE

CRANBERRY APPLESAUCE

BABY CARROTS

GREEN BEANS

POUND CAKE GRAND MARNIER

ZINFANDEL

Have a cozy dinner for four. To enjoy this 30-minutes-to-make dinner, start with the applesauce, then prepare the pork. Use the tenderloin section. It cooks quickly, and as the name implies, it's the most tender cut. Plan on a half tenderloin per person. They are often sold two to a package. Why not make your own applesauce to serve with the meal... homemade really is better. While the applesauce cooks and the pork simmers in its sauce, steam some baby carrots and green beans (frozen are fastest). A fruity zinfandel is a good wine choice. For dessert, serve slices of pound cake with scoops of vanilla or chocolate ice cream, drizzled with Grand Marnier.

PORK TENDERLOIN IN ROSEMARY SAUCE

1 T. butter or margarine
1 T. oil
2 pork tenderloins (¾ lb. each)
1 tsp. dried rosemary leaves, crumbled
½ tsp. dried thyme leaves
½ tsp. salt
¼ tsp. freshly ground black pepper
1 c. dry vermouth
½ c. light cream

In skillet over high heat, heat butter and oil until very hot. Add pork tenderloins (cut in half if necessary to fit in pan) and sear until well browned on all sides. Add rosemary, thyme, salt, pepper and vermouth. Cover; reduce heat to medium-low and simmer about 10 minutes or until juices run clear when tested with a fork. Note: Do not overcook or pork will be stringy and dry. Remove pork from skillet; keep warm. Over high heat, boil vermouth down rapidly until reduced by half. Stir in cream and heat through. Slice pork into ½-inch-thick slices and arrange on plate. Pour sauce over pork. Makes 4 servings.

CRANBERRY APPLESAUCE

3 large cooking apples
⅓ c. water
1 c. whole-berry cranberry sauce

Peel and core apples; cut into quarters. Place apples and water in a medium-sized saucepan. Over high heat, heat to boiling. Reduce heat to low and simmer, uncovered, stirring occasionally, for 10 to 15 minutes, or until tender. Stir in cranberry sauce and heat through. Serve warm or cool. Makes 4 servings.

Rome beauty
McIntosh
Granny Smith

BEST APPLES
FOR MAKING SAUCE

The best apples for cooking are the tart and slightly acid ones. The three shown above are good choices, as are Golden Delicious, Jonathan, York Imperial, Gravenstein or Newton-Pippin. Combine sweet and tangy apples for a delicious sauce.

peasant-style supper

PENNE ALLA VODKA

CHICORY-BACON SALAD

ITALIAN WHOLE-WHEAT BREAD

BRANDY-SPLASHED ORANGES

CHIANTI

Make five friends happy. Invite them for this pretty, palate-pleasing dinner. Penne, ham and peas are tossed in a creamy tomato sauce, laced with vodka and spiked with hot red peppers. Team it with a piquant salad made of chicory and escarole; tuck in bits of bacon for flavor and crunch. Start by boiling the water for the pasta. Then prepare the sauce and cook the bacon for the salad. Mix the salad; use a rich green virgin olive oil in the dressing. Toss the pasta with the sauce. Wine choice: a robust Italian red such as Chianti. For dessert, splash orange sections with brandy and top with chopped almonds.

PENNE ALLA VODKA

1 16-oz. pkg. penne
1 medium onion, diced
4 T. butter or margarine
1 16-oz. can tomatoes, drained
1 8-oz. can tomato sauce
⅔ c. vodka
1 c. heavy or whipping cream
¼ lb. ham, diced
1 c. frozen peas, thawed
¼ to ½ tsp. crushed red pepper
Grated Parmesan cheese

Cook pasta according to label directions. In large skillet over medium-high heat, cook onion in hot butter until tender, about 5 minutes. Add tomatoes and tomato sauce. Add vodka; cook 5 minutes. Blend in cream; heat to boiling. Add remaining ingredients except cheese and heat through. Toss with hot drained pasta. Serve with grated Parmesan cheese. Makes 6 servings.

CHICORY-BACON SALAD

¼ lb. bacon
½ head chicory (curly endive)
½ head escarole,
   or 1 small head romaine
DRESSING:
½ c. olive oil
2 T. red wine vinegar
2 T. Dijon mustard
2 scallions, minced
1 T. minced fresh parsley
Freshly ground black pepper

Cut bacon into 1-inch pieces. Fry until crisp; drain on paper towels. Tear lettuce into bite-sized pieces. Combine all dressing ingredients in a jar with a tight-fitting lid. Shake to blend. Toss with salad. Makes 6 servings.

ABOUT TUBULAR PASTAS:

Tubular pastas are substantial and require a heartier sauce than thin or flat pastas. They are excellent with meaty sauces and sauces with chunky vegetables, or fish sauces. These are the pastas of choice for salads and baked dishes. Here are some favorites:
(1) Rigatoni—stubby, hollow and ridged.
(2) Penne—a narrow, quill-shaped pasta.
(3) Ziti—a short tube, narrow and sometimes ridged.
(4) Bucatini or Perciatelli—looks like thick spaghetti but is hollow in the center.

pasta dinner for spring

ASSORTED SALAMI

PASTA WITH VEGETABLES AND CREAM

GARLIC BREAD

CAFÉ ROMANO

BARDOLINO

Here's an elegant, dinner for four. The star is pasta, brimming with vegetables, all tossed in a creamy sauce. For great nibbling while you fix the pasta, serve your favorite salamis, arrange on a cutting board; let guests help themselves. Then, boil water for the pasta; heat the oven for the bread. Next, melt butter; add garlic and parsley and drizzle over thick, crusty slices of bread. Prepare the vegetables; cook the pasta. Then toss with cream and cheese. The bread can be browning in the oven. The wine—a light, red Bardolino. Finally, a blissfully easy dessert—Café Romano. Fill half a coffee cup with espresso; stir in a little anise-flavored liqueur and top with whipped cream.

PASTA WITH VEGETABLES AND CREAM

½ lb. thin spaghetti (vermicelli)
¼ c. pine nuts or chopped walnuts
2 T. olive or vegetable oil
1 garlic clove, minced
5 medium mushrooms, sliced
1 small zucchini, sliced
1 10-oz. pkg. frozen, chopped
 broccoli, thawed and drained
1 6-oz. pkg. frozen snow peas,
 thawed and drained
3 T. chopped fresh basil
 or 2 tsp. dried
3 T. chopped fresh parsley
½ tsp. salt
¼ tsp. freshly ground black pepper
¼ c. grated Parmesan cheese
½ c. heavy or whipping cream, at
 room temperature
3 T. butter or margarine, softened

Cook pasta according to label directions. Meanwhile, toast nuts in 325° F oven 5 minutes or until golden. In a large skillet over medium-high heat, heat oil. Sauté garlic until lightly golden; add mushrooms, zucchini, broccoli, snow peas, basil, parsley, salt and pepper. Drain cooked pasta. Add sautéed vegetables to pasta. Toss with cheese, cream and butter. Sprinkle with toasted nuts. Makes 4 servings.

GARLIC BREAD

½ loaf Italian bread
⅓ c. butter or margarine
3 large garlic cloves, crushed
¼ c. chopped fresh parsley

With serrated knife cut bread into 8 slices. In small saucepan, heat butter until melted. Add garlic. Reduce heat; cook garlic until golden. Remove and discard garlic. Stir in parsley. Heat oven to 375° F. Drizzle butter over each slice. Bake 10 minutes or until golden. Makes 4 servings.

GET THE MOST FROM GRATED CHEESE

Parmesan or Pecorino Romano are the best grating cheeses for pasta. Pass up the pregrated ones because the cheese loses its flavor within a few hours of grating. Buy a hand grater and use it right at the table.

lunch with sizzle

SPICY SESAME NOODLES

PICKLED CUCUMBERS WITH WATERCRESS

PINEAPPLE WITH KIRSCH

ICED TEA

Serve this splendid cold entrée for a special lunch. The rich nutty flavor of Spicy Sesame Noodles tastes best at room temperature. As a cool, crunchy accompaniment try Pickled Cucumbers with Watercress and a refreshing glass of iced tea made with a Chinese tea, such as Keemun. For dessert, fresh pineapple cut into chunks, with a splash of kirsch and a sprinkle of grated bittersweet chocolate. Here's the cooking plan: Put the water on to boil for the noodles; next make the cucumbers and let stand. Combine the sauce ingredients for the pasta and, finally, create an easy garnish—scallion flowers (see photos). Just before serving, toss noodles with sauce.

SPICY SESAME NOODLES

1 lb. thin linguine or spaghetti
2 T. oriental sesame oil
¼ c. creamy peanut butter
or sesame paste
¼ c. soy sauce
2 T. rice-wine vinegar
1-inch piece fresh ginger, peeled
and minced
¼ tsp. crushed red pepper flakes
1 sweet red pepper,
cut into thin slivers
4 scallions, cut into flowers,
reserving tops and cut into
2-inch pieces

Cook linguine according to package directions; drain. Toss with sesame oil and set aside. In bowl, combine peanut butter, soy sauce, wine vinegar, ginger and red pepper flakes. Toss with noodles. Gently toss in red pepper and cut-up scallion. Serve at room temperature garnished with scallion flowers. Makes 4 servings.

PICKLED CUCUMBERS WITH WATERCRESS

2 medium cucumbers
¼ c. sugar
¼ c. rice-wine or white vinegar
2 T. water
½ tsp. salt
¼ bunch watercress

Peel cucumbers. Cut lengthwise in half and remove seeds. Slice in ¼-inch-thick slices. In small bowl combine sugar, vinegar, water and salt; add cucumbers. Let stand at least 15 minutes at room temperature. Just before serving, remove and discard stems from watercress and add to cucumbers. Makes about 2 cups.

*HOW TO MAKE A
SCALLION FLOWER*

*Trim away root end and all
but 2 to 3 inches of top
greens. Using a small sharp
knife, make several cuts in
both ends of scallion. Be sure
to leave at least 1 inch of
scallion intact in center.
Drop into iced water to open.
Drain on paper towels.*

mini-meal

BUFFALO CHICKEN WINGS

CELERY FANS

BLUE CHEESE DRESSING

BEER

Here's a great idea for munching during a favorite movie, football or baseball game. Instead of just peanuts and popcorn, serve Buffalo Chicken Wings, the invention of Mrs. Theresa Bellissimo, owner of the Anchor Bar in Buffalo, New York. One day in 1964, she received too large a shipment of chicken wings. She fried them up, tossed them with a hot pepper sauce and served them with a tangy blue cheese dressing. You can do the same. Round out the snack with cooling, crisp celery and a selection of cold beers. Perhaps you can suggest that your friends bring their favorites. Start by making the Blue Cheese Dressing. Chill it while you cook the Chicken Wings. Keep the wings hot in the oven while you cook the remaining batches. Pile on a platter; tuck in celery fans and settle in for a great afternoon.

BUFFALO CHICKEN WINGS

4 lbs. chicken wings
Vegetable oil
3 T. butter or margarine
3 T. Tabasco
6 celery stalks, cut into
(directions follow)

Cut chicken wings at joints (see photos). Pour about ½ inch oil into a large heavy skillet; heat over medium-high heat until almost smoking. Add as many chicken wings as will fit in the skillet without crowding. Fry until golden, about 10 minutes, turning once. Heat oven to 250°F. Drain cooked chicken wings on paper-towel-lined baking sheet. Remove paper towel and keep chicken warm in oven while you fry the remaining wings. When all the wings are cooked, pour off all fat from skillet. Reduce heat to low. Allow pan to cool down for a few minutes. Add butter or margarine to skillet and melt. Stir in the Tabasco. Arrange wings on serving plate and drizzle with the hot-pepper butter. Serve with celery fans and Blue Cheese Dressing. Makes 6 servings.

BLUE CHEESE DRESSING

½ c. mayonnaise
½ c. sour cream
⅓ c. crumbled blue cheese
1 garlic clove, minced
1 T. fresh lemon juice

Combine all ingredients in a bowl and beat until well combined. Makes about 1½ cups.

CELERY FANS

Cut four stalks of celery into three-inch lengths. If celery stalks are very large, cut lengthwise in half. To make fans, cut three or four lengthwise slashes through each piece, leaving about 1 to 1½ inches of celery intact. Drop into a bowl of ice water to open. Drain and serve.

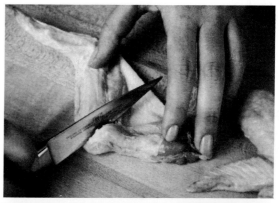

CUT-UP CHICKEN WINGS
_____

Spread wing and cut at each joint. Discard wing tip.

Santa Fé feast

LIME-GRILLED CORNISH GAME HENS
CURRIED CORN WITH RED PEPPERS
SUGAR SNAP PEAS
RUM-LACED PLUMS
GINGERSNAPS
GEWÜRZTRAMINER

S erve this meal full of the flavors of the Southwest for a memorable dinner party. Gutsy ingredients—lime, jalapeño peppers, fresh corn—are combined with an elegant twist, making this a deliciously unusual menu. First, prepare the game hens for broiling or grilling. They can be split in half or opened flat (see photos). Plan on one small hen per person. This is a great recipe for the outdoor grill or indoor broiler—let the weather decide how you cook them. Once the hens are sizzling, begin the Curried Corn. Steam the sugar snap peas for 5 to 7 minutes, just until tender-crisp. Choose a dry, spicy wine such as an Alsatian Gewürztraminer. For dessert, serve sliced plums, splashed with dark rum and sprinkled with cinnamon along with store-bought gingersnaps.

LIME-GRILLED CORNISH GAME HENS

1 large lime
2 T. butter or margarine
⅛ tsp. ground red pepper
4 game hens (about ¾ lb. each), split

Grate rind from lime, then squeeze juice. In small saucepan, melt butter; stir in grated lime peel, lime juice and ground red pepper. Heat broiler. Place hens on broiler pan, skin-side down. Spoon or brush half of lime-pepper butter over hens. Broil, about 5 inches from heat, for 12 minutes. Turn. Spoon remaining butter over hens and broil 7 to 9 minutes more or until fork-tender. Makes 4 servings.

CURRIED CORN WITH RED PEPPERS

2 slices bacon, chopped
2 large sweet red peppers, seeded and cut into slivers
1 fresh jalapeño pepper, seeded and chopped (optional)
1 T. curry powder
¼ tsp. salt
Freshly ground black pepper
½ c. heavy or whipping cream
1 ½ c. corn kernels (about 3 ears)

In saucepan cook bacon until crisp. Add peppers and cook, stirring until tender, 10 minutes. Add curry powder, salt, black pepper and cream. Add corn; heat to boiling. Reduce heat; simmer 3 to 5 minutes. Makes 4 servings.

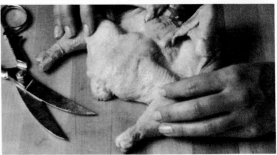

SPLIT A HEN

Score skin and meat with a heavy, sharp knife along breastbone. Then cut through the breast with shears. Turn the opened bird skin-side up and flatten, by pushing down on thighs and wings.

broiled and skewered dinner

**LEMON-BROILED CHICKEN AND
SKEWERED VEGETABLES**

ORZO WITH PARMESAN CHEESE

WHOLE WHEAT BREAD

FRESH PINEAPPLE

CHENIN BLANC

Broiling is one of the fastest, most delicious ways to cook. You get a nice crusty outside and a moist, juicy inside. Here time is saved by broiling the vegetables, too, right alongside the chicken. The game plan for this thirty-minute feast: Heat the broiler. Next combine butter, garlic, lemon juice and parsley to make a "lemon-butter" to baste the chicken and vegetables. Thread the vegetables on a skewer to make cooking them easier. Brush the chicken and vegetables with lemon-butter sauce; pop into the broiler; then start your timer. Meanwhile, cook the orzo (a rice-shaped pasta) following package directions. If you can't find orzo, use rice. For a special touch, toss with freshly grated Parmesan cheese and a sprinkle of parsley just before serving. After you've put the orzo on to cook, turn the chicken and vegetables, brush again and put back for another 10 minutes. You should have enough time now to prepare the pineapple for dessert. (See photos.) Cover it with plastic wrap and refrigerate. Add crusty bread, a chenin blanc wine, three good friends and settle back for a delightful evening.

LEMON-BROILED CHICKEN AND SKEWERED VEGETABLES

3 T. butter or margarine
2 garlic cloves, minced
3 T. fresh lemon juice
¼ c. minced fresh parsley
2 whole chicken breasts, split
VEGETABLES:
1 small red onion, cut into wedges
**2 medium zucchini,
    cut into 2-inch chunks**

Heat broiler. In small saucepan over low heat melt butter or margarine. Add minced garlic, lemon juice and minced parsley to make lemon butter. Place chicken, skin-side down on rack in broiler pan. On two 12-inch skewers, alternately thread onion wedges and chunks of zucchini. Place on broiling rack next to chicken. Brush chicken and vegetables with half of the lemon-butter. Broil 15 minutes. Turn chicken and vegetables; brush with remaining lemon-butter. Broil 10 minutes more. Makes 4 servings.

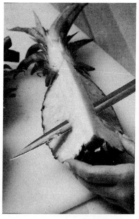

*CUT AND SERVE
FRESH PINEAPPLE*

Lay pineapple on its side. Using a heavy, sharp knife, cut lengthwise in half beginning at base and cutting through leaves at top. Place cut-sides down, cut lengthwise again, making four wedges. Working with one wedge at a time, cut away hard, center core. Work knife under one side, then the other to free pineapple from shell. Do not remove shell. To serve, cut pineapple meat lengthwise in half. Then, crosswise into 1-inch chunks. Stick toothpicks into several pieces of each wedge or serve with a spoon for eating.

champagne dinner for two

**SAUTÉED CHICKEN BREASTS WITH
CHAMPAGNE SAUCE**

POTATO OVALS

WALNUT GREEN BEANS

CHOCOLATE TRUFFLES

CHAMPAGNE

You've barely had a moment alone with him in weeks, so you decide this is the night just for you two— alone. Pop the cork on a bottle of your favorite chilled champagne or sparkling wine and toast one another. To chill quickly, 30 minutes in the refrigerator will do or a mere 15 minutes in a bucket full of half water and half ice. At some point you'll need 30 minutes to get the dinner together—less if he helps. Start by trimming the green beans. Steam them until tender-crisp and set aside until serving time (or simply thaw frozen green beans). Meanwhile, make potato ovals; see photos. About 15 minutes before you want to eat, start to cook the chicken. Then steam the potatoes, and just before serving, complete the Walnut Green Beans. Finish this classic dinner with a few Chocolate Truffles.

SAUTÉED CHICKEN BREASTS WITH CHAMPAGNE SAUCE

2 T. butter or margarine
1 whole chicken breast, boned, skinned and split
2 T. chopped shallots or scallions
⅔ c. champagne or sparkling wine
¼ c. heavy or whipping cream
⅛ tsp. salt

Place each chicken breast half between 2 sheets of waxed paper and using dull side of a heavy knife or with rolling pin pound each to flatten until about ½-inch thick. Over medium-high heat, heat 1 tablespoon butter. Sauté chicken breasts about 5 minutes on each side, until golden and cooked through. Remove chicken; keep warm. Add the shallots to skillet and cook until translucent but not browned. Pour in champagne and cook over high heat until it is reduced by about half. Add the cream and salt, and cook until the sauce thickens slightly. Whisk in the remaining 1 tablespoon butter. Arrange chicken on plates and spoon some sauce over each. Makes 2 servings.

WALNUT GREEN BEANS

½ lb. whole green beans
1 T. butter or margarine
2 T. chopped walnuts

In medium saucepan over medium-high heat, in 1 inch lightly salted water, steam beans until tender-crisp, about 7 to 9 minutes. Drain. In skillet, melt butter. Add beans and walnuts. Toss until heated through. Makes 2 servings.

SHAPE POTATOES INTO OVALS

Cut 2 large potatoes into eight wedges, or cut 3 medium potatoes into six. Taper wedges into small football shapes, using a knife or a swivel-blade vegetable peeler. To prevent darkening, place the potatoes in a bowl filled with water, until ready to cook.

Mediterranean meal

CHICKEN PROVENÇAL

BULGUR WITH PARSLEY

SPINACH WITH OLIVE OIL

MINTED MELON AND STRAWBERRIES

BEAUJOLAIS

The south-of-France flavor of Chicken Provençal combines fresh tomatoes and rosemary sprigs with tangy goat cheese. To accompany it, try mild, nutty bulgur and fresh spinach. Prepare the bulgur, then move on to the chicken. As you finish the sauce for the chicken, steam the spinach leaves just until wilted (but not soggy) to serve with lots of fresh lemon juice and a splash of rich, fruity olive oil. Try a light, red wine, such as Beaujolais. For dessert: Minted Melon and Strawberries. Toss ripe honeydew melonballs with fresh strawberries, a splash of orange juice, a little sugar and a handful of fresh mint leaves.

CHICKEN PROVENÇAL

2 whole chicken breasts, skinned, boned and split
1 T. olive oil
4 T. butter or margarine
4 oz. goat cheese, such as Montrachet, cut into ¼-inch slices
2 to 3 small tomatoes, sliced
1 T. fresh rosemary or ¾ tsp. dried
½ c. dry white wine

Place each chicken breast half between two sheets of waxed paper. With dull side of a heavy knife or with rolling pin, pound each to flatten until ½-inch thick. In a large, heavy skillet over medium-high heat, heat oil and 2 tablespoons butter. Sauté chicken breasts about 3 minutes on each side until golden and cooked through. Arrange alternating slices of cheese and tomato on each chicken breast half. Sprinkle with rosemary. Pour wine around chicken. Cook, cov-

ered, about 3 minutes or until tomato and cheese are heated through; cheese will not melt completely. Remove chicken to warm platter. Over high heat, boil sauce rapidly until it is reduced and thickened. Stir in remaining butter, one tablespoon at a time. Pour sauce over chicken. Makes 4 servings.

BULGUR WITH PARSLEY

1 T. butter or margarine
1 c. bulgur
1 13 ¾-oz. can chicken broth
3 T. minced fresh parsley

In medium skillet over medium heat, melt butter. Add bulgur and sauté 3 to 5 minutes until grains are well coated. Stir in broth; heat to boiling. Reduce heat to low, cover; simmer 10 to 15 minutes until tender and broth is absorbed. Stir in parsley. Makes 4 servings.

ABOUT BULGUR

Also known as cracked wheat, this grain is popular throughout the eastern Mediterranean and the Middle East. It can be baked, cooked as a pilaf or soaked and served as a raw salad, as in the Lebanese salad tabbouleh. Buy bulgur in small quantities and store in a tightly-covered container in a cool place, preferably the refrigerator.

taste of Italy

Prepare this Italian chicken specialty laced with mushrooms and wine for a dinner party with a real gourmet flavor. Traditionally, veal scallops are used, but you can substitute chicken breasts to cut costs. This genuine Italian meal can all be done on top of the stove in 30 minutes. Here's how: Put the water on for the pasta. Then, sauté the chicken breasts. While they cook, you can make the sauce for the pasta. A green bean salad can be put together quickly with frozen whole green beans. Just thaw them under hot running water, then drain and toss with your favorite vinaigrette. Serve the meal with a loaf of crusty, Italian bread. Uncork a bottle of Orvieto, a lovely dry Italian white wine to accompany your meal. Serve pears and a blue cheese like Gorgonzola for dessert. Slice the pears and toss with a splash of lemon juice before dinner and let the cheese warm to room temperature.

CHICKEN MARSALA

4 T. butter or margarine
1 clove garlic, crushed
3 large chicken breasts,
 boned, skinned and split
1 lb. mushrooms, sliced
¾ C. Marsala wine
2 T. chopped parsley

In large skillet over medium heat, heat butter. Add garlic and sauté until golden; discard garlic. Sauté chicken breasts in flavored butter until well browned on all sides. Add mushrooms and Marsala, cover and cook 5 to 7 minutes or until chicken is fork-tender. Remove chicken breasts to warm platter. Over high heat, heat sauce in skillet to boiling, scraping up any brown bits from bottom of pan. Cook until thickened slightly. Stir in parsley and pour over chicken breasts. Makes 6 servings.

FETTUCCINE WITH TOMATOES

1 12-oz. pkg. green fettuccine
2 T. olive oil
1 clove garlic, crushed
2 large tomatoes, seeded and
 chopped (see photos)
½ C. heavy or whipping cream
½ tsp. salt
⅛ tsp. ground nutmeg
½ C. grated Parmesan cheese

Cook fettuccine as label directs. Meanwhile, in large skillet over medium-high heat, heat oil. Add garlic and sauté until golden; discard garlic. Add tomatoes to skillet and sauté 2 minutes. Add cream, salt and nutmeg. Pour cream over hot fettuccine. Toss well. Serve immediately. Pass Parmesan at the table. Makes 6 servings.

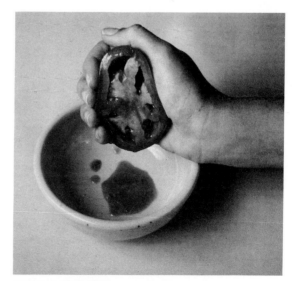

SEED A TOMATO

To remove seeds, simply cut tomato in half or into quarters and squeeze.

country supper

CHICKEN IN APPLE-MUSTARD SAUCE

NEW POTATOES

STEAMED BROCCOLI

SPIRITED ORANGE COCOA

CHARDONNAY

Throw a dinner party for friends you may not have seen lately. Chicken in Apple-Mustard Sauce is a super-easy but delicious choice. The combination of sweet apples and pungent onions makes for a dazzling flavor contrast (the sauce is smooth, and it tastes as though you've simmered it for hours). Small new potatoes, cooked with the skins left on, and broccoli, steamed until bright green, add color and crunch. Start by pounding the breasts. They will cook faster and more evenly if pounded thin. Sauté them quickly to brown, then let them simmer in the appley sauce. Meanwhile, cook the potatoes 15 to 20 minutes in a little boiling water and steam the broccoli. Remove the chicken, quickly reduce sauce by boiling it rapidly and you're finished. Serve with a light, clean Italian Chardonnay. Instead of dessert, try Spirited Orange Cocoa: A cup of hot chocolate with a splash of orange-flavored liqueur; topped with shaved chocolate.

CHICKEN IN APPLE-MUSTARD SAUCE

**4 chicken breast halves,
    boned and skinned
2 T. butter or margarine
1 c. apple juice
1 medium onion, sliced
1 garlic clove, minced
½ tsp. dried thyme leaves
4 tsp. Dijon mustard
1 apple, cored and sliced**

Place each chicken breast half between two sheets of waxed paper. With dull side of a heavy knife pound chicken breasts to flatten to about ½-inch thick. Over medium-high heat, heat butter in a large skillet. Sauté chicken breasts about 3 minutes on each side until golden. Add apple juice, onion, garlic and thyme. Cover and cook 10 to 12 minutes, or until chicken is tender. Remove chicken; keep warm. Heat liquid to boiling. Add mustard to skillet. Stir until well blended. Add apple slices. Pour sauce over chicken. Makes 4 servings.

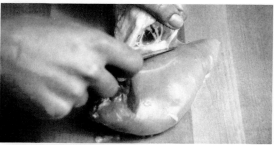

BONE A CHICKEN BREAST

(1) Start with half a chicken breast. Loosen the skin with your fingers. (2) Using a knife, trim away the skin. (3) Hold the meat steady with one hand. Use knife to scrape (don't cut) meat away from the bones. (4) Remove the tendon from the underside of the breast by scraping it free with the knife. Doing this keeps the breast from curling up when cooked.

exotic chicken dinner

SAUTÉED SESAME CHICKEN
SAUTÉED GREEN BEANS WITH COCONUT
RICE
PITA BREAD WITH CASHEW BUTTER
CINNAMON ESPRESSO
GEWÜRZTRAMINER

Try this Indonesian-style menu when your standby chicken dinner leaves you flat. It has all the exotic, wake-up flavor of Chinese cooking without the prep work. Start by marinating the chicken breasts. Next, cook rice. Now, go back to the chicken; coat it with sesame seeds and sauté. Add some pizzazz to the green beans by sautéing them with shredded coconut, fresh if you have time, or packaged. Serve pita bread spread with cashew butter. Chill a bottle of Gewürztraminer, the perfect wine for this many-flavored meal. Brew espresso and toss a couple of broken pieces of cinnamon sticks in with the ground coffee.

SAUTÉED SESAME CHICKEN

3 whole chicken breasts, boned, skinned and split
3 T. soy sauce
2 T. fresh lemon juice
2 T. dark brown sugar
1-inch piece fresh ginger, peeled and minced
1 large garlic clove, minced
¼ tsp. crushed red pepper flakes
⅛ tsp. ground cumin seed
1 2.6-oz. jar sesame seeds (1 c.)
3 T. olive or vegetable oil

With a fork, prick each half chicken breast several times. In large pie plate, combine remaining ingredients except sesame seeds and oil. Add chicken and let stand 10 minutes, turning once. Spread sesame seeds on a sheet of waxed paper; coat chicken. In large skillet over medium-high heat, heat oil until hot. Add chicken breasts and brown. Cover; reduce heat to low and simmer 5 minutes. Makes 6 servings.

SAUTÉED GREEN BEANS WITH COCONUT

2 T. olive or vegetable oil
1 bay leaf
⅛ tsp. crushed red pepper flakes
2 tsp. mustard seed (optional)
2 10-oz. pkgs. frozen whole green beans, thawed
¼ tsp. salt
⅓ c. shredded coconut (fresh or packaged)

In large skillet, heat oil and add bay leaf, red pepper flakes and mustard seed. Fry 30 seconds. Add beans and salt; sauté 2 minutes more. Add coconut. Heat through. Makes 6 servings.

SHRED A COCONUT

● *Punch out the three "eyes" with an ice pick or screwdriver; drain milk. Bake drained coconut in preheated 325°F oven for 15 minutes.*
● *Crack with a hammer; remove meat from the shell and peel away dark skin.*
To grate: Use food processor with metal knife blade; process until flaky. If you're grating by hand, use a medium grater. Place in plastic bag and store up to 6 months in freezer.

island dinner

MACADAMIA NUT CHICKEN WITH RADICCHIO AND ORANGE SECTIONS

SPINACH FETTUCCINE WITH CARROTS

ICE CREAM WITH KAHLUA AND TOASTED COCONUT

PINOT BLANC

Splurge with this delicious meal. Hawaiian macadamia nuts are fairly pricey but because they taste so good they're worth sharing with special friends. First, pound, then coat the chicken with the crunchy bread and nut mixture (see photos). Next, "shave" carrots. Put water on to boil for the pasta. Wash the radicchio (you can use Boston lettuce); cut oranges into slices. Then cook the chicken. Start the pasta now, too: Put on a large pot of lightly salted water. For dessert, serve a scoop of vanilla ice cream topped with a splash of Kahlua and a sprinkling of toasted coconut. Wine choice: a fruity, light pinot blanc.

MACADAMIA NUT CHICKEN

2 whole chicken breasts, skinned, boned and split
⅔ c. dried plain bread crumbs
½ c. finely chopped macadamia nuts
¼ tsp. salt
1 egg
2 T. butter or margarine
2 T. olive or salad oil
½ c. chicken broth
½ c. orange juice
Radicchio or Boston lettuce leaves
Orange sections

Pound chicken breasts until ¼-inch thick. Combine bread crumbs, macadamia nuts and salt on sheet of waxed paper. Beat egg with fork in pie plate. Coat chicken breasts. In large, heavy skillet over medium-high heat, heat 1 tablespoon butter or margarine with oil; add chicken breasts. Cook until golden on all sides. Reduce heat to low; cover and cook 5 to 7 minutes until chicken is fork-tender. Remove chicken and keep warm. Pour chicken broth and orange juice into skillet. Heat to boiling. Cook until sauce is reduced by one third. Blend in remaining butter or margarine, until sauce thickens. Pour over chicken. Serve with radicchio leaves and orange sections. Makes 4 servings.

SPINACH FETTUCCINE WITH CARROTS

2 large carrots
½ lb. spinach fettuccine
2 T. butter or margarine
Grated Parmesan cheese

Scrape carrots. Then, using a vegetable peeler, "shave" carrots into long, thin strips. Cook pasta according to label directions. When just about done, add carrots. Drain; toss with butter and Parmesan cheese. Makes 4 servings.

*HOW TO COAT
A CHICKEN BREAST:*

Place chicken breasts between two sheets of waxed paper. Use the dull side of a heavy knife to pound thinly. Dip breasts into egg first, then into the bread crumbs and chopped macadamia nuts.

Tex-Mex express

CHICKEN BURRITOS

AVOCADO, ORANGE, RED ONION SALAD

PEPPERED MANGOES

SANGRÍA

Here's a Tex-Mex meal that's quick and easy to put together for a hungry group of six. Keep basics on hand—tortillas in the freezer, beans and sauce on the shelf—and you can pull this feast together anytime. You can make Chicken Burritos with leftovers or pick up a roasted chicken on the way home. While the tortillas are heating in the oven, get the burrito ingredients ready so you can assemble them at the last minute. Then, toss together a salad of oranges, red onion and avocados—a flavor mix that complements the spicy burritos. Mix up a batch of your favorite sangría, flavored with lots of fresh orange slices. Finish the feast with juicy, sliced mangoes sprinkled with lime juice and chili powder.

CHICKEN BURRITOS

2 T. olive or vegetable oil
1 medium onion, chopped
1 medium tomato, chopped
1 small green chili, seeded and
　　chopped or 1 4-oz. can green
　　chilies, chopped
1 garlic clove, minced
2 ½ c. cooked chicken, cubed
1 15-oz. can refried beans
1 8-oz. jar taco sauce
12 flour tortillas
Cheddar cheese, grated
1 head romaine lettuce, shredded

In medium skillet over medium heat, heat oil. Add onion, tomato, chili and garlic and sauté until tender, about 10 minutes. Add chicken and heat through. Remove from heat and keep warm. Heat beans and taco sauce in separate saucepans. On each tortilla spread 1 tablespoon beans, top with chicken, a little cheese, then roll up. Place on plate lined with shredded lettuce. Spoon 3 tablespoons taco sauce over each. Makes 6 servings.

AVOCADO, ORANGE, RED ONION SALAD

2 avocados, peeled and sliced
2 oranges, peeled and cut in
　　sections
1 small red onion, thinly sliced
VINAIGRETTE DRESSING:
⅓ c. olive or vegetable oil
2 T. cider vinegar
1 tsp. prepared mustard
Salt
Freshly ground black pepper

Combine avocado, oranges and onion. In small jar with tight-fitting lid, combine vinaigrette ingredients, shaking well to blend. Just before serving toss salad ingredients with Vinaigrette Dressing. Makes 6 servings.

THE POWER OF PEPPERS

Peppers, or chilies, are a key to Mexican cooking. There are over twenty kinds, but you'll probably find only one or two fresh varieties at your local market. The longer, rumpled-looking pepper (1) is "semi-hot." The smaller, smoother one (2) is extremely hot. You may find "fancier" peppers like Jalapeños (3)— the most flavorful of all. Used with the veins and seeds they are very, very hot; without they add a piquant flavor. A rule of thumb: The lighter the green and the blunter the tip, the milder the chili will be. If buying canned peppers, look for the "roasted and peeled" kind for best flavor.
Beware: When handling chili peppers, keep hands away from eyes and afterward wash hands thoroughly. Even the oils and juices from chili peppers can cause burns.

nouveau New Orleans dinner

CHICKEN JAMBALAYA

RICE

CORIANDER CUCUMBERS

FRENCH BREAD

PRALINE SUNDAE

GEWÜRZTRAMINER

Break out of your usual weeknight routine and throw a small dinner party—this colorful feast will take you only a half hour! This Jambalaya is a light, zesty version of the classic. Instead of cooking the chicken with the rice (which is traditional), prepare them separately. While the rice cooks, you can turn your attention to preparing the chicken. Here's the plan: Boil water for the rice (see photos for making perfect rice). Next, fix the cucumbers. Then, turn to the Jambalaya: Sauté the ingredients and make the sauce. Serve with warmed French bread—whole-wheat if you can find it. For the wine, choose a dry Gewürztraminer. Dessert? Try a Praline Sundae: Mix softened vanilla or fudge ripple ice cream with a handful of chopped pecans and a splash of coffee-flavored liqueur.

CHICKEN JAMBALAYA

3 medium oranges
4 T. butter or margarine
½ c. diced Canadian bacon
  or lean ham
3 garlic cloves, minced
2 large onions, thinly sliced
1 sweet green pepper, seeded and
  thinly sliced
1 sweet red pepper, seeded and
  thinly sliced
3 whole chicken breasts, boned,
  skinned and thinly sliced
¼ c. bourbon
¼ tsp. crushed red pepper
½ c. frozen peas, thawed
4 scallions, thinly sliced

Grate peel from 1 orange. Squeeze juice from oranges to make 1¼ cups. In large skillet over medium-high heat, heat 1 tablespoon butter. Add bacon, garlic, onions and peppers. Cook until barely tender; set aside. Heat remaining butter in skillet. Add chicken; cook until it loses its pink color. Add orange juice, bourbon and crushed red pepper. Cover; cook 3 minutes. Remove chicken; set aside. Boil sauce in skillet rapidly until reduced to ⅔ cup. Return bacon and vegetables and chicken to skillet; add peas and scallions. Heat through. Sprinkle with grated orange peel. Makes 6 servings.

CORIANDER CUCUMBERS

4 pickling (Kirby) cucumbers
Juice from 2 lemons
½ tsp. salt
¼ tsp. freshly ground black pepper
¼ tsp. ground coriander

Cut each cucumber into 6 spears and arrange on a platter. Sprinkle with remaining ingredients. Makes 6 servings.

THREE STEPS TO PERFECT RICE

(1) For six ½-cup servings. Put 2 c. water, 1 T. butter or margarine and 1 tsp. salt in medium saucepan over medium heat; bring ingredients to a full boil. (2) Add 1 c. regular long-grain rice (for amount of converted or brown rice to add, follow package directions) and stir. Cover tightly. Reduce heat; simmer 20 mins. (3) Remove from heat, uncover and fluff rice with a fork. Serve.

Oriental express

EGG ROLLS

SZECHWAN ORANGE CHICKEN

STIR-FRIED BROCCOLI

BOILED RICE

FORTUNE COOKIES

OOLONG TEA

Stir-fry means fast cooking, but it usually means lots of time-consuming preparation, too. Not this menu. With these streamlined techniques you can have a fast Oriental-style feast. Here's the game plan: First, start the rice boiling. Next, cut up the chicken, combining it with the spicy-sherry marinade. For a colorful, crunchy accompaniment, cut up some broccoli and red pepper; stir-fry and steam. Heat up egg rolls, either "take-out" or frozen, and then move on to cooking the chicken. Pour the tea, bring out the chopsticks—and enjoy.

SZECHWAN ORANGE CHICKEN

2 whole chicken breasts, boned and skinned
2 T. dry sherry
1 T. soy sauce
4 scallions, cut into 2-inch pieces, including tops
½-inch piece fresh ginger, peeled and minced
1 garlic clove, minced
¼ tsp. crushed red pepper
1 large orange
1 T. cornstarch
½ tsp. sugar
½ tsp. salt
¾ c. orange juice
3 T. peanut or vegetable oil

Cut chicken into thin strips. Combine chicken with sherry and next five ingredients; set aside. With vegetable peeler cut peel, not white membrane, from orange. Cut into 1-inch squares. In a cup combine cornstarch with remaining ingredients except oil. In a large skillet over high heat, heat oil until very hot. Stir-fry orange peel until it just begins to brown around the edges. Remove and drain on paper towels. In flavored oil remaining in skillet, cook chicken and marinade, stirring quickly until it just loses its pink color. Add orange juice and cook until thickened. Stir in orange peel. Makes 4 servings.

STIR-FRIED BROCCOLI

1 medium bunch fresh broccoli
1 small sweet red pepper
3 T. peanut or vegetable oil
1 tsp. sugar
½ tsp. salt
¼ C. water

With vegetable peeler, peel the broccoli. Cut broccoli into 2-inch pieces. Cut red pepper into thin strips. In large saucepan over high heat, heat oil until very hot. Add broccoli and stir until evenly coated with oil. Add sugar, salt and water. Cover and steam 3 to 5 minutes. Remove cover; add red pepper and continue cooking, stirring frequently, until all the water is absorbed. Makes 4 servings.

FOR THE MOST TENDER BROCCOLI

Gently peel only the rough outer skin from broccoli. This will allow it to cook evenly and quickly.

71

dinner for mid-week

TURKEY FORESTIÈRE

WILD AND BROWN RICE

WHOLE-WHEAT PEASANT BREAD

BANANAS AU RHUM

MERLOT WINE

Serve this "turkey dinner," and you'll have to convince your friends that they're not eating veal. Less expensive turkey cutlets are surprisingly similar to high-cost veal when cooked as they are here. Look for them in the meat case, next to other fresh turkey parts. They can also be sliced from the breast. Ask your meat man. The sauce is chock-full of vegetables—no need for an extra side dish. Start by cutting the vegetables. Then prepare your favorite rice mix. Next move onto the turkey. For dessert make Bananas *au Rum.* Do them ahead of time and keep warm, or prepare them after dinner.

TURKEY FORESTIÈRE

4 turkey cutlets (about 1 lb.)
All-purpose flour
1 T. olive or vegetable oil
1 T. butter or margarine
3 scallions, cut into thin slivers
1 carrot, julienned (see photos)
½ lb. mushrooms, sliced (1 c.)
1 tomato, diced
1 tsp. dry rosemary, crumbled
1 c. dry vermouth
1 c. chicken broth
½ tsp. salt
⅛ tsp. freshly ground black pepper
¼ c. heavy cream

Lightly coat turkey cutlets with flour. In large skillet over medium-high heat, heat oil and butter. Sauté turkey until golden, about 2 minutes on each side. Add remaining ingredients except cream. Cover; simmer 7 to 9 minutes, until tender. Remove turkey and vegetables; keep warm. Rapidly boil sauce, reducing to about 1 cup. Stir in cream. Pour over turkey. Serves 4.

BANANAS AU RHUM

3 T. butter or margarine
4 large bananas,
**   cut into 2-inch pieces**
1 T. fresh lime juice
⅔ c. dark rum
¼ c. sugar
½ tsp. ground cinnamon
Vanilla ice cream

In medium skillet over medium heat, heat butter until melted. Add bananas and cook until golden. Add lime juice. In saucepan, heat rum, sugar and cinnamon until sugar dissolves. Pour over bananas. Simmer, uncovered, 5 minutes. Serve with ice cream. Serves 4.

HOW TO JULIENNE
A CARROT

Start with a thick carrot.
Cut it into long, thin diagonal slices, about ⅛-inch thick.
Stack two or three slices and cut into matchstick-thin strips.

no-cook dinner

TURKEY TONNATO

TOMATO, ONION AND BASIL SALAD

BREAD WITH BRIE BUTTER

CANTALOUPE-RASPBERRY COMPOTE

TREBBIANO

When it's so hot that the thought of using even one burner to cook is horrendous, but company's coming, here's a keep-cool meal that's a lifesaver. And no advanced planning is needed. It's a pick-up-on-the-way-home menu. Sliced turkey from the deli counter; tomatoes, onions and dessert from the produce department; some bread and cheese. The plan of attack: Get the wine chilling in a bucket of iced water so it'll be cold. Try a light, crisp Italian trebbiano. Slice the tomatoes and onions and marinate them. Next, make dessert: Toss cantaloupe with fresh raspberries and a dash of crème de cassis; refrigerate. Whirl the Tonnato Sauce in your blender and put it on hold until serving time. Spread the bread with buttery Brie; broil quickly. *Ecco*, an Italian feast ready in thirty cool minutes.

TURKEY TONNATO

1 ½ lbs. sliced roasted turkey breast
1 ½ c. mayonnaise
1 6 ½- to 7-oz. can tuna, drained
½ 2-oz. can flat anchovies, drained
2–3 T. fresh lemon juice
½ tsp. paprika
2 T. capers
1 lemon, sliced for garnish (see photos)

Arrange turkey slices on platter. In blender container or food processor with knife blade, blend mayonnaise, tuna, anchovies, lemon juice, paprika and 1 tablespoon of the capers. Spoon over turkey on platter. Sprinkle with remaining tablespoon capers and garnish with lemon slices. Makes 8 servings.

TOMATO, ONION AND BASIL SALAD

2 large tomatoes
2 large red onions
2 T. chopped fresh basil
  or 2 tsp. dried
⅛ tsp. salt
Freshly ground black pepper
¼ c. olive oil
3 T. red wine vinegar

Thinly slice tomatoes and onions. Alternately arrange tomatoes and onion slices on large platter. Sprinkle with basil, salt and pepper, then oil and vinegar. Cover and let stand at room temperature until ready to serve. Makes 8 servings.

BREAD WITH BRIE BUTTER

1 loaf whole-wheat Italian bread
¼ lb. ripe Brie
2 T. butter or margarine, softened

With serrated knife, slice bread lengthwise in half. Remove rind from Brie. In small bowl, combine Brie with butter. Spread on bread. Broil 3 to 5 minutes or until hot and bubbly. Cut each half into 8 pieces. Makes 8 servings.

SCALLOPED LEMON GARNISH:

Use a zester to remove strips of lemon peel lengthwise. Then cut the lemon into thin slices. The peel will have a scalloped edge.

splurge for spring

TURKEY PICCATA
RICE
ASPARAGUS
ITALIAN CHEESES AND GRAPES
FRASCATI

Celebrate with this wonderful dinner. It's a big splurge—wild rice and asparagus can be pricey—so serve it to only one very special friend. The secret to melt-in-your-mouth turkey cutlets is in the cooking. Make sure the pan is very hot. The cutlets should sizzle when you drop them in. Have the rice and asparagus ready before you start to cook the turkey since these thin scallops will cook quickly. After dinner serve fruit and a selection of cheese, and crusty bread or crackers. Try a fruity white wine, such as Frascati.

TURKEY PICCATA

1 lemon
½ lb. thinly sliced turkey cutlets
  (about ¼-inch thick)
⅓ c. all-purpose flour
¼ tsp. salt
Freshly ground black pepper
1 T. olive or vegetable oil
4 T. butter or margarine
1 T. minced fresh parsley

Cut 5 to 6 very thin (paper thin) slices from lemon; squeeze 1 tablespoon lemon juice from remaining lemon. Set aside. Place cutlets between two pieces of waxed paper and pound slightly with dull side of French knife. Combine flour, salt and pepper on a sheet of waxed paper. Dredge turkey in flour to coat lightly. Meanwhile, in heavy skillet over medium-high heat, heat oil and 2 tablespoons butter until very hot. Add turkey, a few pieces at a time, and sauté quickly until lightly browned, about 45-60 seconds per side. Remove turkey to platter; keep warm. Remove skillet from heat, swirl in lemon juice and scrape any brown bits from bottom of pan. Add remaining 2 tablespoons butter and stir over medium-low heat until melted. Stir in parsley. Pour sauce over turkey. Garnish with lemon slices. Makes 2 servings.

PERFECT ASPARAGUS

Trim ½ pound asparagus spears (see photos). Over high heat, heat about 1-inch lightly salted water in large skillet to boiling. Arrange asparagus in skillet in single layer. Reduce heat to low; cover and simmer 8 to 10 minutes until tender-crisp. Makes 2 servings.

DON'T WASTE ASPARAGUS

Trim ends only where the white part begins to turn green. Trim tiny leaves on each stalk. That's where gritty sand can hide. If large, use vegetable peeler to trim entire stalk for even cooking.

northern Italian treat

RISOTTO WITH SHRIMP AND SAUSAGE

GREENS WITH MUSTARD VINAIGRETTE

BREAD STICKS

AMARETTO TORTA

VALPOLICELLA

Risotto, a one-dish meal made with arborio rice, is flavored here with sweet Italian sausage and shrimp. Making risotto requires about 20 minutes of undivided attention while you add simmering broth to the rice, in small amounts, stirring constantly. As soon as the broth is absorbed by the rice, you add more broth and continue to stir, repeating this process until the rice is creamy and just tender, about 15 minutes of cooking time. Then you add the remaining ingredients. The Italians serve risotto with just enough broth remaining to coat each grain of rice. If you prefer it a bit drier, simmer a minute more. Be sure to have extra Parmesan cheese and a peppermill on the table. Round out the dinner with a simple salad of tossed greens with an olive oil and vinegar dressing. A light red wine such as Valpolicella is the choice for this meal. For dessert, serve an almond-flavored torta.

RISOTTO WITH SHRIMP AND SAUSAGE

1 T. olive oil
2 garlic cloves, minced
8 oz. medium shrimp,
    peeled and deveined
¾ c. chopped, peeled Italian
    tomatoes (drained if canned)
5 c. chicken broth
2 sweet Italian sausages,
    casings removed
⅓ c. butter or margarine
1 medium onion, chopped
1 lb. arborio rice
    or long-grain rice
⅓ c. dry white wine
1 c. frozen peas, thawed
¼ c. chopped fresh parsley

In a medium skillet heat oil over medium-high heat. Add garlic and shrimp; cook until shrimp are pink. Add tomatoes and cook 1 minute more. Set aside. Heat chicken broth to simmering. Crumble sausage into a large saucepan; cook over medium-high heat until browned. Add butter and onion and cook until onion is wilted. Stir in rice and cook 1 minute so that all the grains are coated with butter. Add the wine and stir until the liquid is absorbed. Add ½ cup of the simmering broth and cook, stirring constantly, until it's absorbed. Continue stirring and add ½ cup more broth each time it's absorbed, until rice is just tender, 15 to 20 minutes. Stir in peas, shrimp and tomatoes and heat through. Stir in the parsley and serve. Makes 6 servings.

GREENS WITH MUSTARD VINAIGRETTE

2 T. grainy mustard
2 T. olive oil
1 T. red wine vinegar
⅛ tsp. freshly ground black pepper
3 Belgian endive,
    cut in 1-inch pieces
3 c. curly chicory, rinsed and dried

In a large bowl combine mustard, oil, vinegar and pepper. Whisk until blended. Add greens and toss to coat. Makes 6 servings.

AMARETTO TORTA

½ c. amaretto liqueur
3 c. whipped cream
Angel food cake
Toasted coconut

In small bowl, fold amaretto into whipped cream. Split cake horizontally in half. Spread half of the flavored whipped cream on the bottom layer of cake. Cover with other cake layer and spread remaining cream on top. Sprinkle with toasted coconut. Makes 6 to 8 servings.

Arborio   Long-grain

WHAT IS ARBORIO RICE?

It is stubby short-grain rice. It's more moist, tender and sticky than long-grain rice.

shrimp and rice fiesta

SHRIMP PAELLA

MARINATED ARTICHOKE HEARTS

FRENCH BREAD

FRUIT COMPOTE

ROSÉ WINE

Colorful paella is one of the most wonderful—and delicious—party foods around. This streamlined version of the Spanish classic is scented with spices and packed with shrimp and sausage. Start the meal by cooking artichoke hearts to marinate in vinaigrette. Next, sauté the sausage, onions and garlic; add the rice. Add the shrimp and peas to the paella, simmer, and you're finished. Just slice warmed French bread, and put out in a napkin-lined basket. For a super-easy dessert, combine slices of apples and pears with a sprinkling of brown sugar. Serve the meal with a crisp rosé.

SHRIMP PAELLA

1 T. olive or vegetable oil
½ lb. chorizo (Spanish sausage)
   or Polish sausage, thinly sliced
1 small onion, chopped
1 garlic clove, minced
1 10 ¾-oz. can condensed chicken
   broth
1 8-oz. can tomatoes, chopped
½ tsp. ground cinnamon
¼ tsp. saffron
1 ½ c. long-grain rice
1 8-oz. pkg. frozen shrimp, thawed,
   or ½ lb. shelled and deveined
   fresh shrimp
1 c. frozen peas, thawed

In medium skillet over medium heat, cook sausage, onion and garlic in hot oil until sausage is browned and onion is tender, about 5 minutes. Add broth, tomatoes and their liquid, cinnamon, saffron and rice. Heat to boiling. Cover and simmer 15 minutes. Add shrimp and peas; simmer 5 minutes more. Makes 4 servings.

MARINATED ARTICHOKE HEARTS

1 10-oz. pkg. frozen artichoke
   hearts
3 T. olive or vegetable oil
1 T. red wine vinegar
¼ c. finely chopped parsley
1 garlic clove, minced
1 tsp. Dijon mustard
¼ tsp. freshly ground black pepper

Cook artichoke hearts half the amount of time the label recommends. Drain. Combine remaining ingredients in a jar and shake well. Pour over artichoke hearts. Let stand at room temperature until serving. Makes 4 servings.

SAFFRON: HOW TO USE IT

Saffron is the dried stamen of the saffron crocus. About 75,000 flowers are needed to produce one pound of saffron—which is why it's the world's most expensive spice. But a little goes a long way. Use ground saffron and stem saffron interchangeably. To extract color and flavor from the threads, crumble and add to a hot liquid such as the chicken broth that the rice is cooked in here. That way you'll be getting every bit.

Indonesian meal

INDONESIAN RICE

CUCUMBER SALAD

PITA BREAD WITH CHUTNEY BUTTER

PAPAYA-KIWI SALAD

BEER

Low on funds, but still want to have the crowd over for dinner? Try this version of an exotic Indonesian fried rice. Start with rice as your base and then add bits of cooked meat, fish, vegetables, eggs and fruit, along with spicy seasonings—an easy way to stretch the meal but not your budget. If you're really feeling the pinch, skip the shrimp and add more of something else such as vegetables or eggs. Serve a cool salad of cucumber slices, minced parsley and coriander. Beer, of course, is the perfect beverage. Dessert? Put together a healthy combination of tropical fruits. Layer slices of kiwi fruit and papaya in a shallow glass bowl; sprinkle with kirsch. Chill until serving time.

INDONESIAN RICE

3 T. butter or margarine
2 large onions, chopped
½ lb. ground beef
⅓ c. chopped celery leaves
2 tsp. curry powder
1 tsp. ground cumin
½ tsp. crushed red pepper flakes
¼ tsp. dry mustard
1 lb. cooked shrimp
½ 10-oz. pkg. frozen peas, thawed
1 c. rice, cooked according to package directions, substituting chicken broth for water
2 T. chopped fresh coriander (cilantro), optional

In large skillet over medium-high heat, melt butter. Add onions and sauté until golden. Add beef, celery leaves, curry, cumin, red pepper and mustard. Cook, stirring occasionally, until beef browns. Stir in shrimp and peas. Heat through. Toss with hot rice. Sprinkle with coriander. Serve with pita bread and chutney butter. Makes 6 servings.

CHUTNEY BUTTER

½ c. butter or margarine softened
¼ c. chutney
2 T. chopped parsley

In a small bowl mix together butter, chutney and parsley until well blended. Use to spread on pita bread. Makes ½ cup.

THE SUPERFAST WAY TO CHOP AN ONION

(1) Slice a peeled onion in half, through the root end. Place the flat side on a cutting board. From top to bottom, make slices parallel to board; leave root end intact. (2) Slice vertically through the onion; leave root end intact. (3) Slice from top to bottom, to the root end.

do-ahead dinner

CHILLED LEMON-POACHED SALMON

ZUCCHINI-POTATO SALAD

CUCUMBER-DILL RIBBON SALAD

FRUIT BREADS WITH HONEY BUTTER

MELON WITH LIME

ICED TEA

f you start this meal early in the morning or the night before, all you need to spend in the kitchen that evening is 30 minutes. Do the salmon and potato salad in the morning or the night before. Cover with plastic wrap and refrigerate. Then, in the evening all you'll need to do is make the Cucumber-Dill Ribbon Salad. A stop at your local bakery makes this meal easy, too. Search out fruit breads or muffins; blueberry or an orange-nut would be a good choice. Serve them with a softened sweet (unsalted) butter blended with a little honey. Large glasses of iced tea or your favorite white wine are a wonderful and refreshing accompaniment. For dessert, cut open a succulent melon such as casaba and serve with wedges of lime for a tangy flavor contrast.

CHILLED LEMON-POACHED SALMON

3 c. water
1 c. white wine, or ½ c. dry
   vermouth and ½ c. water
1 lemon, sliced
2 scallions, sliced
¼ tsp. salt
⅛ tsp. freshly ground black
   pepper
4 1-inch-thick salmon or
   halibut steaks

In large skillet combine water, wine, lemon slices, scallions, salt and pepper. Over high heat, heat to boiling; add salmon or halibut steaks. Reduce heat to low; cover and simmer gently 7 to 10 minutes. With slotted spatula remove fish from liquid. Arrange on platter, cover with a plastic wrap and refrigerate until chilled. Makes 4 servings.

ZUCCHINI-POTATO SALAD

3 to 4 red potatoes,
   cut into ¼-inch strips
1 large zucchini,
   cut into 1½-inch chunks
¼ c. olive oil
2 T. dry vermouth
1 scallion, diagonally sliced
2 T. fresh tarragon or ½ tsp. dried
½ tsp. sugar
½ tsp. salt
Freshly ground black pepper

In small saucepan over medium heat, bring 1 inch of lightly salted water to boiling. Add potatoes and cook 7 to 10 minutes until fork-tender.

In another pan in 1 inch of lightly salted boiling water, cook zucchini 5 minutes or until tender-crisp. Drain potatoes and zucchini. In small jar with tight-fitting lid, combine oil with remaining ingredients. Shake to combine. Pour over hot potatoes and zucchini. Toss to coat. Cover with plastic wrap and refrigerate. Makes 4 servings.

CUCUMBER-DILL RIBBON SALAD

1 seedless cucumber*
2 T. white vinegar
¼ c. chopped fresh dill or 1 T. dried
⅛ tsp. ground white pepper
Seedless cucumbers are also known as gourmet cucumbers, usually sold wrapped in plastic.

Cut cucumber lengthwise into very thin slices (see photo). Place in bowl of ice cubes and water to curl. Just before serving, dry on paper towels and toss with vinegar, dill and pepper. Makes 4 servings.

HOW TO MAKE
CUCUMBER RIBBONS

Using a vegetable peeler, cut a seedless cucumber lengthwise into paper-thin slices. When you reach the center, turn and cut from the other side.

elegant fish

BROILED BLUEFISH WITH MUSTARD SAUCE

STEAMED RADISHES AND SCALLIONS

PEACH ICE CREAM WITH AMARETTO PEACHES

MUSCADET OR CHABLIS

You may not have time to go fishing, but you can fillet your own bluefish in about 5 minutes—or you can buy fillets. The bluefish is sweet; the mustard sauce, creamy and tangy. Paired with crisp steamed radishes and scallions, this dinner looks and tastes fabulous. Start by broiling the bluefish. Then, while the fish cooks, make the mustard sauce and steam the vegetables. For a sophisticated presentation, spoon some sauce onto each dinner plate first; then arrange fish and vegetables on top. For dessert: peaches and ice cream amaretto. Toss ripe peach wedges with honey and amaretto liqueur. Serve over peach ice cream with cinnamon cookies.

BROILED BLUEFISH WITH MUSTARD SAUCE

4 bluefish fillets, about 1½ lbs.
1 T. butter or margarine
1 tsp. dried rosemary
½ tsp. dried thyme leaves, crumbled
⅛ tsp. freshly ground black pepper
3 T. Dijon mustard
¼ c. water
2 tsp. fresh lemon juice
¾ c. heavy or whipping cream

Heat broiler. Arrange fish fillets on a foil-lined broiler pan. Dot with butter; sprinkle with rosemary, thyme and black pepper. Broil 8 to 10 minutes or until fish flakes when tested with a fork. Meanwhile, in a small saucepan stir together the mustard, water, lemon juice and cream. Simmer over medium heat for 5 minutes. Spoon ¼ cup sauce onto each plate; arrange fish and vegetables on top. Makes 4 servings.

STEAMED RADISHES AND SCALLIONS

2 bunches scallions, trimmed
2 bunches radishes

Cut scallions into 4-inch lengths. Trim leaves and stems from radishes. Steam scallions over boiling water for 1 minute. Add radishes; steam 2 minutes more. Makes 4 servings.

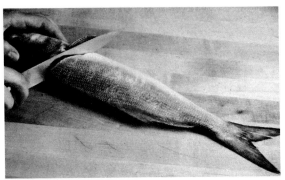

FILLETING A BLUEFISH

● *Make a cut just to the bone just behind the gills.*
● *Hold the knife almost horizontal to the fish; insert in cut and cut along the spine to free the backbone until you reach the tail. Now return to the area behind the gills, drawing the knife gently against the bones to loosen and remove the fillet. Turn fish over; repeat to remove second fillet.*

low-calorie treat

FISH EN PAPILLOTE
SWEET POTATO PURÉE WITH ORANGE ZEST
SNOW PEA PODS
WHOLE-WHEAT PITA BREAD
SPICED GRAPEFRUIT
WHITE WINE

Here's a low-calorie cooking technique to add to your repertoire. *En papillote,* which means "in parchment," seals in moisture and flavor without adding calories. In an expensive French restaurant, parchment paper would be used; this version uses aluminum foil, which works just as well. This fish is subtly seasoned with ginger, scallions, lemon and freshly ground black pepper. Experiment by adding fresh herbs, if you like, such as dill, tarragon or basil and use lime or orange slices instead of lemon. Start by preparing the fish *en papillote,* then make the scrumptious side dish, Sweet Potato Purée. At the last minute, bake the fish and sauté the pea pods. Serve warmed whole-wheat pita and a dry white wine. For dessert, broil grapefruit halves and top with a drizzle of honey, a pinch of nutmeg and cinnamon and a sprinkling of brandy.

FISH EN PAPILLOTE
Calories: 100 per serving

2 firm-flesh fish fillets, about 6 oz. each, such as cod or halibut
1 scallion, julienned
1 lemon, sliced thinly
¼ tsp. minced fresh ginger
Salt
Freshly ground black pepper

Heat oven to 350°F. Place fish on foil. Top with scallion, lemon, ginger, salt and pepper. Seal. (See photos.) Bake fish about 10 minutes per inch of thickness. Makes 2 servings.

SWEET POTATO PURÉE
Calories: 200 per serving

1 large sweet potato
4 tsp. butter or margarine
1 T. orange juice
Zest of ½ orange

Peel and cut sweet potato into 1-inch chunks. In medium saucepan heat 1 inch lightly salted water to boiling. Add potato. Reduce heat to low; cover and simmer about 15 minutes. Place sweet potato and remaining ingredients in a food processor or use a mixer on medium speed. Blend until smooth. Makes 2 servings.

SEAL EN PAPILLOTE

Cut four circles of foil, about 10 inches in diameter, depending on the size of fish. (1) Place each fillet on one of the circles. Distribute the scallion, lemon, ginger and pepper over the fish. (2) Cover each fillet with another piece of foil; crimp edges.

taste of the shore

CRAB CAKES

HOT SLAW

BISCUITS

BUTTER-PECAN ICE CREAM WITH BOURBON

t's late afternoon—time to round up three friends for a cozy, delicious, yet light, supper. This menu features easy-to-make crab cakes and a warm cole slaw that you're sure to love. Mix the crab cake ingredients and refrigerate while you prepare the vegetables for the Hot Slaw. About 10 minutes before you're ready to eat, shape and cook the crab cakes and cook the onion slices for the slaw. Heat biscuits or rolls to serve alongside. For dessert, scoop out butter-pecan ice cream; douse each bowlful with a good splash of bourbon.

CRAB CAKES

**1 lb. fresh crabmeat,
    or frozen crab, thawed
¾ c. fresh bread crumbs
¼ c. chopped fresh parsley
    (see photos)
2 T. finely chopped scallions
2 T. fresh lime juice
½ tsp. Worcestershire sauce
1 egg
3 T. butter or margarine
Lime wedges**

Pick over the crabmeat and remove any shell or cartilage bits. Flake crab into a large bowl. Add remaining ingredients except butter and lime wedges. Mix until combined. (Chill crab while you make the slaw.) Shape into eight 2½-inch patties. In large skillet over medium-high heat, melt butter. Arrange crab cakes in skillet. Reduce heat to medium. Cook crab cakes until golden brown, approximately 4 minutes on each side. Drain on paper towels. Serve with lime wedges. Makes 4 servings.

HOT SLAW

**1 T. olive or vegetable oil
¼ tsp. crushed red pepper flakes
1 medium onion, sliced
4 c. slivered green cabbage
    (¼ large head)
1 medium carrot, peeled, cut into
    matchstick-thin pieces
1 small red pepper, cored, seeded,
    cut into matchstick-thin pieces
1 T. fresh lemon juice**

In a large skillet over medium-high heat, heat oil with red pepper flakes. Add the onion and cook over low heat for 5 minutes. Stir in the vegetables and cook until the cabbage is just wilted and the vegetables are heated through. Toss with lemon juice. Makes 4 servings.

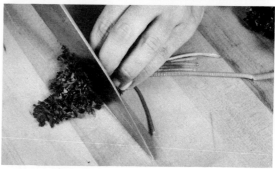

*HOW TO CHOP
FRESH PARSLEY*

*Rinse and dry fresh parsley.
Gather sprigs into a tight
bouquet by twisting stems.
Holding parsley by stems,
chop the leaves finely.*

lobster dinner

LOBSTER TAILS IN CHAMPAGNE SAUCE

PAN-ROASTED POTATOES

GREEN BEANS

ROLLS WITH SWEET BUTTER

ASSORTED CHOCOLATES

CHAMPAGNE

The two of you deserve something special. So, try this very special meal. It's delicious, it's romantic and yes, it's a splurge. Use lobster tails. You can buy them frozen from your fish market. A bottle of champagne or sparkling wine will be festive. Use a little for the sauce, and the rest is for you. Here's how to make this entire feast in thirty minutes. Start with the lobster. While it simmers in the champagne (be sure to keep the rest of the bottle on ice), you'll have time to do the potatoes. Frozen green beans take only 5 minutes to cook, and you can squeeze them in between jobs. To keep things simple, serve your favorite assortment of chocolates for dessert.

LOBSTER TAILS IN CHAMPAGNE SAUCE

3 frozen lobster tails, partially frozen*
⅔ c. champagne or sparkling wine
2 scallions, minced
¼ tsp. salt
¼ c. heavy or whipping cream
4 T. unsalted butter or margarine
2 scallions, cut into very thin strips for garnish
one for you, two for him

Rinse lobster tails. In skillet, combine lobster, champagne, scallions and salt. Over high heat, heat to boiling. Reduce heat to low. Cover and simmer 15 minutes. Remove lobster. Add cream to sauce in skillet. Boil sauce quickly until reduced to about ⅓ cup. With a whisk, beat in butter, one tablespoon at a time, until smooth. Keep warm. Remove lobster from shells (see photos). Slice into medallions. Spoon sauce over each. Sprinkle with scallions. Makes 2 servings.

PAN-ROASTED POTATOES

3 medium potatoes
3 T. butter or margarine
1 T. olive or vegetable oil
¼ tsp. salt
⅛ tsp. freshly ground black pepper

Peel potatoes. Cut each in half. In skillet, melt butter with oil. Add potatoes, salt and pepper; cook over medium heat until browned on all sides. Cover; cook 5 minutes or until fork-tender. Makes 2 servings.

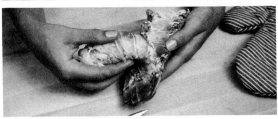

HANDLE A LOBSTER TAIL WITH EASE

The easiest way to unshell a lobster tail is with a good pair of sharp scissors. Start by cutting along the underside of the tail, first on one side, then the other. Gently pull all the meat from the shell. Place the lobster tail flat on a cutting board, then use a sharp knife to cut into ¼- to ½-inch pieces.

low-calorie seafood feast

SCALLOPS PROVENÇAL

RICE WITH PEAS AND PARSLEY

CARROT AND SPROUT SALAD

ICY PINEAPPLE

SPARKLING WATER

Don't feel deprived when dieting. Instead, use lots of fresh ingredients for sensational flavor without lots of fattening butters and sauces. Another trick: Make your meal look special. Dress up your plate with bright green chicory. Start by getting the salad and rice ready, so you can keep a close eye on the scallops while they're cooking. Keep a batch of fresh-frozen fruit on hand for a cool dessert. Try icy pineapple, for example. Cut a pineapple into slices or chunks; place on a cookie sheet and pop into the freezer until just firm.

SCALLOPS PROVENÇAL
Calories: 125 per serving

3 T. butter or margarine
1 lb. fresh sea scallops
 or frozen scallops, thawed
1 garlic clove, minced
2 tomatoes, peeled and chopped
3 T. chopped fresh basil,
 or 1 T. dried
½ tsp. salt
⅛ tsp. freshly ground black pepper
3 scallions, cut into matchstick-
 thin pieces

In large skillet over medium-high heat, melt 2 tablespoons butter. Pat scallops dry on paper towels. Cook scallops in hot butter until opaque and lightly browned. Remove scallops to platter; keep warm. Add remaining 1 tablespoon butter to skillet. Add garlic. Cook 1 minute. Add tomatoes, basil, salt and pepper. Cook until tomatoes render their juices, about 3 to 5 minutes. Return scallops to skillet; add scallions; heat through. Makes 6 servings.

RICE WITH PEAS AND PARSLEY
Calories: 135 per serving

1 c. long-grain rice
½ c. fresh peas, cooked,
 or frozen peas, thawed
½ c. minced fresh parsley

Cook rice according to package directions. When done, stir in peas and parsley; heat through. Makes 6 servings.

CARROT AND SPROUT SALAD
Calories: 20 per serving

3 large carrots, cleaned
1 c. alfalfa sprouts
Salt
Freshly ground black pepper
Fresh lemon juice

Use food processor or coarse grater to shred carrots. Combine with alfalfa sprouts. Sprinkle with salt and pepper and lemon juice to taste. Makes 6 servings.

FASTEST WAY
TO PEEL A TOMATO

Spear the tomato with a fork and lower into a pan of simmering water. Hold it there while you slowly count one-one hundred, two-one hundred, up to ten. Voilà. The tomato won't be cooked, but the skin will slip off easily when you coax it with a knife.

delicious diet dinner

SHRIMP EN BROCHETTE

HERBED RICE

DILLED CARROTS

MELON

MINERAL WATER

Treat yourself like someone really special tonight; make this luscious dinner. "Too much trouble just for me," you say? Nonsense. You're dieting you say? The whole meal, *including* dessert, has about 430 calories. To make this diet meal look not so diet, serve it on smaller plates, such as a luncheon-sized plate; that way the smaller-sized portions will look like more. The first step is to marinate the shrimp. Next, put the rice on to cook. Then cut the carrots into matchstick-thin pieces. Here's how: Cut carrot into ⅛-inch-thick slices. Stack several slices and cut into ⅛-inch-thick strips. Last, thread the shrimp on a skewer and broil. The secret to great shrimp is not to overcook them, so set the timer. While the rice simmers, the shrimp broil and the carrots steam, set a pretty tray. Enjoy a cold glass of sparkling mineral water freshened with lime. Remember to eat slowly and savor every bite. For dessert, cut open a juicy melon and portion a half if small, and a quarter if large for yourself. A squirt of fresh lime will enliven the flavors.

SHRIMP EN BROCHETTE
Calories: 165

**¼ lb. medium shrimp, cleaned and
    deveined (about 6–8)***
6 small mushrooms
2 T. fresh lemon juice
1 garlic clove, minced
1 tsp. olive or vegetable oil
1 tsp. grated ginger
Dash Tabasco
*If using frozen, thaw first

Combine all ingredients in small bowl. Set aside to marinate 10 to 15 minutes. Heat broiler. Thread shrimp and mushrooms alternately on one or two skewers. Reserve marinade. Broil 3 minutes. Turn, baste with reserved marinade and broil 2 to 3 minutes longer until shrimp are pink and opaque. (Don't overcook—the shrimp will become tough.) Makes 1 serving.

HERBED RICE
Calories: 160

½ c. water
⅛ tsp. salt
¼ c. uncooked long-grain rice
1 T. minced scallion
1 T. minced parsley

In small saucepan over high heat, heat water and salt to boiling. Stir in rice. Heat to boiling. Reduce heat to low, cover and simmer 15 minutes or until rice is tender and liquid is absorbed. With fork, fold in scallions and parsley. Makes 1 serving.

HOW TO GRATE GINGER

Grated ginger has a more pronounced flavor than when it's simply minced. Use a Japanese ginger grater and gently yet firmly rub the ginger in small circular motions. The finest side of a regular grater will work, too.

Southwestern feast for two

SPICY SHRIMP IN TORTILLAS

RICE

GARLICKY GREENS

BEER

KIOKE COFFEE

This dinner is bold and gutsy—spicy shrimp in tortillas. It's the kind of meal that you want to roll up your sleeves and get into. Make it with shrimp, but an equal amount of cooked chicken can be substituted, too. For a crunchy and piquant accompaniment, serve the garlic-scented greens; use cabbage or kale or romaine lettuce. To finish in 30 minutes, start with the rice, then make the filling. Mash half an avocado for garnish. Fill the tortillas and keep them warm. Then, sauté the shredded cabbage. Beer is wonderful with this meal. For dessert, Kioke coffee: Add splashes of both brandy and Kahlua liqueur to mugs of coffee, topped with whipped cream.

SPICY SHRIMP IN TORTILLAS

6 flour tortillas
2 T. olive or vegetable oil
1 medium onion, chopped
1 large garlic clove, minced
2 tomatoes, chopped
1 fresh jalapeño, minced,
**   or 1 4-oz. can chilies, drained**
**   and chopped**
½ lb. cleaned and shelled fresh or
**   frozen medium shrimp**
3 T. fresh lime juice
2 T. chopped fresh coriander
**   (cilantro), or 3 T. chopped fresh**
**   parsley plus a pinch of ground**
**   cumin**
½ tsp. salt
½ avocado, mashed with 1 T. fresh
**   lime juice**
2 heaping tablespoons sour cream
1 lime, cut into wedges
2 scallions, sliced

Wrap tortillas loosely in aluminum foil and heat in 300°F oven. Meanwhile in large skillet over medium heat, heat oil. Add onion and garlic and sauté until tender. Add tomatoes, chilies and shrimp. Cook, stirring gently, until shrimp turn pink and opaque. Fold in lime juice, coriander and salt. Working with one tortilla at a time, fill and fold (see photos). Keep warm on a platter in a 200°F oven while preparing the remaining tortillas. To serve, overlap three tortillas on a plate. Garnish each plate with a spoonful of avocado, sour cream, a few lime wedges and scatter with sliced scallions. Makes 2 servings.

GARLICKY GREENS

2 T. olive or vegetable oil
1 garlic clove, crushed
2 c. shredded cabbage
**   (about ¼ medium head)**
**   or other hearty green**
¼ tsp. salt
Freshly ground black pepper

In a large skillet over high heat, heat oil until hot. Add garlic and sauté until golden; discard garlic. Add cabbage to the flavored oil in skillet, and cook until cabbage is just limp, about 3 to 5 minutes. Sprinkle with salt and pepper if desired. Makes 2 servings.

TO FOLD THE TORTILLAS

Spoon some of the sautéed shrimp onto one quarter of a warm flour tortilla. Fold in half and then again in half, making a triangular package.

finger food dinner

CHILLED PICKLED SHRIMP

PEARL HARBORS

AVOCADO, TOMATOES AND CHEESES

MUSTARD MAYONNAISE

MUSCADET

When it's too hot to spend time in the kitchen—here's a cool entrée that's big on taste and short on fuss. Serve Pearl Harbors for cocktails. (They get their name from the Japanese-made liqueur and Hawaiian pineapple.) Start by making Chilled Pickled Shrimp. While the boiled shrimp are cooling, cover a huge platter or tray with crisp lettuce. Then, arrange slices of creamy avocado and juicy tomatoes, cornichon or your favorite pickles, a runny-ripe Brie, a wedge of Havarti with caraway seeds, grapes, crusty bread and sweet butter. Make it as big as you want—one pound of shrimp and two pounds of cheese with the fruit and bread will easily serve six. Try stirring a spoonful of prepared mustard into a cup of mayonnaise to spread on cheeses or to use as a dip for the shrimp. A dry white wine, such as a Muscadet, completes the feast.

CHILLED PICKLED SHRIMP

1 lb. medium shrimp in shells
1 12-oz. can beer
8 peppercorns
1 bay leaf
1 tsp. dried dill weed
1 garlic clove, crushed
½ tsp. salt

In medium saucepan over high heat, heat all ingredients to boiling. Cover and remove from heat. Let stand 4 minutes, covered, or until shrimp curl and turn pink and opaque. Drain. Place in freezer to chill quickly. When cool enough to handle, drain, shell and devein shrimp, (see photos). Makes 6 servings.

PEARL HARBOR

Ice
1 ½ oz. vodka
1 T. melon liqueur
4 oz. pineapple juice
Lime wedge

For each serving, fill a tall glass with ice. Add vodka, melon liqueur and pineapple juice. Stir until mixed. Garnish with lime. Makes 1 serving.

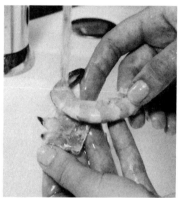

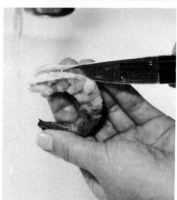

WORKING WITH FRESH SHRIMP

For best flavor, cook the shrimp and then shell: Leave on the tail and adjoining end-shell section for prettiest presentation. Devein with a small sharp knife by cutting a slit down the center of the outer curved side. Rinse.

Salads left to right:
Red Pepper and Snap Bean, page 150
Tabouli, page 151
Bean and Sausage, page 150
Corn and Beef, page 148
Asparagus with Orange Sauce, page 177

Serve a selection of salads and a choice of red or white wine

When it's your turn to
Entertain

This chapter is an indispensable party-planning source for stress-free, foolproof entertaining. Whether you enjoy a large gathering of friends for cocktails, a smaller buffet open house or intimate dinners for two or four, you'll find lots of options here, ranging from dressed-up and classy to down-home and relaxed. To make it simpler for you to choose the type of party you want to throw, this chapter is divided into warm- and cool-weather entertaining. The summer party recipes make the most of the season, using plenty of fresh fruits and vegetables—all are fast and easy. Who wants to spend hours stirring and basting when the tennis court, beach or backyard hammock beckons? The winter parties are hearty and warming. They are sparkling holiday feasts or leisurely cozy meals meant to be shared with friends on cold evenings. Time-saving tips will keep jitters to a minimum, from the planning stages to the last departing guest's goodbye hug. Photographs of the food and how-to preparations will help eliminate the chance of foul-ups in the kitchen. You will see that the meals and dishes are stylish, but not fussy. One last word: Any party you give should have *your* special touch. If you'd like to switch recipes from one party to another or include a favorite family recipe, go right ahead. And don't let the seasonal categories limit you either. There may be a drink or hors d'oeuvre idea in one section that you think would be just as good, or better, in another. By all means switch. It's fun to experiment.

cool-start breakfast

Eggs, scrambled and crowned with caviar and chives

A wonderful beginning to a summer's day, breakfast with friends

LEMON-BLUEBERRY MUFFINS ● BANANA-DATE BRAN MUFFINS

STRAWBERRY-YOGURT MUFFINS ● OATMEAL CHOCOLATE-CHIP MUFFINS

HONEY BUTTER WITH CINNAMON

LEMON CREAM-CHEESE SPREAD

SUCCULENT SUMMER SALAD

SCRAMBLED EGGS WITH CHIVES AND CAVIAR

CAFÉ AU LAIT ● CHAMPAGNE

Gently fold berries into batter

Get the fun going early and fuel up for the activities of the day ahead—in summer you don't want to miss a minute of daylight. The cheery, high-energy fare to prepare: scrambled eggs laced with aromatic chives and crowned with sparkling beads of salmon caviar; a fresh fruit salad that stars the season's best; a muffin sampler of hearty fruit-studded variations. Give your guests a choice of sweet, honey-and-cinnamon-laced butter or citrusy Lemon Cream-Cheese to spread on muffins. Make lots of steaming, bracing Café au Lait. To get the party spirit flowing, have plenty of chilled champagne on hand. Muffins can be baked and frozen up to two months before party time, reheated just before guests arrive. Or bake them the morning of the party to fill the air with the appetizing aroma. Muffin spreads can be made a day ahead and kept refrigerated, the fruit salad can be made the evening before, and that's when to put the champagne "on ice," too. The day of the party, just put out muffins and spreads, fresh fruit salad and champagne on ice, and brew the coffee. Once guests have arrived, scramble the eggs and gather 'round.

LEMON-BLUEBERRY MUFFINS

1¾ c. all-purpose flour
½ c. plus 2 T. sugar
2 tsp. baking powder
¼ tsp. salt
½ c. chopped walnuts
1 tsp. grated lemon peel
2 eggs
1 c. milk
4 T. melted butter or margarine
1 tsp. vanilla
1½ c. blueberries

Heat oven to 400°F. Grease a 12-cup muffin tin or line tin with cupcake papers. In a large bowl combine flour, sugar, baking powder and salt. Stir in walnuts and lemon peel. In a small bowl beat eggs, milk, butter and vanilla. Pour egg mixture into dry ingredients and stir just until flour is moistened (batter will be lumpy). Fold in blueberries. Spoon into muffin cups and bake 20 to 22 minutes or until tops are golden. Makes 12 muffins.

BANANA-DATE BRAN MUFFINS

1 c. All-bran cereal
¼ c. milk
1⅓ c. mashed ripe bananas
1¼ c. all-purpose flour
¼ c. sugar
1 tsp. baking soda
½ tsp. salt
½ c. chopped pitted dates
2 eggs
4 T. melted butter or margarine
1 tsp. vanilla

Heat oven to 400°F. Grease a 12-cup muffin tin or line tin with cupcake papers. In a small bowl combine bran with milk and bananas. Set aside and let stand for 5 minutes. In another bowl stir together flour, sugar, baking soda, salt and dates. Beat eggs, butter, and vanilla into bran mixture and add to dry ingredients. Stir just until flour is moistened (batter will be lumpy). Spoon into muffin cups. Bake 20 minutes or until tops are golden. Makes 12 muffins.

STRAWBERRY-YOGURT MUFFINS

2 c. all-purpose flour
½ c. sugar
1½ tsp. baking soda
½ tsp. salt
2 eggs
1 c. plain, low-fat yogurt
4 T. butter or margarine, melted
1 tsp. vanilla
1 c. chopped fresh strawberries

Heat oven to 375°F. Grease a 12-cup muffin tin or line tin with cupcake papers. In bowl combine flour, sugar, baking soda and salt. In another bowl beat together eggs, yogurt, butter and vanilla until blended. Toss strawberries with dry ingredients. Stir egg mixture into dry ingredients just until flour is moistened. Spoon into muffin cups. Bake 20 to 23 minutes or until tops are golden. Makes 12 muffins.

OATMEAL CHOCOLATE-CHIP MUFFINS

1 c. boiling water
⅔ c. oatmeal (not instant)
4 T. butter or margarine, cut into cubes
1½ c. all-purpose flour
½ c. brown sugar
1 tsp. baking powder
1 tsp. baking soda
½ tsp. salt
½ tsp. cinnamon
½ c. semisweet-chocolate pieces
2 eggs
1 tsp. vanilla

Heat oven to 400°F. Grease a 12-cup muffin tin or line tin with cupcake papers. In small bowl stir together boiling water, oatmeal and butter. Set aside and let stand for 20 minutes. In a large bowl combine flour, brown sugar, baking powder, baking soda, salt and cinnamon. Add chocolate pieces. Beat eggs and vanilla into oatmeal. Stir oatmeal mixture into dry ingredients just until flour is moistened (batter will be lumpy). Spoon into muffin cups. Bake 20 minutes or until tops are golden. Makes 12 muffins.

Note: To make ahead, cool muffins completely. Wrap individually in aluminum foil and freeze up to two months. To reheat, place unwrapped muffins in heated 325°F oven for 10 minutes or until heated through.

SUCCULENT SUMMER SALAD

1 small ripe honeydew melon
2 ripe cantaloupe melons
4 oranges
2 c. strawberries, hulled
1½ c. blueberries

Halve, seed, peel and cut melons into 1-inch chunks. Peel oranges, leaving no white membrane, and slice horizontally into rounds. Combine melon chunks, oranges, strawberries and blueberries in large bowl and chill until serving time. Makes 8 servings.

HONEY BUTTER WITH CINNAMON

1 lb. unsalted butter, softened
2 T. honey
½ tsp. ground cinnamon

With wooden spoon or in a food processor with knife blade attached, combine butter with honey and cinnamon until smooth. Makes 2 cups.

LEMON CREAM-CHEESE SPREAD

2 8-oz. pkgs. cream cheese, softened
1 T. freshly grated lemon peel
1 T. fresh lemon juice

With wooden spoon or in a food processor with knife blade, combine cream cheese with peel and juice until smooth. Makes 2 cups.

CAFÉ AU LAIT

1 qt.(4 c.) milk
1 qt. (4 c.) hot, strong coffee or espresso

In saucepan over medium-high heat, heat milk until foam begins to form around the edges of pan. Pour equal parts of heated milk and hot coffee into 8 large mugs or cups and serve. Makes 8 servings.

Sparkling fruit; sparkling wine

Quiche spiked with peppers, sausage flecked with cilantro

brunch for a balmy day

LEMON-FLAVORED VODKA WITH TOMATO OR ORANGE JUICE

JALAPEÑO QUICHE WITH SALSA

PORK SAUSAGE WITH CILANTRO

EARLY SUMMER SALAD

CORN BREAD STICKS

RASPBERRY TART WITH CRÈME FRAÎCHE

Raspberries in a nutted crust

LEMON-FLAVORED VODKA

Cut the rind from one large lemon, being careful not to peel off the bitter white part. Place the rind in one liter of vodka and let steep for 48 hours at room temperature. Refrigerate or place in freezer. Serve well-chilled straight up or mixed with tomato or orange juice.

JALAPEÑO QUICHE

CRUST:
12 T. butter or margarine
1½ c. all-purpose flour
½ tsp. salt
4-6 T. cold water
FILLING:
1 medium onion, chopped
1 sweet green pepper, seeded and
**   chopped**
1 sweet red pepper, seeded and
**   chopped**
2 fresh jalapeño peppers, seeded
**   and chopped, or 1 4-oz. can**
**   chilies, drained and chopped**
2 T. butter or margarine
1 c. sharp Cheddar cheese,
**   shredded**
4 eggs, beaten
1 c. heavy or whipping cream
1 ½ tsp. salt
Salsa (recipe follows)

With fingertips, cut butter into flour and salt until mixture is the consistency of coarse corn meal. Add only enough cold water to hold dough together. Shape into ball. Roll dough out into 12-inch circle. Lay in 9-inch tart pan with removable bottom; trim edges (see photos, page 22). Prick bottom and sides with fork. Line with foil, fill with dried beans or pie weights. Heat oven to 400°F. Bake 10 minutes. Remove pie weights and foil, prick again and bake 5 minutes longer or until pastry begins to brown. Cool on wire rack. Reduce oven to 375°F. In skillet over medium-low heat, cook onion, peppers and chilies in hot butter or margarine until onion is tender. Sprinkle half the cheese in bottom of cooled pie shell. Top with onions and peppers. Sprinkle on remaining cheese. In bowl, beat eggs, cream and salt together. Pour over cheese. Bake 35 to 40 minutes or until set. Cool for 5 minutes before cutting. Serve with Salsa and hot sauce if desired. This is enough for 4 to 6 servings. To serve 8, make two.

Wake up to a lazy day—Sunday is always a good choice—with this brunch menu. The recipes are easy to adjust to any size party. Make one or two quiches, depending on the number of guests. This is a party that's high on satisfaction, easy on your energy. Do the cooking in stages, and on the day of the brunch your work will be a snap. For example, make the crusts for the quiche and the Raspberry Tart the day ahead. The sausage can be mixed the night before, too. Shape the sausage into patties and wrap well in plastic wrap. Refrigerate them until ready to cook. Make the Lemon-Flavored Vodka up to one month ahead. Store it in the freezer until the party—it will get richly syrupy. Serve it straight up, mixed with orange juice or splashed into tomato juice. You can simplify by buying the corn sticks, or make your own in advance and freeze. Be sure to have lots of butter for the cornbread. The salsa recipe included in this menu is simple and fast, but store-bought is fine, too. Have extra hot sauce to spike up the already spicy quiche for the fire-eaters among your friends, and plenty of juices to cool off heated palates.

SALSA

1 16-oz. can tomatoes
6 jalapeño peppers, seeded and
  chopped or 2 4-oz. cans chilies,
  drained and chopped
1 T. red wine vinegar
1 tsp. salt

Put tomatoes and their liquid in a medium saucepan and break them up with a wooden spoon. Add chili peppers, vinegar and salt. Simmer, uncovered, stirring frequently until slightly thickened. Serve with Jalapeño Quiche. Makes about 1 cup.

PORK SAUSAGE WITH CILANTRO

1⅓ lbs. lean ground pork
⅔ lb. pork fat
2 tsp. salt
1 tsp. freshly ground black pepper
½ tsp. ground red pepper
1 c. chopped fresh coriander
  or ½ c. chopped parsley plus
  ½ tsp. ground cumin
About ¼ c. oil

In bowl, combine all ingredients except oil. Pinch off small portions and fry in a little oil until no longer pink. Taste for seasoning, adding more salt and pepper if necessary. (Never taste raw pork.) Shape heaping tablespoons into patties. Heat small amount of oil in large skillet. Cook patties 5 to 7 minutes per side until no pink remains in center, adding more oil if necessary. Drain on paper towels; serve hot. Makes 8 servings.

EARLY SUMMER SALAD

2 large bunches fresh spinach
  (about 1½ lb.)
1 small head radicchio (or red
  lettuce)
2 small heads Belgian endive
VINAIGRETTE:
½ c. olive oil
2 T. lemon juice
2 scallions, minced
2 T. minced fresh parsley
½ tsp. salt
¼ tsp. freshly ground black pepper

Wash and dry greens. Place in salad bowl. In small jar with tight fitting lid, combine vinaigrette ingredients. Shake until well combined. Toss with greens. Makes 8 servings.

RASPBERRY TART

CRUST:
1 c. walnuts
½ c. unsalted butter or margarine,
  softened
3 T. sugar
1½ c. all-purpose flour
1 egg yolk, beaten
½ tsp. vanilla
FILLING:
1 pts. fresh raspberries
1 pkg. unflavored gelatin
2 T. black raspberry liqueur
1 10-oz. jar red currant jelly
Crème Fraîche (recipe follows)
  or unsweetened whipped cream

Mix ground nuts and remaining crust ingredients until just blended. Press into buttered 9-inch tart pan with removable bottom. Chill 1 hour. Heat oven to 350°F. Bake 15 to 20 minutes or until crust begins to brown. Cool completely on wire rack. Fill tart shell with berries. In small saucepan, combine gelatin and liqueur; let soften 1 minute. Add jelly and stir over low heat until smooth and gelatin has dissolved. Remove from heat, cool slightly and spoon over berries. Refrigerate 1 hour or until set. Serve with crème fraîche or unsweetened whipped cream. Makes 8 servings.

CRÈME FRAÎCHE

2 c. heavy or whipping cream
1 T. buttermilk

Pour the cream into a clean glass jar. Stir in the buttermilk. Cover tightly with lid or plastic wrap. Let stand at room temperature 12 hours or overnight or until cream has thickened to the consistency of lightly whipped yogurt. Place in refrigerator and use within two weeks. Makes 2 cups.

summer dinner party

Spiked berries and sherbet and macaroons

SALMON PÂTÉ WITH HERBED MAYONNAISE

CHILLED FINO SHERRY

BASIL-STUFFED BREAST OF VEAL

NUTTED WILD RICE

TOMATOES WITH FRESH DILL

GREEN BEAN AND ONION SALAD

FRENCH BREAD

ORANGE ICE WITH TEQUILA SOAKED STRAWBERRIES

CHOCOLATE MACAROONS

COFFEE

CALIFORNIA MERLOT WINE

A dazzling dinner bursting with color

Romance your guests with this dinner party of make-ahead foods. Dine outdoors or inside with plenty of pretty and summery plants. All recipes serve eight. You and your guests will probably be most comfortable served at the dining table or on large buffet plates atop TV tables. Start with the Salmon Pâté and homemade mayonnaise. It really isn't hard to make if you have a food processor. If not, stir the flavorings—watercress, parsley and scallions into store-bought mayonnaise. The main course, a veal breast rolled around basil, spinach and tomatoes, is best served at room temperature. Make it ahead and refrigerate. On the day of the party take it out of the fridge and let it lose its chill before serving. The rice salad, too, can be made the day before and actually benefits from the extra time that the flavors have to blend. Slice or cut the summer's juiciest, brightest tomatoes to toss with dill and olive oil...select a dark green, fruity olive oil for this salad. The salad and the green beans should be prepared as close to serving time as possible. A hearty Merlot wine is the choice here. The flavors in the meal are assertive and can handle this mellow red. Or, if you prefer, select a full-flavored white such as a California Chardonnay. Marinate the strawberries in a tequila bath in the morning, before the party. The macaroons can be made ahead, too, if you store them in an air-tight tin. Check the weather forecast...if high humidity is on the way, instead of macaroons, which could get soggy, buy chocolate sugar cookies or try the recipe for Chocolate Heart Cookies on page 206.

SALMON PÂTÉ

**1½ lb. fresh salmon,
   skinned and boned
½ c. heavy or whipping cream
6 large eggs
1 tsp. fresh lemon juice
¼ tsp. salt
⅛ tsp. freshly ground pepper
Herbed Mayonnaise
   (recipe follows)
Radishes, for garnish**

Purée salmon in food processor or blender with remaining ingredients except mayonnaise and radishes. Heat to 350°F. Butter 8- by 4-inch loaf

pan; line bottom with waxed paper. Pour in salmon mixture, cover with foil. Place loaf in large baking dish. Pour in hot water to come 2 to 3 inches up the side of loaf pan. Bake 50 minutes or until set. Cool to room temperature; refrigerate, covered with foil, overnight with several soup cans on top (this weights pâté to make a firm texture that's easy to slice). To serve, run a knife around the edges; invert to unmold. Cut 16 slices. Serve with Herbed Mayonnaise, and garnish with radishes. Makes 8 servings.

HERBED MAYONNAISE

**2 large egg yolks, at room
   temperature
1 T. fresh lemon juice
¼ tsp. salt
⅛ tsp. freshly ground pepper
2 c. vegetable oil
1 c. watercress leaves, chopped
¼ c. chopped fresh parsley
4 scallions, finely chopped**

In food processor with knife blade in place or in blender container, combine egg yolks, lemon juice, salt and pepper. With motor running, starting with ¼ cup oil, add ½ teaspoon at a time, until it emulsifies and thickens. Add remaining oil in very fine stream. Work in watercress, parsley and scallions until mayonnaise turns green. Makes about 2½ cups.

BASIL-STUFFED BREAST OF VEAL

**3-4 lb. boneless breast of veal
2 T. unsalted butter or margarine
1 medium onion, chopped
1 garlic clove, minced
1 10-oz. pkg. frozen spinach,
   thawed and squeezed until
   very, very dry
1 c. tightly packed fresh basil
   leaves
¼ tsp. freshly ground black pepper
⅓ c. grated Parmesan cheese
1 egg
1 6½-oz. jar (6 tomatoes),
   oil-packed
   sundried tomatoes, julienned,
   or substitute 6 canned roasted
   red peppers, cut into thin strips
2 c. chicken broth**

Note: Have your butcher bone veal breast and prepare for rolling. You will need 3 to 4 pounds of meat after boning. Have the butcher trim every bit of fat. If not well trimmed, it will be fatty and unappetizing.

In skillet in hot butter, sauté onion until limp. Reduce heat, add garlic and cook, stirring constantly, about 3 minutes. Add spinach, basil, pepper, Parmesan, egg and dried tomatoes. Spread on the breast evenly, leaving a ½-inch border. Roll up lengthwise (not too tightly) and secure with skewers. Heat oven to 400°F. Place roast on rack in a pan. Pour broth into pan. Cover tightly with foil. Roast for 30 minutes. Reduce heat to 350°F and roast 1½ hours longer. Insert tip of a knife into the thickest part of breast. Juice should run clear. (May be made up to this point up to one day ahead. Cool and refrigerate, return to room temperature before serving.) Remove to carving board or platter and let rest at least 25 minutes before slicing. Remove skewers and carve into ½-inch thick slices. Makes 8 servings.

NUTTED WILD RICE

1 c. (½ lb.) raw wild rice
5½ c. chicken broth or water
1 c. pecan halves
1 c. golden raisins
Grated rind of 1 large orange
¼ c. olive oil
⅓ c. fresh orange juice
1½ tsp. salt
Freshly ground black pepper

Put rice in strainer and rinse under cold water. Combine rice with chicken broth in heavy medium saucepan. Heat to boiling. Reduce heat to low, and simmer, uncovered, 30 to 35 minutes or until rice is tender, but not too soft. Drain. In medium bowl, toss rice with remaining ingredients. Cover and let stand 2 hours for flavors to develop. Makes 8 servings.

TOMATOES WITH FRESH DILL

6 large ripe tomatoes
¼ c. olive oil
¼ c. minced fresh dill or 2 T. dried
1 tsp. salt
¼ tsp. freshly ground black pepper

Cut tomatoes into wedges. Toss with remaining ingredients. Makes 8 servings.

GREEN BEAN AND ONION SALAD

2 lbs. green beans,
** washed and trimmed**
1 medium red onion, thinly sliced
VINAIGRETTE:
½ c. olive oil
1½ T. red wine vinegar
1 tsp. Dijon mustard
½ tsp. salt
¼ tsp. freshly ground black pepper

In steamer or in saucepan in 1 inch lightly salted boiling water, steam beans until tender-crisp, about 7 to 8 minutes. Drain. In medium bowl, combine beans and onion. Combine vinaigrette ingredients. Toss vinaigrette gently with beans. Makes 8 servings.

ORANGE ICE WITH TEQUILA SOAKED STRAWBERRIES

1 pint fresh, ripe strawberries
¼ c. best-quality tequila
3 T. orange-flavored liqueur
2 pints orange sherbet or sorbet

Wash, then hull strawberries. Toss with tequila and liqueur. Refrigerate up to 6 hours, tossing occasionally. To serve, top sorbet with strawberries. Drizzle with syrup. Makes 8 servings.

CHOCOLATE MACAROONS

3 egg whites, room temperature
½ tsp. cream of tartar
1 c. sugar
⅓ c. unsweetened cocoa
1 c. flaked coconut

Heat oven to 300°F. Cover cookie sheet with foil. Beat whites until foamy. Beat in cream of tartar. Beat in sugar, 2 tablespoons at a time, until stiff, glossy peaks form. Stir in cocoa and coconut. Drop by tablespoonfuls onto baking sheets. Bake for 20 to 25 minutes. Allow to cool slightly before removing foil. Makes 1 dozen cookies.

hands-on crab feast

Old fashioned shortbread with chocolate

SPICY CRAB BOIL

SAUSAGE AND PEPPER BISCUITS

SWEET POTATO AND APPLE SALAD

CORN ON THE COB ● FRESH CUCUMBER PICKLES

CHOCOLATE-DIPPED PECAN SHORTBREAD

BEER ● COLA

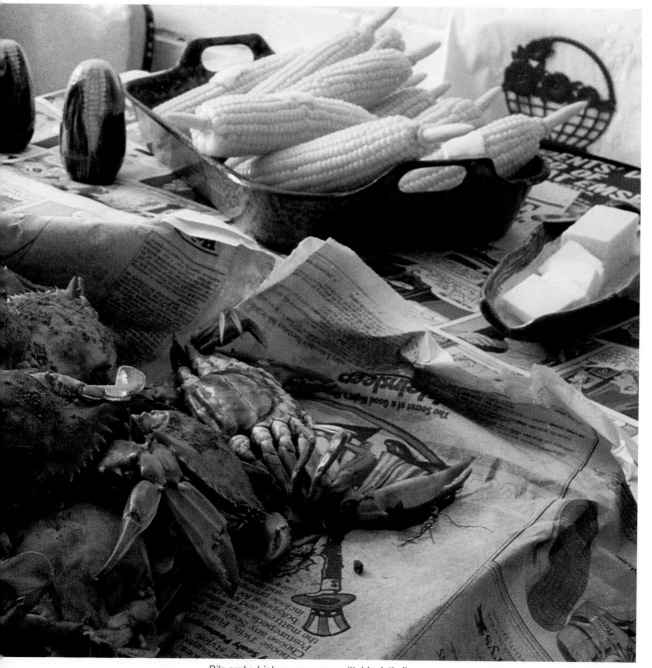

Pile crabs high on newspaper "tablecloths"

SPICY CRAB BOIL

Juice of 1 lemon
2 T. mustard seeds
3 T. ground red pepper
3 bay leaves
1 T. each salt, whole cloves, allspice, coriander seeds and ground ginger
3 dozen hard-shell crabs or 4 lbs. large shrimp, unshelled, or about 12 dozen 6-inch-long crayfish
SPICY COATING:
2 T. salt
2 T. freshly ground black pepper
2 T. chili powder
2 T. ground cumin
1 T. plus 1 tsp. ground red pepper
1 T. garlic powder

Over high heat, heat a large saucepan of water to boiling. Add the lemon juice and remaining ingredients except crabs and Spicy Coating. Add the crabs and cook for about 15 minutes or until their color changes to bright red and the triangular "apron" on underside of crab loosens. (If using shrimp or crayfish, cook 6 to 8 minutes or until shrimp curl and turn opaque or crayfish turn bright red.) Remove crabs from water. Meanwhile, in a small bowl combine ingredients for Spicy Coating. While crabs are hot, toss with Spicy Coating. Serve hot. Makes 6 to 8 servings.

HOW TO EAT A CRAB

Start by pulling off the legs and claws of the crab; set them aside to enjoy later. Turn the crab over, belly-side up. Lift up, remove and discard the triangular-shaped "apron." Now turn the crab over, belly-side down, and lift off the top shell. Set the body aside. Everything in the top shell is edible. Now go back to the crab body. Remove the feathery gills and the small sac at the bottom. Discard them. Hold the crab body on both sides and snap it in half. There'll be a nice piece of meat in the back—don't miss it. Use your fingers or a seafood pick to dig out the meat in the small compartments in the body shell. Now go back to the claws. Use a mallet and knife and nutcrackers to crack the shell in several places. You can then pull or dig out the meat. The legs make tasty sucking.

Ahh, summer . . . and the messy fun of a seafood feast! A party built on the seasonal abundance of land and sea—hard-shell crabs (you can substitute crayfish or shrimp, depending on what's available where you live); savory Sausage and Pepper Biscuits; Sweet Potato and Apple Salad, with a tangy poppy-seed dressing to spoon over it; homemade pickles; and fresh-from-the-farmers'-market corn on the cob. The sweet finale—Chocolate-Dipped Pecan Shortbread. The cooked crabs are piled high on newspaper "tablecloths" (no serving platters here). Wooden mallets and seafood picks as well as side dishes are all within arm's reach. Station lots of deep bowls or big platters for guests to discard crab-shells as they eat. There's something about eating with your fingers that makes spirits soar. This party has the appeal of a beach clam/seafood bake with the convenience of a meal prepared indoors. Planning is the key. In addition to plotting out food, have plenty of newspapers and utensils, and determine ahead of time how much tabletop room you'll need to accommodate all menu items and guests. Use a card table to hold extras—individual plates, glasses, napkins. As guests gather for the feast, take them through a sample crab-cracking so they'll know how to get to the sweet meat. (How-to-eat directions are included with the recipe.) Enjoy this feast for lunch or an early supper.

SAUSAGE AND PEPPER BISCUITS

1 lb. sweet Italian sausage
4 c. all-purpose flour
2 T. baking powder
1 tsp. baking soda
1 tsp. salt
½ tsp. freshly ground black pepper
⅔ c. solid vegetable shortening
1⅓ c. buttermilk

Heat oven to 450°F. Remove casings from sausages. Crumble sausage into saucepan and cook over medium-high heat until it loses its pink color, about 10 minutes. Cool slightly. In a large bowl combine flour, baking powder, baking soda, salt and pepper. With fingertips, rub in shortening until the mixture resembles coarse crumbs. Crumble sausage into flour mixture, adding any pan drippings. Pour in buttermilk and stir until dough comes together. On a well-floured surface, knead dough 2 or 3 times, then pat out to ¾-inch thickness. Cut out biscuits with 2½-inch biscuit cutter. Place on ungreased cookie sheets. Bake 12 to 15 minutes. Serve warm. Makes 24 biscuits. To reheat biscuits, wrap loosely in aluminum foil, then warm in 250°F oven 10 to 15 minutes.

SWEET POTATO AND APPLE SALAD

7 large sweet potatoes
3 Granny Smith apples
3 scallions
POPPY SEED DRESSING:
½ c. orange juice
2 T. cider vinegar
2 T. Dijon mustard
1 T. minced onion
1 T. grated orange peel
1 tsp. salt
1 c. light olive oil
1 T. poppy seeds

In a saucepan, heat 4 inches of water to boiling. Add sweet potatoes. Reduce heat to low, cover and simmer 30 minutes or until tender. Drain and cool. Peel, cut in half lengthwise, then slice. Quarter apples, core and then cut into horizontal slices. Slice scallions and combine with apples and sweet potatoes. Make the dressing: In blender combine orange juice, vinegar, mustard, onion, orange peel and salt. With blender running, slowly drizzle in oil until fully incorporated. Stir in poppy seeds. Toss with fruit and vegetables. Makes 12 servings.

FRESH CUCUMBER PICKLES

1½ c. kosher salt
1 gallon water
4 lbs. pickling (kirby) cucumbers
1½ qt. cider vinegar
1 T. mustard seed
1 whole clove
3 garlic cloves
2-inch piece peeled ginger root
2 T. sugar, firmly packed
2 bay leaves
1 dried chili pepper, or ½ tsp. crushed red pepper flakes

In very large bowl, non-aluminum saucepot or in large crock, combine salt and water. Add cucumbers (they should be weighted down with a plate to stay submerged). Cover and let stand for 24 hours. Drain cucumbers and cut into 2-inch slices. Place cucumber slices in a heatproof jar or jars. In a large non-aluminum saucepan over high heat, heat the vinegar with remaining ingredients to boiling. Pour hot vinegar over cucumbers in jars. Cool; cover and refrigerate up to 1 month. Makes 2½ quarts.

CHOCOLATE-DIPPED PECAN SHORTBREAD

½ c. pecans, finely chopped
2 c. all-purpose flour
¼ c. brown sugar, firmly packed
¼ c. granulated sugar
¾ c. butter or margarine, cut into cubes
6 oz. semisweet-chocolate pieces

In bowl with mixer at medium speed combine pecans with flour and sugars. Add butter, several pieces at a time; mix until dough begins to clump together. On floured surface knead 3 or 4 times until dough holds together. Divide dough. Wrap and refrigerate for 30 minutes. Roll out one half of dough about ¼ inch thick. Cut with 3½-inch heart-shaped cookie cutter. Transfer to ungreased cookie sheets. Prick with a fork at ½-inch intervals. Refrigerate cookies on sheet for 30 minutes. Roll, cut and refrigerate remaining dough. Heat oven to 325°F. Bake cookies for 20 to 25 minutes until undersides are pale golden. Transfer cookies to wire racks to cool. In double boiler top over hot, not boiling, water, melt chocolate. Stir until smooth. Dip cookies so that one half is covered with chocolate. Dry on wire racks. Store in an airtight container, layered with sheets of waxed paper, up to 1 week. Makes about 1 dozen cookies.

Chicken Gumbo and brown rice served with beer

supper for a mid-summer night

Pound cake flavored with fresh ginger

CRUDITÉS PICKLES

MONTEREY JACK CHEESE BOARD

CHICKEN-SAUSAGE GUMBO

BROWN RICE

YAM BISCUITS

GINGER POUND CAKE WITH LEMON SAUCE

BEER

This party menu is the perfect close to a summer day—a twilight supper shared with good friends. Start with Crudités Pickles, served with Monterey Jack cheese. The secret to a really good gumbo is in the roux (the fat and flour that flavors the stew). It must be cooked over high heat, until it is deep red-brown or the gumbo's flavor will be weak. Serve the gumbo with a scoop of brown rice in the center of the bowl...it's more interesting than plain white rice. The bread here is a biscuit made with yams. Serve with apple butter. Make the Ginger Pound Cake a day ahead and refrigerate it. It will slice more easily. Save any leftovers to toast in the morning. Have lots of different icy beers along with dinner. With the quickly setting sun, the chirp of unseen crickets, the reminiscences of the day's events—this is the setting for fine entertainment.

Homemade pickles with crunch and snap

CRUDITÉS PICKLES

PICKLING MIXTURE:
2 qts. cider vinegar
1½ qts. water
1½ c. sugar
⅓ c. mixed pickling spice
3 T. mustard seeds
2 tsp. dried crushed red pepper or 5 whole small dried chili peppers
RADISHES:
2 dozen small radishes (about 2 bunches)
1 tsp. cumin seeds
1 medium onion, quartered
CARROTS:
2 dozen baby carrots (about ¾ lb.)
1 tsp. dried tarragon leaves
1 tsp. celery seeds
ASPARAGUS:
3 dozen thin asparagus spears (about 1¼ lbs.)
4 shallots, sliced
2 tsp. chopped fresh chives
MUSHROOMS:
3 dozen small mushrooms (about ¾ lb.)
2 garlic cloves, halved
1 tsp. dill seeds
OKRA:
3 dozen small okra pods (about 1½ lbs.)
2 garlic cloves, halved
1 tsp. coriander seeds

In large saucepan over high heat, combine all pickling mixture ingredients and heat to boiling. Reduce heat to low; cover and simmer for 30 minutes. Meanwhile, in steamer over boiling water or in saucepan with 1 inch boiling water, steam radishes for 1 minute. Rinse in cool water and pack into canning jar with cumin seeds and onion. Repeat steaming, rinsing and packing with remaining vegetables and corresponding spices. Steam vegetables according to the following: 3 minutes for carrots, 2 minutes for asparagus, 1 minute for mushrooms, 2 minutes for okra. Pour the hot pickling liquid over the vegetables and seal jars. You should have enough liquid to fill five 1-quart jars. Store jars in refrigerator for at least 1 week before serving.

CHICKEN-SAUSAGE GUMBO

½ tsp. salt
½ tsp. garlic powder
½ tsp. ground red pepper
1 chicken (3 lbs.), cut up
2 medium onions, chopped
2 medium sweet red peppers, cut into strips
1 c. chopped celery
1¼ c. all-purpose flour
½ c. vegetable oil
6 c. chicken broth
1 bay leaf
½ tsp. dry mustard
½ tsp. ground cumin
2 garlic cloves, minced
½ lb. kielbasa (smoked Polish sausage), sliced diagonally
2 c. cooked brown rice (recipe follows)

Rub salt, garlic powder and red pepper on all sides of chicken pieces; set aside. Combine onions, peppers and celery; set aside. Reserve ½ cup flour; dredge chicken in remaining flour. In a large heavy skillet heat oil and fry chicken until golden on all sides, about 8 to 10 minutes per side. Drain on paper towels. With a metal spoon, scrape the pan to loosen any brown bits. Place pan over high heat. Using a wire whisk, gradually stir in the reserved ½ cup flour. Cook, whisking constantly until the roux is a dark red-brown, about 3 to 4 minutes. Remove from heat and add the vegetables, stirring constantly until the roux stops cooking. Return pan to low heat and cook, stirring constantly, until vegetables are soft, about 3 to 4 minutes. Transfer vegetables to a 5-quart Dutch oven or saucepan; add chicken broth, bay leaf, mustard, cumin, garlic and kielbasa. Heat to boiling, stirring and scraping pan often. Reduce heat to low and simmer, uncovered, for 45 minutes. While gumbo is simmering, remove and discard skin and bones from chicken; cut chicken into 1-inch pieces. Add to gumbo and heat through. Remove bay leaf before serving. To serve, mound about ⅓ cup cooked brown rice in center of soup bowl; ladle about 1¼ cups gumbo around rice. Makes 6 servings.

BROWN RICE

½ c. brown rice
1¼ c. water
⅛ tsp. salt

In medium saucepan over high heat, heat rice, water and salt to boiling. Reduce heat to low, cover and simmer about 45 minutes or until rice is tender and all the liquid is absorbed. Makes about 2 cups.

YAM BISCUITS

2 c. all-purpose flour
4 tsp. baking powder
1 tsp. salt
¾ c. cooked mashed yams
   or sweet potatoes
¼ c. solid vegetable shortening
1 T. minced onion
1 T. chopped fresh parsley
1 c. milk

Heat oven to 425°F. In medium bowl, combine flour, baking powder and salt. Add yams, shortening, onion and parsley. Beat on low speed with electric mixer until crumbly, about 2 minutes. With wooden spoon gradually stir in milk, stirring just until mixed. Use ¼-cup measure to spoon batter onto an ungreased cookie sheet. Bake 15 to 17 minutes or until lightly browned. Makes 1 dozen biscuits.

GINGER POUND CAKE WITH LEMON SAUCE

⅔ c. butter or margarine, softened
1 c. sugar
3 eggs
2-inch piece fresh ginger, peeled
   and grated
½ tsp. vanilla
2¼ c. all-purpose flour
1 tsp. baking powder
1 tsp. salt
½ c. milk
Lemon Sauce (recipe follows)
Slivered crystalized ginger
   for garnish

Heat oven to 325°F. Grease a 9- by 5-inch loaf pan; set aside. In medium bowl with mixer at medium speed, cream butter and sugar until light and fluffy. Add eggs, 1 at a time, beating well after each addition. Beat in ginger and vanilla. Add dry ingredients to creamed mixture, alternating with milk. Spoon into loaf pan. Bake 1 hour and 10 minutes or until a toothpick inserted in center comes out clean. Cool on wire rack 10 minutes before removing from pan. Cool completely on wire rack before serving. Serve with a dollop of Lemon Sauce and a few slivers of crystalized ginger. Makes 1 loaf.

LEMON SAUCE

2 eggs
½ c. sugar
¾ tsp. grated lemon peel
¼ c. fresh lemon juice
½ c. butter or margarine, melted

In mixing bowl combine eggs and sugar. Beat with mixer at medium-high speed, until light and fluffy, about 5 minutes. Gradually beat in lemon peel, lemon juice and butter. Beat until thoroughly mixed. Transfer mixture to top of double boiler. Cook over hot, not boiling, water, stirring constantly, until thickened and the consistency of sour cream, about 7 to 9 minutes. Cool; refrigerate. Makes about 1½ cups.

late-night supper

An unexpected pairing; Goat cheese and chilies

MANGO DAIQUIRIS

ROASTED CHILIES STUFFED WITH GOAT CHEESE ● AVOCADO RELISH

GAME HENS WITH GREEN SALSA

SKILLET-GRILLED VEGETABLES

THREE-BERRY NAPOLEONS

WHITE WINE ● COFFEE

A buffet of foods to serve at room temperature

115

ecause almost everything can be eaten at room temperature—and made ahead of time—this evening buffet has a feeling of unhurried calm. On the menu: dishes that toast summer's bounty in their straightforward simplicity of color, texture and flavor. Exotic Mango Daiquiris set the mood. Make them in batches so you don't have to worry about tending bar. The sweet mango takes the edge off guests' hunger until the main-event begins. The bill of fare is lush: Sweet-spicy Roasted Chilies Stuffed with Goat Cheese and served with Avocado Relish make an unexpected "salad." Make the roasted game hens special by serving them on a bed of Green Salsa—a delightfully cool yet spicy sauce. Easy Skillet-Grilled Vegetables—summer squash, zucchini, red onions and potatoes—are blackened for an authentic, just-off-the-coals taste. For dessert, a simple yet impressive Three-Berry Napoleon—a layered confection of puff pastry, lime custard and strawberries, blueberries and raspberries. This Napoleon is actually very easy to assemble. Bake the pastry and make the custard the morning before the party. This buffet is the perfect end to a summer day.

MANGO DAIQUIRIS

2 c. ripe, cubed mango
½ c. light rum
2 T. freshly squeezed lime juice
2 T. sugar
3 c. crushed ice

Combine all ingredients in blender. Blend on high until smooth. Makes 4 servings.

ROASTED CHILIES STUFFED WITH GOAT CHEESE

8 Anaheim chili peppers
    or sweet Italian peppers
4 oz. goat cheese,
    such as Montrachet
1 scallion, finely sliced
8 radicchio leaves
Avocado Relish (recipe follows)

Heat broiler. Broil peppers, turning frequently, until skin is blackened all over. Place the peppers in a paper bag and close. Set aside for 20 to 25 minutes. (This makes the peppers very easy to peel.) Peel. Make a vertical slit down each pepper. Carefully remove the seeds. In a small bowl, crumble the goat cheese and mix with the scallion. Use to stuff peppers. To serve, arrange a radicchio leaf on each of 8 plates. Spoon some Avocado Relish onto each. Place one pepper on each plate. Serve at room temperature. Makes 8 servings.

AVOCADO RELISH

1 avocado, peeled and cut
    into ½-inch pieces
½ cucumber, washed and cut
    into ½-inch pieces
4 tomatoes, seeded and cut
    into ½-inch pieces
1 medium onion, chopped
½ tsp. dried ground cumin
Salt and freshly ground black
    pepper to taste
1 T. olive oil
1 tsp. fresh lemon juice.

Combine all ingredients in a small bowl.

GAME HENS WITH GREEN SALSA

8 game hens
⅓ c. vegetable oil
⅓ c. fresh lime juice
1 T. dried ground cumin
1 tsp. salt
Green Salsa (recipe follows)
Coriander leaves for garnish
Lime slices for garnish

With poultry shears or a sharp heavy knife, cut along each side of backbone of hens. Remove and discard backbones. Flatten hens. In large shallow roasting pan combine remaining ingredients except salsa, coriander and lime slices. Add hens and turn to coat. Cover with plastic wrap. Refrigerate 4 hours or overnight, turning occasionally. Heat oven to 425°F. Pat the hens dry and place breast-side down in clean roasting pans or jelly-roll pans. Bake for 10 minutes. Turn hens and roast for an additional 20 to 25 minutes or until skin is golden and crisp and hens are fork-tender. To serve, spoon some Green Salsa onto a plate. Place hen on top of salsa. Garnish with coriander and lime slices. Makes 8 servings. Note: If you do not have oven room to roast the hens split, then marinate them whole and roast at 375°F for 1 hour.

GREEN SALSA

1 sweet green pepper
2 c. fresh or canned tomatillos*,
   diced
¼ c. chopped onion
⅓ c. fresh coriander leaves,
   (cilantro) (optional)
3 fresh jalapeňo peppers, seeded
3 garlic cloves, crushed
1 T. fresh lime juice
¼ tsp. salt
*Available in Latin markets
or in Mexican food section of
supermarkets.

Heat broiler as manufacturer directs and broil green pepper until blackened on all sides. Place roasted pepper in a brown paper bag; set aside for about 15 minutes. (This makes the pepper very easy to peel.) Use a small knife to peel the pepper; remove and discard seeds and stem. Combine peeled pepper, tomatillos and remaining ingredients in a blender or food processor and process until chunky. Makes about 2½ cups.

SKILLET-GRILLED VEGETABLES

About ¼ c. salad oil
8 small new potatoes,
   steamed and halved
2 medium zucchini, halved, then
   quartered lengthwise
1 large red onion,
   cut into ½-inch-thick slices
1 medium yellow squash,
   cut into ½-inch-thick slices
¼ c. olive oil
Salt
Freshly ground black pepper

Over high heat, heat a cast-iron skillet until very hot. Add 1 to 2 tablespoons salad oil and cook the vegetables in a single layer until they are quite browned on all sides. Repeat until all vegetables are grilled. If necessary, more oil may be added to the skillet. Drizzle with olive oil. Sprinkle with salt and pepper. Serve at room temperature. Makes 8 servings.

THREE-BERRY NAPOLEONS

Lime Custard (recipe follows)
1 sheet frozen puff pastry
1 pt. fresh strawberries,
   hulled and cut into slices
1 c. blueberries
½ pt. raspberries

Three-berry dessert with lime cream

Make Lime Custard and cool completely. Thaw pastry according to label directions. Meanwhile, cut sheet of puff pastry into thirds. On well-floured surface, with floured rolling pin, roll each strip into a 13- by 5-inch rectangle. Arrange on cookie sheets and prick with a fork at ½-inch intervals. Refrigerate for 10 minutes. Heat oven to 400°F. Bake pastry until golden, about 12 to 15 minutes. Cool on wire racks. Up to 3 hours before serving, assemble the napoleon. Spread one layer of pastry with one third of the custard. Arrange strawberry slices in single layer on top. Add another layer of pastry, spread with one third more of custard. Top with a single layer of blueberries. Place another pastry layer on top. Spread with remaining custard and arrange raspberries on top. Cover and refrigerate until serving time. To serve, use a serrated knife to cut 8 slices. Makes 8 servings.

LIME CUSTARD

2¾ c. milk
½ c. sugar
¼ c. cornstarch
2 eggs, lightly beaten
1 T. grated lime peel
¼ c. fresh lime juice

Heat milk in a medium saucepan over medium heat until small bubbles form around edges; remove from heat. In another saucepan combine sugar and cornstarch until blended. Add eggs and beat with wire whisk until smooth. Pour in the heated milk and stir until combined. Cook over medium-low heat, stirring constantly, until custard comes to a boil. Boil 1 minute. Remove from heat. Stir in lime peel and juice. Transfer to a mixing bowl and place sheet of waxed paper or plastic wrap directly on surface of custard. Refrigerate until completely chilled.

cocktail dinner buffet

GARLIC SHRIMP

BLUE CHEESE DIP

CHORIZO ON BREAD

BEEF KABOBS

SPICY CHICKEN WINGS

TUNA EMPANADAS

CHOCOLATE-DIPPED ORANGES

POPPY SEED SPICE COOKIES

RUM PUNCH

A cocktail party in which the hors d'oeuvres become the meal has many benefits besides offering a nibble of everything on the menu. You don't need a huge dining room table, matching set of dishes or room to seat all your guests to pull off this festive cocktail dinner party. Substantial, self-contained and not too messy are the criteria for appetizers served at a cocktail dinner party. Foods that easily go from hand to mouth without worry about spilling on a silk blouse or pale rug are best. Also, appetizers that don't require silverware and can be hand-held in a napkin make it easier to juggle drinks. Design your appetizers as you would a dinner party—in courses. Serve a first course of cold appetizers, ready when guests arrive. Garlic shrimp, the blue cheese dip and chorizo (a spicy Spanish sausage) on bread all taste best cold or at room temperature. The second course is the hot appetizers. Complete the meal with light, sweet nibbles for dessert. Count on about twelve to sixteen appetizer servings per person for a substantial appetizer dinner. Make your invitations specific. Tell your guests you plan to serve a meal of appetizers. This way guests will arrive on time and won't make dinner plans for later.

A meal made of hors d'oeuvres

BLUE CHEESE DIP

2 T. olive oil
2 tsp. red wine vinegar
1 large garlic clove, minced
2 tsp. grated onion
¼ lb. crumbled blue cheese
1 c. sour cream
Fresh fennel and Belgian endive
for dipping

In a small bowl combine oil, vinegar, garlic and onion; mix well. Add cheese and beat until almost smooth. Stir in sour cream. Serve with fennel and endive for dipping. Makes 1½ cups.

BEEF KABOBS

2 to 2½ lbs. London broil
½ c. olive oil
3 T. vinegar
3 T. honey
2½ tsp. ground cumin
1 tsp. paprika
¼ c. minced scallions
½ tsp. salt

Slice meat into ¼-inch-thick strips; place in large bowl. Combine oil and remaining ingredients. Pour over meat. Cover and marinate in refrigerator at least 3 hours, tossing occasionally. Skewer meat by threading onto long bamboo skewers that have been soaked in water for 20 minutes. Heat broiler. Place skewers on broiler pan. Cook 3 to 5 minutes, basting with marinade. Serve hot. Makes about 40. To reheat: Place on baking sheet, cover loosely with aluminum foil and heat in 350°F oven for about 20 minutes, or microwave on HIGH (700 watts) in microwave-safe dish, for 1 minute.

SPICY CHICKEN WINGS

20 chicken wings, about 3 lbs.
Vegetable oil for frying
3 T. fresh lime juice
3 T. dry sherry
1 T. chopped fresh parsley
1 tsp. grated onion
¼ tsp. garlic powder
¼ tsp. ground red pepper
⅛ tsp. salt

Cut chicken wings at joints. Cut off and discard wing tips. Pour ½ inch oil into a large skillet; heat over medium-high heat until almost smoking,

GARLIC SHRIMP

1½ lbs. medium, fresh shrimp,
or ¾ lbs. cleaned frozen*
¼ c. olive oil
2 T. butter or margarine
4 garlic cloves, sliced
2 T. minced onion
¼ tsp. hot red pepper flakes
3 T. fresh lemon juice
¼ tsp. salt
2 T. chopped fresh parsley
If using frozen shrimp, do not thaw before cooking.

Peel shrimp, leaving tails on, and devein. In large skillet over low heat, heat oil and butter. Add garlic and onion and cook 3 minutes without browning garlic. Add shrimp and pepper flakes. Increase heat to medium and cook, tossing constantly 3 minutes or until shrimp just turn pink and begin to curl. Transfer shrimp and sauce to bowl. Add lemon juice, salt and parsley; toss well. Cover with plastic wrap and refrigerate shrimp at least 2 hours before serving to blend flavors. Makes 45 to 50.

about 375°F on deep-fat thermometer. Add as many chicken wings as will fit in the skillet without crowding. Fry until golden, about 6 to 8 minutes, turning once. Heat oven to 250°F. Drain cooked chicken wings on paper-towel-lined baking sheet. Keep chicken warm in oven while frying remaining wings. When all wings are cooked, transfer to serving platter. Combine remaining ingredients; mix well. Drizzle over warm chicken wings. Makes 40 pieces. To reheat: Place on baking sheet, cover loosely with aluminum foil and heat in 350°F oven for about 20 minutes, or microwave on HIGH (700 watts) in microwave-safe dish for 1 minute.

TUNA EMPANADAS

2 T. olive oil
1 small onion, chopped
½ sweet green pepper, chopped
1 6 ½-oz. can oil-packed tuna, drained and flaked
1 8-oz. can tomato sauce
1 T. chopped fresh parsley
½ tsp. salt
¼ tsp. freshly ground black pepper
1 hard-cooked egg, chopped
DOUGH:
2 c. all-purpose flour
½ tsp. salt
½ c. vegetable shortening
5-6 T. cold water
Vegetable oil for frying

In skillet over medium heat, heat oil. Add onion and green pepper; sauté until tender, about 5 minutes. Add tuna, tomato sauce, parsley, salt and pepper. Reduce heat to low and simmer, uncovered, for 10 minutes, stirring occasionally. Add chopped egg. Set aside. In medium bowl, combine flour and salt. Cut in shortening with fingertips until mixture resembles coarse crumbs. Sprinkle in water and mix with a fork until dough forms a ball. Divide dough in half. On a floured surface roll each half out about ⅛-inch thick. Using a 3-inch biscuit cutter, cut 20 circles. Repeat with remaining dough. Spoon 1 teaspoon of tuna filling onto each dough circle. Using your finger, dab water around edges of pastry. Fold over and press edges together with a fork. Pour 2 inches of oil into a deep skillet or Dutch oven. Heat to 375°F on deep-fat thermometer. Fry a few at a time, until golden brown. Drain on paper towels. Makes about 30. To reheat: Place on baking sheet, cover loosely with aluminum foil and heat in 350°F oven for about 20 minutes, or on paper towels in microwave on HIGH (700 watts) for 1 minute.

CHOCOLATE-DIPPED ORANGES

24 oz. semisweet-chocolate pieces
¼ c. solid vegetable shortening
6 oranges, divided into sections

In double boiler top over hot, not boiling, water, melt chocolate and shortening; remove from heat. Dip orange sections into chocolate; place on waxed-paper-lined cookie sheets. Refrigerate 30 minutes. Keep refreigerated until serving time. Makes 50 to 60 pieces.

POPPY SEED SPICE COOKIES

¾ c. butter or margarine, softened
¾ c. light brown sugar, firmly packed
½ c. granulated sugar
1 tsp. vanilla
2 eggs
3 T. milk
3 c. all-purpose flour
1½ tsp. baking powder
½ tsp. salt
1 tsp. grated nutmeg
1 tsp. ground cinnamon
2 T. poppy seeds

In large bowl with electric mixer on medium-high speed, cream together butter, brown and white sugar and vanilla until light and fluffy. Add eggs and milk and blend well. In another bowl combine flour, baking powder, salt, spices and poppy seeds. Blend dry ingredients into sugar and butter until well combined. Wrap dough in waxed paper and refrigerate for easier handling. Heat oven to 350°F. On lightly floured surface roll out dough to ¼ inch thick; cut with cookie cutter and place 2 inches apart on ungreased cookie sheets. Bake 10 to 12 minutes or until cookies turn light golden brown. Cool cookies 1 minute; remove from cookie sheets. Cool on wire racks. Makes 2½ to 3½ dozen cookies.

RUM PUNCH

3 c. unsweetened pineapple juice
2 c. fresh orange juice
Juice of 4 large limes
1 c. dark rum
1-1½ c. grenadine

Combine juices, rum and grenadine and serve. For a layered effect, mix all ingredients except grenadine and pour into glasses, then add 2 to 3 tablespoons grenadine to each glass. The grenadine will sink to the bottom of the glass; juices will float on top. Makes 8 servings.

winter open house

APPLES AND CHEDDAR CHEESE

UNSHELLED NUTS

BEER BEEF STEW

PEASANT FISH STEW

CHEDDAR-BEER BISCUITS

FOCACCIA

PROSCIUTTO BREAD

CHOCOLATE-WALNUT PIE

OPEN BAR

Biscuits and Flatbread round out the meal

A stew of beef and young vegetables

This is a party plan for quiet winter Sundays. It's a great idea for the holidays or even a mid-winter, February-March leisurely weekend. Invite guests to arrive in staggered hours, especially if your place is small. Invite some of your guests to arrive at one, others at three and at five o'clock. Plan to have a selection of stews. Serve only one variety if your guest list is less than the 50 planned for here. Have pots of the stews simmering on the stove. The breads, which you can make the day before, can be piled in baskets. Scatter bowls of mixed nuts and platters of sliced apples and cheese throughout your apartment or house. Select a friend to play bartender—it will take the heat off you. Suggest that guests eat whatever they want in whatever order they want. For example, the apples and Cheddar cheese make a good dessert or an appetizer. If some have already eaten, just Chocolate-Walnut Pie and coffee will fit the bill for them. Have all the food accessible. Paper or plastic dishes are a must at this kind of party. Don't forget to plan for trash stations that are easy to get to but still out of the way—in a niche in the kitchen or in a corner is a good idea.

BEER BEEF STEW

**8 lbs. lean stewing beef,
    trimmed and cut into 2-inch
    pieces
Salt
Freshly ground black pepper
About 2 c. flour
About ⅔ c. vegetable oil
8 medium onions,
    peeled and chopped
7 13¾-oz. cans beef broth
1⅓ c. dry red wine
1½ 6-oz. cans tomato paste
Bouquet garni: 3 bay leaves, 12
    sprigs parsley and 1 tsp. dried
    thyme leaves
2 lbs. new potatoes,
    peeled and quartered
2 10-oz. pkgs. frozen peas
2 lbs. baby carrots,
    trimmed and peeled**

Pat beef dry with paper towels, sprinkle with salt and pepper, then dredge in flour. Set aside. In a large sauce-pan over medium-high heat, heat 3 tablespoons oil. When very hot, add just enough beef to cover bottom of pan without crowding. Brown beef well on all sides; remove to colander to drain while you brown remaining beef, adding more oil as needed. To oil remaining in pot, add onions and cook over low heat 15 minutes or until soft. Return beef. Add broth, wine, tomato paste and bouquet garni. Over high heat, heat to boiling. Reduce heat to low and simmer, partially covered, for 2 hours or until beef is tender, stirring occasionally, adding more liquid if necessary. Skim and discard fat. Add potatoes, peas and carrots and simmer 25 to 30 minutes or until tender. Makes about 4 gallons.

PEASANT FISH STEW

**2 lbs. bacon, cut into 1-inch pieces
8 medium onions, chopped
14 garlic cloves, minced
8 medium sweet green peppers,
    seeded and chopped
8 medium sweet red peppers,
    seeded and chopped
8 8-oz. bottles clam juice
6 13¾-oz. cans chicken broth
4 c. (1 qt.) dry white wine
Generous pinch saffron threads
1 qt. (4 c.) heavy or whipping cream
4 lbs. thick, firm, fresh or frozen
    fish* such as cod or haddock
4 lbs. medium fresh or frozen
    shrimp*, peeled (tails intact,
    if desired) and deveined
4 lbs. fresh or frozen scallops*, cut
    into halves or quarters if large**
**If using frozen seafood do not
thaw before cooking.*

In large, heavy skillet over medium-low heat cook bacon until golden but not browned. Drain bacon on paper towels. Set aside. Pour off all but ⅓ cup bacon drippings from skillet and reserve remaining drippings for later use. In skillet with ⅓ cup bacon drippings over medium heat cook onions uncovered about 10 minutes or until soft and golden. Add garlic to the skillet and cook about 1 minute over low heat until garlic just releases its fragrance. Remove onions and garlic to a large kettle. Add ¼ cup of reserved bacon drippings to skillet. Add peppers and cook uncovered over low heat about 5 minutes or until barely tender. Add bacon, peppers, clam juice, chicken broth, wine, saffron and cream to kettle and bring to a boil. Add fish, shrimp, and scallops and simmer about 5 minutes or until just cooked through. Taste for seasoning. Note: To keep warm, keep soup just below a simmer as it sits on the stove so seafood will not become tough or overcooked. Makes about 5 gallons.

CHEDDAR-BEER BISCUITS

2⅓ c. buttermilk baking mix
¾ c. shredded cheddar cheese
⅔ c. flat beer
Flour

Heat oven to 450°F. Combine baking mix and ½ cup cheese. Stir in beer until soft dough forms. Beat vigorously 30 seconds. Turn out onto floured board. Roll to ½-inch thick. Cut with 3-inch cutter dusted with flour. Transfer to ungreased baking sheet. Sprinkle with remaining ¼ cup cheese. Bake 8 to 10 minutes. Makes 1 dozen biscuits. Note: For best results do not double recipe. To make enough for open-house party make biscuits three times.

FOCACCIA
(Italian flatbread)

6-6½ c. all-purpose flour
2 T. sugar
4 tsp. salt
2 pkgs. active dry yeast
2 c. water
¾ c. olive oil
2 tsp. coarse salt
1½ tsp. dry rubbed sage
2 garlic cloves, minced

With mixer on low speed combine 3 cups flour, sugar, salt and yeast. In saucepan over low heat, heat water and ¼ cup oil until very warm (120°F to 130°F). With mixer on low speed, add liquid to dry ingredients. Beat 2 minutes. Add 2 cups flour and beat on high speed 2 minutes. Stir in enough additional flour to make a stiff dough. Turn onto lightly floured surface and knead until smooth and elastic, 8 to 10 minutes. Place in greased bowl, turning to grease top. Cover; let rise until doubled in bulk, about 45 minutes. Punch dough down. Divide in half. Spread each half in a greased jelly roll pan. Heat oven to 425°F. Cover; let rise 30 minutes. Make lots of indentations on dough with thumb. Sprinkle each pan of dough with ¼ cup olive oil. Sprinkle with salt, sage and garlic. Bake 25 to 30 minutes or until golden brown. Makes 2 loaves.

PROSCIUTTO BREAD

2 T. sugar
4 tsp. salt
2 pkgs. active dry yeast
6-6½ c. all-purpose flour
2 c. water
¼ c. olive oil
1½ c. chopped prosciutto or ham
1½ tsp. dried basil
1½ tsp. dried oregano
Olive oil

In large bowl with mixer on low speed, combine sugar, salt, yeast and 3 cups flour; mix well. In saucepan over low heat, heat water and oil until very warm (120°F to 130°F). With mixer at medium-low speed, gradually add liquid to dry ingredients. Beat 2 minutes. Add 2 cups flour and beat on high speed 2 minutes. Stir in enough additional flour to make a stiff dough. Turn onto lightly floured surface and knead until smooth and elastic, 8 to 10 minutes. Place in greased bowl, turning to grease top. Cover; let rise until doubled in bulk, about 45 minutes. Punch dough down. Knead in prosciutto, basil and oregano. Divide dough in half. Roll each piece into a 15-inch-long loaf. Transfer to greased baking sheet. Make diagonal slits along top of loaf. Cover; let rise 30 minutes. Bake in a 425°F oven for 20 to 25 minutes. Remove from oven and brush with olive oil. Makes 2 loaves.

CHOCOLATE-WALNUT PIE

3 squares semisweet-baking
**   chocolate**
3 T. butter or margarine
4 large eggs
½ c. sugar
1 c. light corn syrup
3 T. Kahlúa
2 c. walnuts (large pieces or halves)
1 9-inch unbaked pie crust

Heat oven to 350°F. In top of double boiler over hot, not boiling, water, melt chocolate and butter. Remove from heat and set aside to cool completely. In a medium bowl with fork, beat eggs with sugar and corn syrup until light and fluffy. Blend in chocolate. Stir in nuts and Kahlúa. Pour into pie shell and bake about 40 minutes or until center is set. A toothpick will not come out clean when inserted in center. Pie will firm up as it cools. Let stand at least 1 hour at room temperature before serving. Can be made 3 to 4 days in advance. Cover with plastic wrap and refrigerate. Note: For a party of 50, make 5 pies.

Salmon spread flecked with dill

Tri-color vegetable pâté

Broiled Negi Maki, cold Kappa Maki and almonds

bring your own champagne feast

JAPANESE-STYLE MARINATED CARROTS

SALMON TERRINE

FRENCH TOMATO TURNOVERS

KAPPA MAKI

NÉGI MAKI

VEGETABLE PÂTÉ

SAUTÉED ALMONDS

CHAMPAGNE

One-bite tomato tarts

Marinated for flavor, cut with style

Whether you prefer to invite all your friends for a huge, festive gathering or just a close few for a quiet and special evening, you'll find this the perfect mid-winter celebration. Add or subtract items from the menu to match the size of your gathering. It's a classy twist on the Bring-Your-Own-Beer party—but this time it's Bring-Your-Own-Champagne. Suggest a $15.00 per bottle limit to spare budgets. When guests arrive, have a large bucket full of ice to chill the champagne, or make room in the refrigerator. You'll need to have lots of glasses (plastic ones are available, or rent crystal flutes from a party supply store). The food is all do-ahead. Serve carrots cut and twisted into triangles instead of the usual sticks and marinate them Japanese-style. You'll find do-ahead and freezing directions for making the turnovers. The vegetable pâté can be made up to a day ahead. The Kappa Maki (pronounced Cap-a-ma-kay) is a cucumber sushi roll. It can be made ahead, too, and sliced just before serving. Make the almonds anytime and store them in an air-tight container until the party. The presentation should be special too. Use sophisticated colors to complement the food, such as black and turquoise, brass and copper.

127

JAPANESE-STYLE MARINATED CARROTS

1½ c. rice wine vinegar
1½ c. water
6 T. soy sauce
¼ c. sugar
3 lbs. carrots (about 24 medium carrots)

In large saucepan over high heat, heat vinegar, water, soy sauce and sugar to boiling; remove from heat and cool to room temperature. Meanwhile, cut carrots into diagonal slices, about ⅛ inch thick. Cut into a "z" shape by making a slit on one side, then on the other. Then twist and tuck ends to make a triangle. Toss with vinegar mixture. Refrigerate overnight. Drain before serving. Makes 3 pounds.

SALMON TERRINE

2 7½-oz. cans salmon, drained
½ lb. smoked salmon, minced
10 T. butter or margarine, softened
3 T. dry white wine
2 tsp. finely minced fresh dill
or ¾ tsp. dried
Fresh dill, for garnish
1 16-oz. pkg. thinly sliced pumpernickel bread
1 16-oz. pkg. thinly sliced rye bread

Combine canned and smoked salmon with butter until well blended. Blend in wine and dill. Taste, adding more butter for a smoother texture, more dill and wine if a more pronounced flavor of either is desired. Cut bread diagonally into quarters. Garnish with fresh dill and serve with bread triangles. Makes about 3 cups.

FRENCH TOMATO TURNOVERS

2 T. olive oil
2 T. butter
1 large onion, minced
4 large garlic cloves, minced
1 35-oz. can plum tomatoes, drained, seeded and chopped
1 tsp. rosemary, crumbled
2 T. finely minced fresh parsley
¼ tsp. crushed red pepper flakes
½ tsp. salt
¼ tsp. freshly ground black pepper
2 5¼-oz. pkgs. pie crust mix, made according to pkg. instructions

In heavy saucepan over medium heat, heat oil and butter. Add onion and cook over medium-low heat until soft, about 10 minutes. Add garlic and cook 1 minute until it releases its fragrance. Add remaining ingredients except pie crust and simmer over medium-low heat, uncovered, for 30 minutes, stirring frequently. Mixture should be very thick. Heat oven to 350°F. Roll dough out to ⅛ inch thick. Cut into 2½-inch circles. Place rounded ½ teaspoon of filling in center. Fold over and press to seal. Moisten edges with a little water if necessary. Crimp edge with a fork; prick top with a small knife. Bake on ungreased cookie sheet 10 minutes or until golden. Makes 40 to 45 turnovers. To do ahead: Do not bake. Wrap well in aluminum foil. Freeze. Bake, frozen in 400°F oven 15 minutes or until golden and heated through.

KAPPA MAKI
(Cucumber Sushi Roll)

About 8 sheets (8- by 8-inch) roasted *nori**
1 recipe vinegared rice (recipe follows)
¼ c. toasted sesame seeds, tossed in a dry skillet 3 to 4 minutes until golden
3 T. *wasabi** mustard powder mixed with just enough water to make a paste
3 large, firm cucumbers, unpeeled and cut diagonally, then into julienne strips
*Available where Oriental groceries are sold.

Cut each *nori* sheet in half to make 16 8- by 4-inch pieces. Place half sheet of *nori* on a sheet of waxed paper, long side facing you. With wet fingers firmly press about ⅓ cup rice along the long side of sheet of *nori*, to cover about ⅔ of the sheet. Make a "ditch" in the center of the rice with a wet finger tip. Spread about ¼ teaspoon *wasabi* along the "ditch." Sprinkle ¼ teaspoon seeds on top of wasabi. Place about 10 to 15 pieces of cucumber along the the "ditch." Then, holding cucumbers in place with finger tips, roll *nori* over rice to form a cylinder. Use waxed paper to help you roll if necessary. Seal edge with a little water. Trim ends with a wet knife; cut into 1½-inch pieces and place cut side up on a serving dish. Makes about 100 pieces.

NÉGI MAKI
(Scallion-Stuffed Beef Rolls)

⅓ c. sugar
½ c. soy sauce
½ c. rice vinegar
1-inch piece fresh ginger, peeled
    and minced
2 lbs. partially frozen lean beef
    (such as London broil), 1½-inches
    thick
About 6 bunches scallions,
    trimmed and cut into 1½-inch
    lengths including green tops

Heat broiler; in a saucepan over moderate heat, dissolve sugar in soy sauce and vinegar. Add ginger, increase heat to high and boil mixture until reduced to 1 cup. Set aside. Using a sharp knife, cut beef into paper-thin strips 5- by 1½-inch. Place 5 to 6 scallion pieces (some white bottoms and some green tops) at one end of beef strip. Roll up tightly and place seam-side down on lightly oiled, heavy broiling pan. Pour glaze over rolls. Broil 8 to 10 inches from heat 4 to 5 minutes or until browned. Insert skewers or toothpicks and serve warm or at room temperature. Makes about 50 pieces. Watch carefully as beef broils—marbling may cause splattering.

VEGETABLE PÂTÉ

1½ lbs. carrots (about 12 medium)
    peeled and cut into ½-inch
    pieces
1 medium yellow onion, chopped
2 T. butter or margarine
1 10-oz. pkg. frozen chopped
    broccoli, thawed and well
    drained
2 tsp. dried chives
5 large eggs
1½ c. heavy or whipping cream
½ c. grated Parmesan cheese
½ tsp. salt
¼ tsp. freshly ground pepper
¼ tsp. grated nutmeg
1 16-oz. can beets (not pickled),
    drained
½ tsp. dried thyme leaves
4 5¾-oz. pkgs. flatbread crackers

Grease sides and bottom of a 9- by 5-inch loaf pan. Line sides and bottom with waxed paper. Grease again and set aside. In steamer or in 1-inch lightly salted boiling water, cook carrots for about 10 minutes, or until very tender. Drain and set aside. In a medium skillet over medium heat, cook onion in hot butter or margarine 10 minutes or until soft and tender. Add broccoli to onions. Cook 1 to 2 minutes to blend flavors; stir in chives. Set aside. In a medium bowl, beat eggs with 1 cup of the cream. Add cheese, salt, pepper and nutmeg. Set aside. Purée beets in food processor or blender with ½ cup of egg mixture. Pour into loaf pan, spreading evenly with a spatula. Rinse work bowl or blender jar. Purée broccoli mixture with ¾ cup egg mixture and ¼ cup cream. Spoon gently on top of beets, spreading evenly. Purée carrots with remaining ¾ cup egg mixture and remaining cream. Add thyme; spoon gently on top of broccoli, spreading evenly. Place loaf pan in a roasting pan. Fill roasting pan with enough boiling water to come half way up sides of loaf pan. Bake 60 to 75 minutes or until pâté is firm to the touch in the center. Remove from roasting pan and cool. To serve, unmold onto serving platter and remove waxed paper. Slice and serve on flatbread crackers. Can be made 24 hours in advance. Makes 72 2½- by ¼-inch slices.

VINEGARED RICE

1⅓ c. raw long- or short-grain rice*
⅓ c. rice vinegar
4 tsp. sugar
1¼ tsp. salt
*Long-grain rice may be used,
but do not rinse as in first step.

In large bowl cover rice with cold water. Stir, pour off water, and continue in this manner 9 to 10 times until water runs clear. Drain rice then combine in a saucepan with 2 cups water and let stand uncovered for 30 minutes. Over high heat, heat to boiling. Cover; reduce heat to low and simmer 10 minutes. Remove from heat and let stand, covered, 15 minutes. Meanwhile, in small saucepan, combine vinegar, sugar and salt. Over low heat, cook, stirring constantly, until sugar is dissolved. Set aside to cool. Slowly add vinegar to warm rice, stirring gently. Rice can be made up to 12 hours ahead. Cover with damp cloth and store at room temperature.

SAUTÉED ALMONDS

2 T. butter or margarine
1½ lbs. whole, blanched almonds
2 T. salt

In heavy skillet over medium heat, heat butter. Add almonds. Reduce heat to low and cook, stirring constantly until lightly browned. Toss with salt. Makes 1½ pounds.

grand finale dessert party

CHOCOLATE-CINNAMON TORTE

**FRESH PEAR CAKE
WITH BRANDY SAUCE**

LEMON MOUSSE TART

TIRAMI SU

COFFEES

LIQUEURS

Give a desserts-only affair—it's truly a winter party made in heaven. Planning a party around different desserts is a rich twist on after-dinner, after-theater and afternoon gatherings. Everything is "do-ahead," so there's no last-minute rushing. Plan ahead and make these desserts a day in advance, so you can relax when guests arrive. Choose desserts that offer variety in taste and texture. Balance a rich, decadent dessert, such as Chocolate-Cinnamon Torte, with a dessert featuring fruit or tangy flavors, such as the Lemon Mousse Tart. Serve a creamy dessert, such as Tirami Su (pronounced tier-a-me-sue). Balance it with a lighter-tasting but rich-in-flavor cake, such as the Fresh Pear Cake with Brandy Sauce. Serve slivers or small portions of each dessert to start, beginning with the tangy one, then serve a sinfully rich sweet, ending with a lighter choice or fruit. Have freshly brewed coffee or espresso available, both regular and decaffeinated, and an assortment of teas. Cordials are always nice to serve afterward or to splash into coffee; use rock-candy swizzle sticks instead of passing the sugar bowl. Be specific on your invitations: Tell your friends it will be a dessert party so they are not expecting a full-course dinner or late brunch.

A selection of confections plus liqueurs

Heat oven to 350°F. Grease and flour two 9-inch round cake pans. Prepare torte: In double boiler top, over hot, not boiling, water, combine chocolate and water; stir until melted and smooth. Remove from heat; set aside. In large bowl, combine flour, cinnamon, baking soda and salt. In another large bowl, with mixer at high speed, combine butter, sugar and vanilla until creamy. Add eggs 1 at a time, beating well after each addition. Blend in chocolate. Gradually add dry ingredients alternately with water. Stir in pecans. Pour into pans. Bake 30 to 35 minutes or until toothpick inserted in center comes out clean. Cool 10 minutes; remove from pans and cool completely on wire racks. With serrated knife, cut each layer horizontally in half. Prepare filling: In small saucepan, melt chocolate and butter over low heat. Stir until smooth; remove from heat. Add milk and vanilla, mix until well blended and transfer to bowl. With mixer at medium speed gradually add confectioners' sugar; mix until smooth and creamy.

Prepare frosting: In medium bowl with mixer at medium-high speed, cream butter and sugar together. Add eggs, vanilla and cinnamon and beat until thick and smooth. To assemble torte, place one cake layer on cake plate. Spread with one third of filling; top with second cake layer and spread with one third of filling; top with third layer and spread with remaining filling. Place fourth layer on top. Frost torte with Cinnamon Frosting. Press chopped pecans around side. Using a pastry bag or a spoon, place 16 dollops of frosting, around top of cake. Place a pecan half on each dollop. Makes 16 servings.

CHOCOLATE-CINNAMON TORTE

TORTE:
6 oz. semisweet chocolate or 1 c.
 semisweet-chocolate pieces
¼ c. water
2½ c. all-purpose flour
2 tsp. ground cinnamon
1 tsp. baking soda
½ tsp. salt
¾ c. butter or margarine, softened
1½ c. sugar
1 tsp. vanilla
3 eggs
1 c. water
¾ c. finely chopped pecans
FILLING:
4 oz. semisweet chocolate or ⅔ c.
 semisweet-chocolate pieces
¼ c. butter or margarine
3 T. milk
1 tsp. vanilla
3 c. confectioners' sugar
FROSTING:
6 T. butter or margarine, softened
4½ c. confectioners' sugar
2 eggs
1½ tsp. vanilla
1½ tsp. ground cinnamon
2 c. chopped pecans
16 pecan halves for garnish

FRESH PEAR CAKE WITH BRANDY SAUCE

3 c. peeled, cored and finely
 chopped fresh pears
 (about 4 to 5 pears)
1½ c. sugar
¾ c. chopped hazelnuts
⅔ c. vegetable oil
1 tsp. vanilla
2 T. brandy or cognac
½ c. milk
3 eggs, slightly beaten
3 c. all-purpose flour
½ tsp. salt
2 tsp. baking soda
1 tsp. dried ground ginger
Brandy Sauce (recipe follows)

Heat oven to 350° F. Grease and flour a 12-cup fluted tube or bundt pan. In large bowl with wooden spoon combine pears, sugar and hazelnuts. Stir in oil, vanilla, brandy, milk and eggs. In another bowl, combine flour, salt, baking soda and ginger; gradually add to pear mixture. Stir with wooden spoon until well combined. Pour batter into pan. Bake 50 to 60 minutes, or until toothpick inserted into cake comes out clean. Cool cake in pan for at least 25 minutes; invert onto wire rack to cool completely. Serve with Brandy Sauce. Makes 16 servings.

BRANDY SAUCE

2 c. milk
2 T. sugar
3 egg yolks, lightly beaten
½ tsp. dried ground ginger
½ tsp. vanilla
2 T. brandy or cognac

In a medium saucepan over low heat, combine milk and sugar. Heat stirring gently until small bubbles form around side of pan. Remove from heat. In double boiler top over hot, not boiling, water, with wire whisk beat eggs with ginger and gradually add milk, a few tablespoons at a time. Cook, stirring constantly, about 5 minutes or until sauce thickens and lightly coats a spoon. Remove from heat and add vanilla and brandy. Cool, then place a piece of waxed paper directly on top of sauce to prevent film from forming. Refrigerate until chilled. Serve with Fresh Pear Cake. Makes 2¼ cups.

LEMON MOUSSE TART

2½ c. finely ground gingersnaps
(about ⅔ of a 1-lb. box)
⅔ c. butter or margarine, softened
1 envelope unflavored gelatin
2 T. cold water
½ c. fresh lemon juice
1½ c. granulated sugar
7 egg whites, at room temperature
1 c. heavy or whipping cream
Grated peel of 3 lemons
½ c. water
6 lemons, thinly sliced
3 T. apricot preserves

Heat oven to 375°F. In medium bowl combine gingersnap crumbs with butter until well blended. Press into two buttered 8-inch tart shells with removable bottoms. Bake 10 to 12 min-utes, or until firm. Cool completely on wire racks. In small heavy saucepan soften gelatin in 1 tablespoon cold water. Add lemon juice and 1 cup sugar. Heat, stirring constantly, over low heat until gelatin is completely dissolved. Do not boil. Remove from heat and cool completely. Beat egg whites until stiff, but not dry, peaks form. Gently fold gelatin into egg whites, until completely incorporated. With mixer at high speed, whip the cream until stiff; fold into egg whites. Fold in lemon peel. (Make sure all ingredients are well incorporated, but be careful not to deflate egg whites.) Spoon into tart shells, cover with plastic wrap and chill 3 to 4 hours or until set. In large skillet over high heat, heat ½ cup sugar and water to boiling. Add lemon slices and simmer gently until tender, about 8 minutes. Transfer to paper towels and drain well. In small saucepan over medium heat, melt apricot preserves with 1 tablespoon water. Lay cooled lemon slices in overlapping pattern to cover tops of tarts completely. Spoon on preserve glaze and chill until ready to serve. Makes 2 tarts, 8 servings each.

TIRAMI SU

4 large eggs, separated
3 T. granulated white sugar
1½ c. mascarpone* cheese,
at room temperature
2 c. slightly sweetened espresso,
cooled
1 7-oz. pkg. of *savoiardi* biscuits**
(24 biscuits) or pound cake cut
into 4- by 1- by ½-inch strips
2 T. unsweetened cocoa

*Mascarpone is a soft, creamy cheese from Italy, available at specialty food shops. Or, substitute drained ricotta cheese.
**Available at gourmet food shops.

In a clean grease-free bowl with mixer at high speed, beat egg whites until stiff, but not dry, peaks form; set aside. In another bowl with mixer at medium-high speed beat together sugar and yolks, then beat in cheese until smooth. With rubber spatula fold beaten whites into beaten cheese-yolk mixture. Place coffee in a wide bowl or pie plate. Dip biscuits or pound cake quickly into coffee, then arrange in bottom of 2-quart dish. Shape to cover bottom of dish completely. Top with cheese mixture. Cover and refrigerate at least 6 hours. Just before serving, dust top evenly with powdered cocoa. Makes 16 servings.

Let your mood be your guide to wonderful things to eat

When you're
in the mood for...

Craving a bite of something sinfully sweet or longing for comfort food like macaroni and cheese or a bowlful of chicken soup? This chapter has a wealth of recipes designed to hit any spot, no matter what taste or mood you're looking to satisfy. There are some pretty special ideas for brunch and breakfast, ranging from Double-Hot Chocolate to Individual Cheese Soufflés to a Vegetable Tart. There is a group of sizzlers filled with lots of spicy Moroccan, East Indian, Mexican and Cajun fire. Add to these: seductive appetizers and other good foods to nibble; wonderful desserts—some rich, others sweet and fruity, and just about anything in between. When you want to create your own memorable meal for an evening of good friends and good food, turn to this section. Most of the recipes include referenced suggestions for foods to balance the meal. Use them as guidelines or devise your own combination of dishes.

You'll also find indispensable charts that summarize information on buying and enjoying fruits, or spotting the ideal vegetable from snap beans to zucchini. There's a chart to help improve your barbecuing technique, one of chicken dinners ready in thirty minutes, a page of quick pasta recipes and even a how-to page on marinating. Like all the recipes in this book, these are pared down and uncomplicated. Enjoy thumbing through this section, finding old favorites and new temptations.

When you're in the mood for... great breakfasts and brunches

Banish boring breakfasts with this section in hand. There is plenty here to tempt the appetite, whether you are entertaining at brunch, serving breakfast to weekend guests or grabbing a bite as you run out the door. For nutritious, quick ideas for yourself, turn to the chart on page 141. It's full of fast, interesting ideas to turn a ho hum breakfast into a real eye-opener. Many of the recipes in this section include *serve-with* suggestions; you can turn out a whole party meal without a lot of fuss and bother. Brunch is an inexpensive yet elegant way to entertain. Eggs are cheap and can be stretched to serve any number of people, but they're also special when jazzed up with extra ingredients (see the Sausage and Pepper Frittata, below and Mexican Scrambled Eggs, right). At brunch don't worry about premeal drinks or bottles of wine if you don't want to, a pitcher of Bloody Marys will do it. Or, serve a pitcherful of Peach Wake-Up Tonic, page 141 or a potful of Doubly-Rich Hot Chocolate, page 141. For more ideas for breakfasts don't forget pages 12 through 15 in the Gourmet on the Run section. If you like to see friends often, but are short on cash, brunch is the way to go.

A frittata is an Italian omelet. Ingredients are mixed in with the eggs and it is served flat, without folding, unlike the French omelet.

SAUSAGE AND PEPPER FRITTATA

8 eggs, slightly beaten
½ tsp. salt
¼ tsp. freshly ground black pepper
2 T. vegetable oil
1 small onion, chopped
1 clove garlic, minced
2 oz. diced pepperoni (½ c.)
½ c. each chopped red and green pepper

In a bowl, combine eggs, salt and pepper. Beat to blend; set aside. Heat 1 T. oil in a large skillet over medium heat; add onion and remaining ingredients except eggs. Cook until golden, 2 minutes. Reduce heat to medium-low. Pour in eggs. As eggs set around edges, lift so the uncooked portion flows underneath. When frittata has set and is lightly browned on bottom (about 10 minutes), place a large platter upside down over the skillet, then flip both so the frittata falls gently onto the plate. Set aside. Add remaining oil to skillet. Slide frittata back into pan, browned side up. Continue cooking 2 to 3 minutes over low heat until lightly browned on bottom. Cool. Cut into wedges and serve. Makes 4 to 6 servings.
SERVE WITH
● *Café au Lait, page 97*
● *Sliced Papaya with Lime Cream, page 30*
● *Whole-wheat French or Italian bread*

For a very special and pretty brunch idea, serve eggs baked into the bread! Use small store-bought brioche, substitute dinner rolls if brioches are unavailable. Be sure to have extra sparkling wine to serve along with the eggs.

EGGS IN BRIOCHE

6 store-bought brioches
 or ready-to-serve dinner rolls
6 eggs
4 T. butter or margarine, melted
Champagne Sauce (recipe follows)

Heat oven to 400°F. Slice tops off brioches about ⅓ of the way down; arrange on cookie sheet and set aside. Carefully scoop out inside of each brioche, leaving enough room (about 2 inches wide and 1 inch deep) to hold 1 egg. Set brioches in muffin tins and brush insides with butter or margarine. Bake tops and "cups" 2 to 3 minutes. Remove from oven; set aside. Break 1 egg into each brioche "cup." Return brioches to oven and bake 8 to 10 minutes or until eggs are set. Remove from muffin tins and place on plate. Spoon Champagne Sauce over each and place lid on top. Makes 6 servings.

CHAMPAGNE SAUCE

2 T. butter or margarine
2 T. all-purpose flour
¼ tsp. salt
½ c. milk
½ c. champagne or sparkling wine
1 T. chopped fresh parsley

In medium saucepan over medium heat, melt butter. With wire whisk, blend in flour and salt. Gradually add milk. Cook, stirring constantly, until sauce thickens and boils. Just before serving, stir in champagne and parsley. Makes about 1 cup.
SERVE WITH:
● *Bloody Marias, page 30*
● *Gingered Fruit Salad, page 14*
● *Irish Coffee, page 197*

A recipe that will wake up even the most sluggish palates, these scrambled eggs are filled with fiery jalapeños and savory bell peppers. Cheddar cheese and avocado make them creamy.

MEXICAN SCRAMBLED EGGS

2 T. butter or margarine
1 small sweet red pepper,
seeded and chopped
1 jalapeño pepper, seeded and
minced or 1 small sweet green
pepper, seeded and chopped
1 small onion, chopped
12 eggs
2 T. water or milk
½ tsp. salt
½ tsp. freshly ground black pepper
½ c. grated Cheddar cheese
GARNISH:
1 ripe avocado, sliced
1 medium tomato, sliced
Fresh coriander (cilantro)

Over medium heat, in medium skillet, melt butter or margarine. Add peppers and onion; sauté until tender. Remove with slotted spoon and set aside. In a bowl beat eggs with water, salt and pepper until frothy. Pour into skillet, and reduce heat to low. Cook, stirring lightly as eggs begin to thicken. Fold in vegetables and cheese. Serve immediately. Garnish with avocado, tomato and coriander. Makes 6 servings.
SERVE WITH:
● *White Wine Sangría, page 198*
● *Bread with Brie Butter, page 74*
● *Chocolate Decadence, page 37*

Here's a suggestion for an intimate, very special brunch for two. Don't let the word soufflé intimidate you. It's a lot easier than you think. Just be sure to keep the oven door closed until it's done. Opening the door will make it fall.

SPINACH-CHEESE SOUFFLÉ

3 T. butter or margarine
3 T. all-purpose flour
½ tsp. salt
1 c. milk
1 c. grated Cheddar cheese
3 eggs, separated
1 10-oz. pkg. frozen chopped
spinach, thawed and well-
drained
½ tsp. Tabasco

Grease 1½-qt. soufflé dish. Heat oven to 350°F. In saucepan, over medium heat, melt butter or margarine. With wire whisk, blend in flour and salt until smooth. Stir in milk and cook, stirring constantly until sauce is thickened and has boiled 2 minutes. Stir in cheese until melted. Stir a small amount of hot cream sauce into egg yolks. Blend yolks back into sauce, stirring constantly. Blend in spinach and Tabasco. Remove from heat. With mixer at high speed, beat egg whites until stiff. Fold cream sauce into egg whites. Pour into soufflé dish. Bake 40 to 50 minutes until golden. Makes 2 breakfast servings.
SERVE WITH:
● *Fresh Fruit Cup, page 15*
● *Gingerbread Muffins, page 140*
● *Doubly-Rich Hot Chocolate, page 141*

To cut down on time, bake this soufflé in individual ramekins. And remember the recipe when you need a dramatic first course, too.

CHEESE SOUFFLÉ

3 T. butter or margarine
3 T. all-purpose flour
1 c. milk
4 eggs, separated,
at room temperature
½ tsp. salt
Pinch ground nutmeg
Pinch ground red pepper
½ c. grated Gruyère or Swiss or
Cheddar cheese
½ c. freshly grated Parmesan
cheese

Heat oven to 400°F. In medium saucepan over medium heat, melt butter or margarine. With wire whisk, blend in flour and cook, stirring constantly, for 2 minutes, or until boiling. Whisk in milk. Cook, stirring constantly for 1 minute, until mixture boils and becomes very thick. Remove saucepan from heat. Whisk in egg yolks, one at a time. Blend in salt, nutmeg and red pepper. Fold in cheeses; set aside. In large mixing bowl with mixer at high speed, beat egg whites until stiff. With rubber spatula or wire whisk, stir ¼ of egg white into cheese sauce. Then, gently fold in remaining egg whites. Pour into six 4-ounce soufflé dishes. Place in oven and immediately reduce heat to 375°F. Bake 15 to 20 minutes or until soufflé is puffed, golden and soft, but set. Makes 6 servings.

SERVE WITH:
- *Smoked salmon or trout with horseradish mixed with mayonnaise*
- *Bagels*
- *A green salad*
- *Chocolate-Dipped Strawberries, page 200*

Tired of quiche? Need an idea for brunch? Try this vegetable tart. It's full of savory things like mushrooms and leeks and ham.

VEGETABLE TART

CRUST:
2 c. all-purpose flour
¼ tsp. salt
½ c. butter or margarine
¼ c. vegetable shortening
3 to 4 T. cold water
FILLING:
2 T. butter or margarine
4 large leeks, split, well rinsed, and sliced (4 c. sliced)
2 c. sliced mushrooms
4 oz. baked ham, chopped (¾ c.)
¼ tsp. dried thyme leaves
⅛ tsp. grated nutmeg
3 eggs
½ tsp. salt
¼ tsp. freshly ground black pepper
1 c. half-and-half

Make the pastry: In a large bowl combine the flour and salt. With pastry blender or with fingertips, cut in the butter or margarine and vegetable shortening until the mixture resembles coarse crumbs. Sprinkle on enough water, while mixing, to allow you to gather the pastry into a ball. Wrap the pastry in plastic wrap and chill for 30 minutes. Meanwhile, in large skillet over medium heat, melt the butter or margarine. Add leeks and sauté until tender, about 5 minutes. Add the mushrooms, ham, thyme and nutmeg, and cook until moisture from mushrooms is evaporated. Set aside. Heat oven to 400°F. Roll out the pastry to fit a 12-inch tart pan. Arrange pastry in pan and trim any excess pastry away. Prick with fork at 1-inch intervals. Line the pan on top of the pastry with foil and fill with beans or pastry weights. Bake for 15 minutes. Remove foil and weights and bake 5 minutes more. Beat the eggs with the salt and pepper and half-and-half. Add the vegetable mixture. Pour into the tart shell and bake 25 to 30 minutes more, or until pale golden and slightly puffed. Makes 12 servings.

SERVE WITH:
- *Fuzzy Navels, page 197*
- *Sour Cream Coffee Cake, page 139*
- *Winter Compote, page 144*

A Southern favorite, ham biscuits make good breakfast, picnic or party food.

HAM BISCUITS

1 ¾ c. all-purpose flour
½ tsp. salt
3 tsp. baking powder
4 T. butter, cut into four pieces
¾ c. milk
2 T. butter or margarine
½ lb. baked ham, thinly sliced, each slice cut in half

Heat oven to 450°F. In large bowl combine flour, salt and baking powder. With fingertips, cut butter into dry ingredients until it resembles coarse cornmeal. Add milk; stir just until dough is free from sides of bowl. Turn onto a lightly floured surface; knead 12 times. Pat out to ¼ inch thick. Cut out with a 2-inch cutter lightly dipped in flour. Place on ungreased cookie sheet. Bake for 12 to 15 minutes, until lightly browned. Meanwhile, melt butter or margarine in medium skillet. Add ham and sauté until heated through. Split biscuits and sandwich a slice of ham in each. Makes about 24 biscuits.

SERVE WITH:
- Scrambled eggs
- Nectarine-Blueberry Compote, page 18
- Pecan Shortbread, page 207

This version of French toast is even better if you can find sourdough bread. It's a delicious way to start the day.

HONEYED FRENCH TOAST

2 eggs, lightly beaten
½ c. plain or vanilla yogurt or milk
¼ tsp. ground cinnamon
2 T. honey
4 slices bread
4 T. softened butter or margarine

In a shallow bowl combine eggs, yogurt or milk, 1 tablespoon of the honey, and cinnamon. Blend well. Dip bread into mixture to coat each side. In a skillet heat 2 tablespoons of the butter. Add bread slices and sauté over medium heat 2 to 3 minutes per side. In a small bowl mix remaining honey and butter until blended, and serve with French toast. Makes 2 servings.
SERVE WITH:
- Canadian bacon or sausage links
- Wake-Up Juice, page 13

These rolls may be time consuming, but they are not diffucult to make. Plan to make them a day ahead. They can be warmed in a 325°F oven for 10 to 15 minutes before serving.

CINNAMON ROLLS

3 T. sugar
1 tsp. salt
1 package (½ oz.) quick-rising yeast
3 ½ c. all-purpose flour
½ c. water
¼ c. milk
4 T. butter or margarine
1 egg, at room temperature
¼ c. light brown sugar,
   firmly packed
¾ tsp. ground cinnamon
ICING:
1 c. confectioners' sugar
5 tsp. milk

Heat oven to 375°F. Grease a 9-inch round cake pan; set aside. In large bowl, mix sugar, salt, yeast and 2½ cups flour. In saucepan, heat water, milk and 3 tablespooons butter or marga-

rine until very warm (125°F to 130°F). Stir into dry ingredients. Mix in egg and enough extra flour to make a soft dough. Turn onto a lightly floured surface and knead 8 to 10 minutes, or until smooth. Put dough into a greased bowl and turn to grease top. Cover; let rise in a warm place until doubled in size, about 35 minutes. Punch down. Roll dough into a 14- by 8-inch rectangle. Melt remaining 1 tablespoon butter and spread over dough. Sprinkle with brown sugar and cinnamon. Roll up lengthwise and pinch to seal long edge. Cut across into 12 slices. Arrange, cut side up, in cake pan. Cover; let rise until doubled, about 30 minutes. Bake 20 to 25 minutes. Remove from pan and cool on wire rack. Combine icing ingredients and drizzle or spread over top. Makes 12 rolls.

Bake this coffee cake when you're asked to bring something to add to a brunch. It travels well. Cool in pan, then remove and return to a clean tube pan and cover; remove and slice when ready to serve.

SOUR CREAM COFFEE CAKE

¾ c. walnuts, finely chopped
2 tsp. ground cinnamon
⅓ c. sugar
CAKE BATTER:
¾ c. butter or margarine
1 ½ c. sugar
3 c. all-purpose flour
1 ½ c. sour cream
3 eggs
1 ½ tsp. baking powder
1 ½ tsp. baking soda
1 ½ tsp. vanilla

Heat oven to 350°F. Grease 10-inch tube pan. In small bowl, combine walnuts, cinnamon and ⅓ c. sugar. Use about ⅓ of this mixture to "dust" inside of tube pan. Set the rest aside for use later. In large bowl with mixer at medium speed, beat butter or margarine with 1½ c. sugar until light and fluffy. Add flour and remaining ingredients (do not include saved nut and sugar mixture); beat at low speed until blended, constantly scraping bowl with rubber spatula. Increase speed to medium; beat 3 minutes. Spread half of batter in pan; sprinkle with half of reserved nut mixture. Spoon in remaining batter, then sprinkle with remaining nut mixture. Bake 60 to 65 minutes, until cake pulls away from sides of pan. Cool cake in pan completely on wire rack. Makes 20 servings.

Bran Muffins are packed with fiber from the bran, flour, raisins and nuts. These are on the large side, made in custard cups instead of muffin tins. Bake them, cool, wrap individually in foil and freeze. Reheat in a 375°F oven, 10 minutes.

THE ULTIMATE BRAN MUFFIN

1 c. bran cereal
¾ c. whole-wheat flour
½ c. all-purpose flour
1 tsp. baking soda
1 tsp. baking powder
½ tsp. salt
2 T. vegetable oil
3 T. honey
½ c. golden raisins
¼ c. slivered almonds
1 c. buttermilk
1 egg, beaten

Heat oven to 375°F. Grease twelve 2-inch muffin cups or six 1-cup custard cups. In large bowl combine bran, flours, baking soda, baking powder and salt. Add oil, honey, raisins, almonds, buttermilk and egg; stir until just combined. Spoon into muffin cups and bake 15 to 20 minutes for medium muffins or 20 to 25 minutes for larger ones or until golden brown. Makes 12 medium or 6 large muffins.

Bake these muffins in mini-muffin cups. They make great go-alongs with any brunch menu. You can also serve them with salad for lunch.

GINGERBREAD MUFFINS

3 c. all-purpose flour
¼ tsp. salt
1 ½ tsp. baking soda
1 tsp. ground ginger
1 tsp. ground cinnamon
½ tsp. ground coriander
¼ tsp. ground cloves
1 T. finely chopped candied ginger
½ c. chopped pitted dates
¾ c. molasses
½ c. butter or margarine
½ c. sugar
1 egg
1 ¼ c. buttermilk

Heat oven to 375°F. Grease 12 regular or 24 mini-muffin cups. In a large mixing bowl, combine dry ingredients, add the candied ginger and dates; set aside. In a small saucepan heat the molasses and butter or margarine until the butter is melted. Stir in the sugar. Beat the egg into the buttermilk and stir into molasses. Pour into the dry ingredients and mix just until smooth. Pour into muffin cups. Bake 20 minutes for large or 12 for small, or until tops are springy in center. Makes twelve 2 ½-inch muffins or 24 smaller muffins.

Any morning becomes special, if you wake up your usual toast or breakfast muffin with these tastes.

FRENCH CINNAMON SUGAR

1 c. confectioners' sugar
2 T. ground cinnamon

In shaker or in small bowl, combine sugar and cinnamon. Sprinkle on buttered toast.

STRAWBERRY BUTTER

½ c. butter or margarine, softened
1 c. strawberries,
   washed and hulled
   or 1 c. frozen strawberries,
   thawed

In blender or in food processor, process butter or margarine and strawberries until smooth. Spoon into a small crock.

When mornings leave no time for a full breakfast, start your day with one of these blender drinks. They cut corners on time, but not on flavor or nutrition.

QUICKIE BLENDER SHAKE

½ c. fresh or frozen fruit, such as
   pineapple, peach, strawberry or
   blueberry
½ banana
½ c. flavored yogurt
1 T. wheat germ

Combine all ingredients in blender container. Whirl on high until smooth. Makes 1 serving.

PEACH WAKE-UP TONIC

⅔ c. cold buttermilk
¼ pkg. frozen unsweetened
    peaches (about ½ c.)
1 egg
2 tsp. maple syrup

Place all ingredients in a blender container. Blend on high speed until thick and frothy. Makes 1 serving.

Hot cocoa will never have quite the same meaning after you try this one. Instead of adding whipped cream to the chocolate make a rich chocolate whipped cream and add hot, simmering milk . . . yum!

DOUBLY-RICH HOT CHOCOLATE

2 1-oz. squares semisweet
    chocolate
2 T. light corn syrup
¼ tsp. orange extract or 2 T.
    orange liqueur
2 c. milk
½ c. heavy or whipping cream

Make chocolate syrup: In double boiler top over hot, not boiling, water, melt chocolate with corn syrup. Remove from heat; stir in orange extract and cool. In heavy saucepan, heat milk until small bubbles form (do not boil). Beat heavy cream with the cooled chocolate syrup until soft peaks form. Spoon some chocolate whipped cream into each of 4 cups. Pour in hot milk. Stir to melt cream. Makes 4 servings.

GREAT REASONS TO GET OUT OF BED IN THE MORNING

Whether you're a no-time-for-breakfast, a grab-it-on-the-run type, or just find breakfast boring most mornings, there's a way to work in a nutritious, interesting morning meal to fit your own pace. Take a look at the chart here to see what a little imagination can do to enhance breakfast. Your reward: you'll feel better all day, avoid that mid-morning slump and start forming a healthier eating habit.

IF YOU USUALLY HAVE	TRY THIS	WITH A LITTLE EXTRA EFFORT
Toast	Toast 2 slices of bread; spread one slice with apple butter, the other with chunky peanut butter. Sprinkle with raisins and coconut. Make a sandwich.	Sprinkle a corn tortilla with grated Cheddar cheese. Top with tomato slices and minced chilies. Broil.
English Muffin	Mash avocado with ricotta cheese. Spoon onto muffin; sprinkle with sesame seeds.	Top with a slice of ham, alfalfa sprouts, a slice of Swiss cheese and a pineapple ring.
Bagel	Spread bagel with chunky peanut butter and top with sliced bananas.	Blend canned salmon with cream cheese and spread on toasted bagel. Top with sprouts and Muenster cheese.
Just coffee	Have a mug of cream of tomato soup.	Make instant oatmeal; flavor with brown sugar and walnuts.
Croissant	Split and fill croissant with a slice of ham, a smear of honey and papaya wedges.	Split and spread croissant with tuna salad flavored with curry; top with an apple slice.
Bowl of cereal	Combine cereal with fruited yogurt instead of milk.	Top cereal with a scoop of ice cream; sprinkle with sunflower seeds and almonds.
Danish	Spread orange marmalade and cream cheese on a slice of date nut bread. Top with orange sections.	Spread bran muffin with ricotta cheese, dates and a spoonful of honey. Sprinkle with wheat germ.
Yogurt	Blend cucumber slices and tomato chunks in yogurt.	In a blender container, combine plain yogurt, chopped apricots, a splash of orange juice, a pinch of ground ginger and cinnamon and ice cubes. Whirl until frothy.

141

When you're in the mood for... the refreshing taste of fruit

Fruit picked at the height of the season, whether it's a blushing mid-summer peach or a crisp autumn apple, has a flavor which is astonishingly true, and these recipes let that flavor shine through. Sorbets, for winter or summer, compotes using dried or fresh fruits, and even popsicles make fabulous desserts. Some of these recipes are extraordinarily simple, such as the Frozen Fruit on Skewers, below. Others, the Glacéed Oranges with Sugar Straws, right, for instance, demand a little more time. Note the charts on all types of fruits that tell you what to look for, how to store and what to serve them with. You'll learn all you need to know about optimum flavor and freshness.

This icy cold refresher is a favorite with kids and adults on steamy days. Substitute cantaloupe and peaches for the honeydew and nectarines, if you like.

FROZEN FRUIT ON SKEWERS

1 fresh pineapple
½ medium honeydew melon
3 nectarines
½ pint strawberries, washed and hulled
2 T. honey
2 T. fresh lemon juice

Cut pineapple into 4 wedges, then into ½-inch crosswise slices. Cut melon in half; seed, then cut into 2-inch thick wedges. Cut wedges horizontally in half. Cut each nectarine in half, discard pits and cut each half into 3 wedges. In small bowl, combine honey and lemon juice. Dip pieces of fruit into honey and lemon. Thread fruit on 6 skewers, alternating the different fruits. Place on jelly-roll pan and freeze until the fruit is firm, about 3 hours. Let stand about 10 minutes to soften slightly before serving. Makes 6 servings.

Toss together three of the best flavors and colors of summer—succulent blueberries, raspberries and blushing peaches.

BLUEBERRY-PEACH COMPOTE WITH RASPBERRY SAUCE

3 c. blueberries
3 peaches
Raspberry Sauce (recipe follows)

Pick over and rinse blueberries and slice peaches. In a bowl, toss fruits together; cover with plastic wrap. To serve, divide among 6 goblets or bowls. Top with Raspberry Sauce. Makes 6 servings.

RASPBERRY SAUCE

1 pint fresh raspberries*
2 T. sugar
¼ c. cassis (black currant liqueur)
*Or use 1 10-oz. pkg. frozen raspberries, thawed and omit sugar

In food processor or blender, purée raspberries, sugar and liqueur. Press through fine sieve to remove the seeds. Chill.

Making sugar straw is a little tricky. But, you can make it ahead alone in the kitchen without the worry of waiting guests.

GLACÉED ORANGES WITH SUGAR STRAW

6 navel oranges
Water
4 c. sugar
6 T. orange liqueur

Use a vegetable peeler to peel oranges, being careful not to cut off any of the white pith. With sharp knife, cut about 20 very thin strips of peel; discard remaining peel. Drop strips into boiling water for 5 minutes. Remove, drain and cool. With sharp knife, cut away and discard outer white membrane from oranges. Cool to room temperature. In heavy saucepan over medium heat, cook sugar and 1⅓ cups water. Do not stir. When sugar is dissolved, cover pan and boil 5 minutes. Remove cover and continue cooking until temperature reaches 250°F on a candy thermometer, or hard-ball stage (when a small amount of syrup dropped into cold water forms a hard-ball). Reduce heat to very low. Working quickly, spear an orange on the tines of a fork and coat with syrup. Place on serving plate. Repeat with remaining oranges. To make sugar straw: Remove saucepan from heat. Allow remaining syrup to cool and begin to set. Using the tines of a fork, pull sugar into thin strands. (Keep checking temperature. If too hot, the strands will not form; if too cool, you won't be able to pull the sugar.) Pile straw around oranges. Pour about 1 tablespoon orange liqueur over each orange just before serving. Scatter strips of peel over each. Makes 6 servings.

Keep this recipe on hand to sweeten up less than perfect melons: Cantaloupe, a honeydew, Cassaba, Crenshaw or watermelon.

FRESH FRUIT MARSALA

SAUCE:
1 c. Marsala wine
¼ T. honey
2 2-inch strips lemon peel
2 2-inch strips orange peel
4 whole cloves
1 4-inch stick cinnamon
¼ c. fresh orange juice
FRUIT:
1 small honeydew melon (or other)
1 pint strawberries
2 papayas

In medium saucepan over medium-low heat, heat all sauce ingredients except juice until honey melts; do not boil. Remove from heat, stir in juice. Let stand 1 hour. Cut melon into 4 wedges; remove seeds. Cut each wedge horizontally in half, then in thin slices lengthwise; trim off rind. Wash, then hull strawberries. Cut berries in half. Seed and peel papaya. Cut into chunks. In large bowl combine fruit and sauce. Chill before serving. Makes 6 servings.

Not for drizzling over ice cream only, this fruit sauce is excellent ladled over pancakes or thick slices of buttery pound cake. Remember this too, for gifts. Pack into jars, label and refrigerate for up to a month.

SPICED BLUEBERRY SAUCE

¼ c. sugar
¼ c. water
½ tsp. ground cinnamon
¼ tsp. ground cloves
¼ tsp. grated nutmeg
1 pt. blueberries

Combine sugar, water, cinnamon, cloves and nutmeg in small saucepan. Over high heat, heat to boiling. In small bowl, crush 1 cup blueberries with fork; add to syrup. Cook 4 to 5 minutes, until mixture is thick. Stir in remaining 1 cup whole blueberries and cook for 2 minutes more. Let cool slightly. Serve over ice cream. Makes about 1 ½ cups.

THE JUICY DETAILS
When selecting oranges or tangerines, look for fruit that is firm and heavy for its size. Once you get the fruit home, refrigerate it until ready to use.

VARIETY	LOOK FOR...	TRY THEM FOR A...
Navel	thick-skinned, extra-large fruit. Peels easily. Best supply: Nov.–Jan.	salad: Thinly slice 4 oranges (peeled) and 2 small onions; arrange on a platter. Sprinkle with dried mint and oil/vinegar dressing.
Valencia	large fruit with smooth, thin skin, deep color. Usually seedless. Best supply: Apr.–May.	soup: Combine 2 cans tomato soup with ½ c. dry white wine, 1 c. orange juice and 1 tsp. sugar. Heat through.
Temple	medium to large fruit with deep orange color. Peels easily. Best supply: Jan.–March.	salad: Peel and section 2 oranges and toss with 2 avocados, peeled and sliced. Sprinkle with 2 tsp. minced onion, ¼ tsp. salt, ¼ tsp. chili powder. Sprinkle with oil.
Tangelo	large fruit, cross between tangerine and grapefruit. Resembles an orange. Best supply: Jan.	dessert: Grate rind from 1 tangelo. Mix with 2 T. butter, 3 T. brown sugar. Layer 2 tangelos, peeled and sliced with 2 bananas, peeled and sliced. Dot with orange butter. Bake 10 minutes at 400°F.
Tangerine	small or medium fruit with flattened ends, deep color. Peels and sections easily. Best supply: Dec.–Feb.	snack: Peel and section tangerine. Dip each section into honey, then chopped walnuts. Freeze on a tray until firm. Eat while still frozen.

Try this recipe for a romantic evening just for the two of you—the strawberries give it exactly the right color for Valentine's Day.

STRAWBERRIES SABAYON

2 egg yolks
⅓ c. sugar
⅓ c. brandy
½ pt. fresh strawberries, hulled

In double-boiler top over hot, not boiling, water, beat egg yolks, sugar and brandy with wire whisk until very thick. Set double-boiler top in bowl of icewater and continue beating until mixture is cold. To serve, halve berries if large; place in 2 wine glasses. Spoon sauce over berries. (Sauce can be made ahead. Cover and refrigerate until time to serve.) Makes 2 servings.

Flambéing always causes a sensation. (See page 199). Keep ingredients on hand, and you can delight guests at a moments notice.

SAUTÉED BANANAS

2 firm bananas, peeled and cut in
half lengthwise
2 T. butter or margarine
1 tsp. grated lemon peel
2 T. sugar
2 T. brandy

In large skillet over medium heat, sauté bananas in hot butter or margarine for 2 minutes. Add lemon peel, sugar and brandy. Ignite and serve at once. Makes 2 to 4 servings.

This recipe combines all the spicy goodness of the season.

WINTER COMPOTE

2 c. apple juice
½ c. prunes
½ c. dried apricots
¼ c. golden raisins
¼ c. bourbon
3 thin lemon slices
¼ tsp. ground ginger
1 Granny Smith apple, peeled,
cored and cut into wedges

1 pear, peeled, cored and
cut into wedges
¼ c. wheat germ, for garnish

In a heavy saucepan heat apple juice, prunes, apricots and raisins to boiling. Add bourbon, lemon and ginger. Reduce heat to low, cover and simmer 15 minutes. Add apple and pear and simmer 5 to 7 minutes more, or until apple and pear are tender but still hold their shape. Remove lemon; cool slightly before serving. Sprinkle with wheat germ. Makes 4 servings.

A GUIDE TO PERFECT MELONS

Are you intimidated when picking out a melon? Then use this chart for disappointment-free choosing and enjoy.

MELON	LOOK FOR...	GOOD USES
Cantaloupe	smoothly rounded depression at ends; webbing protruding from yellowish surface. Slight pleasant aroma when ripe; stem end yields to pressure.	Halve in saw-tooth pattern. Scoop out seeds; fill with blackberries; sprinkle with cassis.
Casaba	golden-yellow, ridged skin; large, round shape. Pointed end softens slightly when ripe.	Serve wedges with blue cheese and salami as light lunch or appetizer.
Crenshaw	pear shape, either bright yellow or yellow and green. Pleasant aroma; yields to pressure on ends when ripe.	Combine chunks with hearts of palm, fresh raspberries and slices of avocado. Serve with your favorite vinaigrette.
Honeydew	creamy white or pale yellow color. For better quality and more edible fruit, buy large (5–7 lbs.) size.	Purée ¾ melon. Stir in 2 c. pineapple juice, ⅓ c. fresh lime juice, 3 T. honey and remaining ¼ melon, cubed. Chill. Add 2 c. chilled white wine. Garnish with lime slices.
Watermelon	creamy color on underside, rounded, filled-out ends and smooth, not shiny surface.	Blend on high: 5 c. cubed and seeded watermelon, ½ c. orange juice, ⅓ c. melon liqueur and 2 T. grenadine. Add ice cubes, 1 c. at a time, until thick.

Fresh, unadorned raspberries served with crisp sparkling wine

Jazz up your favorite type of pear— even canned— with this super simple recipe.

PEARS IN RASPBERRY SAUCE

**4 pears, washed, peeled, cored
   and thinly sliced
1 T. fresh lemon juice
1 10-oz. pkg. frozen raspberries,
   thawed
¼ c. orange liqueur
   or fresh orange juice
1 8-oz. container vanilla yogurt**

Sprinkle lemon juice over pears. Arrange in individual bowls. Purée raspberries in blender; combine with liqueur and yogurt in a bowl. Spoon over pears and serve. Makes 4 to 6 servings.

Five recipes to satisfy any sorbet craving—any time of the year. Some are made with winter fruits, others with summer.

APPLE SORBET

**3 large apples, peeled,
   cored and chopped
Juice of 1 lemon
⅔ c. sugar
½ c. water
2 c. apple juice or cider**

In blender or food processor with knife blade attached, purée apples and lemon juice; set aside. In medium saucepan combine sugar and water. Over high heat, heat to boiling. Cook 5 minutes or until thickened slightly. Add apple juice and remove from heat. Add apple purée. Cool. Pour into ice cream maker and freeze according to manufacturer's directions or pour into metal baking dish and freeze. When frozen, scoop into food processor (or into a bowl using an electric hand mixer), process to break up ice crystals. Freeze again. Reprocess and serve. Makes 5 cups sorbet.

RASPBERRY SORBET

**2 pts. raspberries
1 c. sugar
½ c. water
1 T. fresh lime juice**

In a bowl, with wooden spoon, mash the berries with sugar and let stand for 30 minutes. Press through a fine sieve, discard seeds. Add water and lime juice. Pour into ice cream maker and freeze according to manufacturer's directions or pour into metal baking dish and freeze until almost firm. Scoop into food processor (or into a bowl using an electric hand mixer) and process until smooth. Freeze again. Reprocess and serve. Makes 3 cups.

CRANBERRY SORBET

**⅔ c. sugar
⅔ c. water
3 c. fresh or frozen cranberries
1 c. chilled cranberry juice
Grated peel of 1 orange
1 egg white**

In small saucepan over medium heat, combine sugar and water. Cook, stirring constantly, just until mixture starts to boil. Remove from heat. Cool, then cover and refrigerate until chilled. In food processor with knife blade attached, or in blender, purée cranberries. Add chilled syrup and remaining ingredients except egg white. Process until well combined. Pour into ice cream maker and freeze according to manufacturer's directions or pour into metal pan and freeze. When frozen, scoop into food processor (or into a bowl using an electric hand mixer); add egg white and process to break up crystals; freeze again. Makes 4 cups.

BANANA SORBET

**⅔ c. sugar
⅔ c. water
2 large ripe bananas, chilled and
   peeled
1 c. fresh orange juice, chilled
2 T. fresh lemon juice**

In small saucepan over medium heat, combine sugar and water. Heat, stirring constantly, just until mixture starts to boil. Remove from heat, cool and chill. In food processor with knife blade attached, or in blender, purée bananas. Add chilled syrup and remaining ingredients and process until smooth. Pour into ice cream maker and freeze according to manufacturer's directions or pour into metal pan and freeze. Remove from freezer. Scoop into processor (or into a bowl using an electric hand mixer) and process to break up crystals. Refreeze. Makes 4 cups.

LIME SORBET

1 lime, quartered
Water
1 ⅓ c. sugar
3 T. fresh lime juice
1 egg white
Green food coloring
(optional)

In small saucepan, combine quartered lime with enough water to cover. Heat to boiling. Cover and simmer 10 minutes, or until tender. Remove from heat and strain, reserving liquid and lime. In food processor with knife blade attached or in blender, purée lime with ⅓ cup sugar. With machine running, gradually add ½ cup reserved liquid. Return mixture to saucepan and simmer slowly, stirring often, until thick and syrupy, about 25 minutes. Remove from heat. Stir in lime juice; cool; chill. Meanwhile, in another small saucepan, combine 1 cup water and remaining 1 cup sugar. Cook, stirring constantly, just until mixture starts to boil. Remove from heat. Cool, then chill. When both lime mixture and syrup are chilled, process together. Pour into ice cream maker and freeze according to manufacturer's directions or pour into metal pan and freeze. When frozen, remove from freezer. Scoop into food processor (or into bowl with electric hand mixer) and process, adding egg white and a few drops of food coloring until smooth; freeze again. Makes 4 cups.

GOURMET FRUIT SHOPPERS GUIDE

Fresh fruits tempt your senses with their luscious colors, shapes, juices and fragrances. Here, how to pick, store, serve and enjoy some special fruits.

FRUIT	LOOK FOR...	STORE...	ENJOY...
Apricots	glowing golden-yellow color and distinct fragrance. The stronger the color, the sweeter the fruit.	refrigerated. Use as soon as possible. Wash only when ready to use.	sliced into a bowl; top with honey, yogurt and sprinkle with chopped almonds or wheat germ.
Blackberries	brightness and shine—dull skin means overripe fruit. Avoid green spots. Berries without stems have fullest, richest flavor.	unwashed in a covered bowl and use within a day or two of purchase.	berries gently folded into heavy or whipped cream (or yogurt) and sprinkle with grated orange peel.
Cranberries	plump, dry berries. A good one will bounce if dropped; damaged ones won't.	refrigerated and use within one to two weeks. Cranberries freeze perfectly in plastic bags.	chopped raw cranberries in a sweetened orange or apple salad with a few chopped walnuts.
Cherries	firmness. The darker the color, the sweeter the taste. Cherries with green, healthy stems last longer.	unwashed in sealed plastic bags and refrigerate. They will keep for about 3 days without losing flavor.	pitted and sliced cherries, folded into softened vanilla ice cream. Sprinkle with kirsch.
Figs	figs that are soft to the touch with unblemished, unbruised skin. Overripe ones have a sour odor.	unwashed figs in sealed plastic bags. Use within 36 hours of purchase.	halved figs draped with thin slices of prosciutto or ham. With a glass of wine, it's a perfect lunch.
Peaches	fully ripe peaches with a reddish blush on a creamy yellow background. Pick plump, spherical, medium-sized ones.	at room temperature for 3–4 days to fully ripen them. Then store in sealed plastic bags in refrigerator for 1–2 days.	sliced and marinated for an hour in red or white wine. Serve in a goblet with a bit of wine spooned over each.
Plums	firm fruit, but soft enough to yield to slight pressure. Look for a glossy skin, uniform color.	if ripe, in sealed plastic bags in refrigerator. To ripen, keep at room temperature for a day then store in refrigerator for 3–5 days.	with a creamy rich cheese such as, Camembert or blue, on the side—a great warm-weather dessert.
Pome-granates	firmness, heaviness for its size, and a shiny skin. Large are better—the kernels are bigger and juicier.	in vegetable bin of refrigerator and use within a week	whole kernels sprinkled into a fresh fruit salad.
Raspberries	firmness and plumpness with uniform color. Stems are a sign of immature fruit.	unwashed in refrigerator. It is best to use them the same day as purchased.	as a traditional strawberry shortcake, substituting raspberries for strawberries.

When you're in the mood for... crisp and crunchy salads

Gone are the days when salad meant a run-of-the-mill bowl of iceberg lettuce doused in thousand island dressing. Salads these days can be simple but sophisticated such as the Golden Tossed Salad, page 151, hearty and filling pastas, or a healthy mix of pick-of-the-season vegetables. There are several different bean salads and a Middle Eastern grain salad. Salads make a terrific first course, or a palate cleanser after a rich meal. They can even become great lunches, brunches and dinners on their own. Dressings can be jazzed up with peanut butter, exotic oils and vinegars and/or an abundance of fresh herbs. Remember: A salad's flavor should snap with freshness, never drown it in dressing, just toss with enough to coat lightly. This collection of salads filled with seasonal goodness will take you throughout the year. To ensure mistake-proof salads every time, follow the dressing basics and green tips on pages 152 and 153.

Some exotic ingredients are used to create this salad. If unavailable in your market, experiment. Substitute other kinds of salad ingredients such as celery, Boston lettuce, or just use one kind of pepper. Cod or halibut can stand in for scallops.

INCREDIBLE SEAFOOD SALAD

8 radishes
2 sweet red bell peppers
1 sweet yellow bell pepper
1 sweet green bell pepper
3 plum tomatoes
1 lb. sea scallops, sautéed in butter or margarine
1 lb. shelled cooked shrimp
½ jicama or ½ c. sliced waterchestnuts
½ head chicory
1 large head romaine
¼ lb. mâche or Boston lettuce
1 pkg. radish sprouts or cress
½ c. black beans
Carribean Dressing (page 152)

Slice or chop vegetables; tear lettuce into bite-sized pieces. Combine all ingredients and toss with dressing. Makes 6 to 8 meal-sized servings.

This delicious salad makes a dazzling presentation served in its own bowl made from a whole loaf of bread (page 33).

CORN AND BEEF SALAD IN BREAD BOWL

BREAD BOWL:
1 large (10" in diameter by 4" high) round loaf of bread
2 eggs, beaten
2 T. milk
SALAD:
½ c. olive oil
2 T. vinegar
2 tsp. ground cumin
½ tsp. salt
1 lb. cooked sirloin cut into 1- by 1½-inch pieces
4 c. corn kernals (fresh or 2 pkgs. frozen corn, thawed)
¼ c. chopped fresh coriander (cilantro) or parsley
2 c. small fresh spinach leaves (or coarsely chopped, if large)
4 to 5 slices red onion (optional)

To make bread bowl, cut a "lid" from the bread using a serrated knife. Cut around the inside circumference of the loaf to remove the inside (reserve to make bread crumbs or croutons), leaving about ¾ inch thick crust all around. Preheat oven to 350°F. Beat eggs and milk together. Brush inside of loaf with egg glaze. Wrap outside of loaf with foil to prevent browning, leaving the inside open and exposed. Place on a cookie sheet. Bake for about 20 minutes or until egg glaze is cooked and inside of loaf is firm and dry. Cool. Combine oil, vinegar, cumin and salt. Combine beef, corn, coriander, spinach and onions in a bowl and toss with dressing to coat. Spoon into bread bowl. Makes 8 servings.

An exotic combination of shellfish and greens make an incredible seafood salad

This potato salad is a sophisticated version of its mayonnaised cousin. Cook the beans only until tender-crisp so they'll give the salad some crunch.

DILLED POTATO-BEAN SALAD

1 lb. new potatoes
¾ lb. fresh green beans,
    cut into 2-inch pieces
¼ C. olive oil
2 T. dry vermouth
1 scallion, minced
1 T. chopped fresh dill
1 T. chopped fresh parsley
½ tsp. sugar
½ tsp. salt
⅛ tsp. freshly ground black pepper

In medium saucepan over high heat, heat potatoes and 1 inch lightly salted water to boiling. Reduce heat to low; cover and simmer 20 minutes or until fork-tender. Drain. In another saucepan bring beans, and 1 inch lightly salted water, to boiling. Simmer 3 minutes or until tender-crisp. Drain and rinse with cold water to stop cooking. When potatoes are cool enough to handle, peel and cut into ¼-inch strips. Add to beans. In small bowl, combine olive oil with remaining ingredients. Pour over potatoes and beans. With rubber spatula, gently toss until well coated. Cover and refrigerate until cold and flavors mellow, about 2 hours. Makes 6 servings.

This dazzling salad is a wonderful choice during the holiday season—but don't wait for winter to enjoy it.

RED PEPPER
AND SNAP BEAN SALAD

3 bottled roasted red peppers
2 lbs. green beans, trimmed
VINAIGRETTE:
½ C. olive oil
1 ½ T. red wine vinegar
1 ½ tsp. Dijon mustard
2 scallions, minced
1 T. minced fresh parsley
Dash freshly ground black pepper

Cut roasted peppers into thin slivers. In steamer or in saucepan in 1 inch water, steam beans

until tender, 7 to 10 minutes. Rinse under cold water to stop cooking; drain. Combine vinaigrette ingredients in jar with tight-fitting lid; shake. Toss with roasted red peppers and green beans. Makes 8 servings.

Serve this salad year round. It's hearty enough to make a meal or pair it with grilled chicken or fish.

BEAN AND SAUSAGE SALAD

⅓ C. olive or salad oil
⅓ C. chopped onion
⅓ C. minced parsley
3 T. white wine vinegar
1 to 2 garlic cloves, minced
1 tsp. freshly ground black pepper
½ tsp. salt (or to taste)
1 20-oz. can white kidney beans,
    drained (about 3 cups)
½ lb. salami, (use small type, slice
    into rounds)
Lettuce leaves

Combine oil, onion, parsley, vinegar, garlic, pepper and salt in a jar. Shake well; pour over beans. Toss gently to coat and let stand covered at room temperature about four hours. Fold in salami. Serve on lettuce leaves. Makes 8 servings.

This pasta will absorb less oil if you drain the cooked tortellini; rinse them well with cold water and chill before tossing with dressing.

TORTELLINI SALAD

4 oz. feta cheese
1 5-oz. pkg. frozen tortellini,
    cooked and chilled (1 ½ c.
    cooked)
½ C. pitted black olives, halved
1 tomato, diced
DRESSING:
¼ C. chopped fresh parsley
3 T. chopped fresh basil
    or 2 tsp. dried
⅓ C. olive oil
⅛ tsp. freshly ground pepper
Dash nutmeg

Cut cheese into ½-inch cubes. In large bowl,

combine all ingredients. Toss with dressing. Good served chilled or at room temperature. Makes 4 servings.

Pair this salad with barbecued lamb and sliced juicy tomatoes. It can be made a day ahead.

TABOULI

1 ½ c. raw bulgur
1 c. boiling water
4 c. cold water
Juice of 1 lemon
½ c. red wine vinegar
1 garlic clove, minced
2 tsp. prepared mustard
Salt and freshly ground black
    pepper to taste
½ tsp. ground cumin
¾ c. olive oil
1 bunch scallions, sliced
½ c. minced fresh parsley
½ c. chopped fresh mint
2 tomatoes, chopped
1 cucumber, peeled and diced

Place bulgur in bowl and pour boiling water over it. Let stand a few minutes; add cold water. In small bowl combine lemon juice, vinegar, garlic, mustard, salt, pepper and cumin. Whisk in oil and pour over bulgur. Combine remaining ingredients. Add to bulgur. Let stand ½ hour before serving. (If bulgur hasn't absorbed the liquid, pour off excess.) Makes 8 servings.

Lightly dressed with an herby dressing, this crunchy and colorful salad is great paired with Dill-Potato Salad (page 150) and served with a roasted chicken or burgers.

ASPARAGUS-CARROT SALAD

¾ lb. asparagus,
    cut into 2-inch pieces
¾ lb. carrots,
    thinly sliced on the diagonal
¼ c. olive oil
2 T. lemon juice
1 garlic clove, crushed
1 T. chopped fresh basil
    or ½ tsp. dried
1 T. fresh thyme leaves
    or ¼ tsp. dried
¼ tsp. sugar
¼ tsp. salt
Dash cracked black pepper

In medium saucepan heat asparagus and 1 inch lightly salted water to boiling. Cook asparagus 3 to 5 minutes, or until tender-crisp. Remove and run under cold water to stop cooking. Repeat with carrots. Combine remaining ingredients in small bowl. While vegetables are still warm, toss with dressing. Cover and refrigerate until cold and flavors are mellow, about 3 hours. Discard garlic before serving. Makes 6 servings.

When your dinners need a lift, serve this salad—it's dramatically colored and hearty.

GOLDEN TOSSED SALAD

DRESSING:
3 T. white wine vinegar
1 T. olive oil
1 T. honey
1 T. toasted sesame seeds
⅛ tsp. dry mustard
SALAD:
1 10 oz. bag fresh spinach leaves
1 head romaine lettuce
½ head leafy lettuce
1 small red onion
1 navel orange,
    peeled and cut into wedges
¼ c. walnuts, toasted

In small bowl with wire whisk, combine dressing ingredients until well mixed; set aside. Wash well and dry spinach, romaine and leafy lettuce. Tear into bite-sized pieces. Peel onion and thinly slice; separate into rings. Combine greens with onion, orange and walnuts. Add dressing; toss until well coated. Makes 6 servings.

This salad packs lots of fiber with its crunch. Toss in a can of tuna for a healthy meal.

WINTER GARDEN SALAD

4 c. spinach leaves
2 c. watercress leaves
½ c. snow peas, lightly steamed
½ c. cooked black beans
½ c. sliced radishes
¼ c. walnut halves
1 grapefruit,
    peeled and cut into sections
8 ears canned baby corn, drained
Olive oil and vinegar, for dressing

Arrange ingredients on a large serving platter or on 4 individual plates. Drizzle with oil and vinegar. Makes 4 servings.

DRESSINGS

This is a basic recipe for vinaigrette. You can experiment with different kinds of oils and adjust the kinds and amounts of vinegars too, to make it your own signature dressing.

THE TASTIEST VINAIGRETTE

½ c. olive oil
1 ½ T. red wine vinegar
1 ½ tsp. Dijon mustard
2 scallions, minced (1 T.)
1 T. minced fresh parsley
Freshly ground black pepper

Combine all ingredients in jar with tight-fitting lid. Shake vigorously. Makes about ¾ cup.

A more pungent vinaigrette, this one is best used on a simple green salad, one with few competing ingredients.

PUNGENT VINAIGRETTE

¼ c. red wine vinegar
⅔ c. olive oil
2 tsp. Dijon mustard
1 T. chopped fresh tarragon leaves
    or ½ tsp. dried
½ tsp. salt
¼ tsp. freshly ground black pepper

Combine ingredients in a jar with tight-fitting lid. Shake vigorously. Makes about 1 cup dressing.

Use this very heady, pungent dressing on salads such as shrimp or chicken.

CARIBBEAN DRESSING

¼ c. fresh lime juice
⅔ c. olive oil
¼ c. chopped fresh coriander
    (cilantro)
½ tsp. ground cumin seed
¼ to ½ tsp. red pepper flakes
½ tsp. salt
⅛ tsp. freshly ground black pepper

Whisk together lime juice and olive oil. Blend in remaining ingredients and mix well. Makes about 1 cup dressing.

This is a thick and creamy dressing. Use it on greens tossed with apple or pear slices for a different kind of winter salad.

CHEDDAR DRESSING

1 c. shredded Cheddar cheese
1 T. prepared horseradish
¼ c. apple juice or apple cider
1 c. sour cream

In small bowl with whisk combine all ingredients. Chill until ready to serve. Makes 2 cups dressing.

Use this dressing on grain salads, like rice or pasta. It is also very good on fresh fruit salad. You can vary the flavor with the kind and amount of curry you use.

CURRIED CITRUS DRESSING

½ c. safflower oil
¼ c. fresh lemon or lime juice
1 T. apricot jam
1 tsp. curry powder

In a small jar with tight-fitting lid, combine oil, lemon or lime juice, apricot jam and curry powder. Cover and shake until well combined. Makes ¾ cup.

GET THE MOST FROM YOUR GREENS

● *Refrigerate them in perforated plastic bags so air can circulate. Use iceberg within two weeks, romaine within five days and all others within two days.*
● *Wash lettuce gently in cold water. Dry thoroughly either in a salad spinner or by blotting with a paper towel. For better crunch, loosely pack in a bag and refrigerate one hour before dressing.*
● *Tear lettuce into bite-sized pieces, just before serving. Cutting lettuce can bruise it.*
● *To avoid soggy salads, put dressing on just before eating.*
● *For extra crisp and snappy salads, try this: Wash and dry greens and other salad ingredients well. Refrigerate. About 10 minutes before serving, toss salad with dressing and place in freezer for five minutes.*

HOW TO MIX GREENS

Any salad that starts and stops with iceberg lettuce is missing out, not only on taste but on texture. A good salad includes a mix of mild and assertive greens to add texture, taste and color. Here, greens you're most apt to see and use.

MILD GREENS	LOOK FOR...	FLAVOR	TEXTURE
Boston (Butterhead)	tightly packed heads with light green outer leaves and light yellow leaves inside.	Subtle and sweet	Soft and tender
Bibb	deep, rich green color; whitish-green toward core.	Delicate and buttery	Slightly crisper than Boston
Romaine	long head with narrow leaves.	Mild and sweet	Crispy, but not tough
Red-Edged Ruby	large, loosely packed, red-tipped leaves.	Mild and sweet	Crisp and delicate
Spinach	rich green color with young tender stems.	Musky flavor	Coarse and hearty
Corn Salad (mâche or lambs lettuce)	dark green leaves about 2–3 inches long; comes in small clusters rather than heads.	Sweet	Very delicate

ASSERTIVE GREENS	LOOK FOR...	FLAVOR	TEXTURE
Escarole	broad-ribbed leaves, loosely packed.	Very bitter	Crisp and hearty
Belgium Endive	white to whitish-green color; compact pointed cylinders.	Strong and somewhat bitter	Snappy
Arugula (rocket)	bunches of oak-shaped leaves; light green color.	Pungent, tart and faintly lemony	Gently crispy
Watercress	fresh, bright color; long stems with small thick leaves.	Pungent and peppery	Crisp
Chicory (curly leaf endive)	bunchy heads with narrow, curly leaves.	Center has milder taste than dark green bitter outer leaves	Crisp and hearty
Raddichio	tight, small deep purple-red heads with white ribs.	Emphatic and bitter	Hearty and cabbage-like

DRESSING BASICS

Consider some of these suggestions for a new twist to your old favorite dressing recipes.

● A rich green, fruity olive oil is an excellent choice for most green salads. Use mild-flavored peanut, corn and safflower oil to combine with a more potent one like a nut oil, strong heady olive oil or sesame oil.

● Blend walnut or hazelnut oil with peanut oil—wonderful with chicken salads. Sesame oil mixed with safflower oil is marvelous with seafood and vegetable salads.

● Vinegars can change the character and flavor of a dressing. A basic vinaigrette (such as the one on page 152) is transformed when you substitute different kinds of vinegar. For example, a vinaigrette made with red wine vinegar is delicious on meat salads and tart greens; white wine vinegar is best for mild lettuce like Boston and Bibb; Sherry vinegar adds pizazz to fruit salad. Balsamic vinegar needs robust greens. Rice wine vinegar is the choice for fish salad. Herb vinegar (tarragon and dill) can be used on greens and chicken salad. Or, substitute lemon or lime juice for vinegar in fish and chicken salads.

● Add zing to dressings with a good pinch of one or more of the following. Experiment with chopped shallots, sliced scallions, minced garlic, grated or minced fresh ginger, grainy mustard, toasted sesame seeds, sautéed nuts, capers or snips of fresh herbs.

When you're in the mood for... small and tasty treats

The recipes here are versatile enough to fit into almost any entertaining situation. There are fabulous hors d'oeuvres for cocktail parties or to get gatherings off to the right start: Beer Cheese, right, for the gang while watching the Superbowl; Pork Rillettes, right, to serve before a warming meal of roast chicken; Herbed Olives, page 157, with a glass of wine while waiting for the pizza to be delivered. You'll also find the perfect nibble for late-night snackers — Sugared Almonds on page 159 are particularly tempting. Look at page 155 for an exotic Humus or Middle Eastern Eggplant Dip, page 156. For unusual, lunch ideas there's Caviar-Filled Artichokes, Spinach Cheese Squares, Baguette au Fromage St. André, as well as a sensational Pizza with Fresh Herbs and Plum Tomatoes. There are lots of spreads to serve with crackers and plenty of dips for chips.

A wonderful warm-weather change from the usual crudités, serve these asparagus arranged on a large platter with cocktails. They're best eaten with your fingers.

PROSCIUTTO-WRAPPED ASPARAGUS

24 asparagus spears, washed and trimmed
12 thin slices prosciutto or smoked ham
Lemon wedges
Freshly ground black pepper

Steam asparagus 8 to 10 minutes, or until tender-crisp. Drain and cool. Cut prosciutto or ham slices crosswise into halves. Wrap each half around a spear. Serve with lemon wedges and black pepper. Makes 24 spears.

Great finger food: Asparagus dressed in prosciutto sprinkled with lots of freshly ground pepper and lemon

This is the cheese spread to make when time is short; only two ingredients.

BLUE CHEESE SPREAD

1 c. cottage cheese
¼ c. crumbled blue cheese

In a small bowl with fork, combine ingredients. Chill until serving time. Makes 1 ¼ cups.

Plain crackers and sparkling wines are best to serve with this cheese spread.

LIPTAUER CHEESE SPREAD

2 8-oz. packages cream cheese, softened
½ c. butter or margarine, softened
½ 2-oz. can flat anchovies (about 4), chopped
2 scallions, chopped
4 tsp. paprika
1 tsp. caraway seed
1 tsp. Worcestershire sauce

In a food processor or blender, combine all ingredients and process until smooth. Cover and refrigerate until ready to serve. Makes 2 cups.

Adding blue cheese makes this a really pungent spread. Serve it with icy-cold beer. Try it with whole-wheat crackers or crudités.

BEER CHEESE

½ lb. Cheddar cheese, finely shredded
¼ lb. blue cheese, crumbled
3 oz. cream cheese, softened
2 tsp. Worcestershire sauce
1 tsp. dry mustard
½ c. beer

In small bowl, combine all ingredients until blended. Makes about 2 ½ cups.

Serve this hearty spread with French or Italian bread. It also pairs well with raw vegetables.

CHUTNEY CHEESE SPREAD

½ c. grated Cheddar cheese
3 oz. cream cheese, softened
1 garlic clove
½ c. mango chutney, chopped

In blender container or in food processor, combine cheeses with garlic and chutney. Process until smooth. Pack into a small crock. Chill 3 hours or overnight. Makes about 1 ½ cups.

Select a soft, mellow goat cheese like a Montrachet or Boucheron, one that blends easily and is not too pungent.

HERB GOAT CHEESE SPREAD

8 oz. goat cheese, softened
3 oz. cream cheese, softened
1 T. chopped fresh parsley
½ tsp. dried thyme leaves
¼ tsp. dried rosemary
1 garlic clove, minced

Combine all ingredients. Makes 1 ⅓ cups.

With humus, a Middle Eastern spread, serve pita bread instead of crackers. Cut the bread into triangles, spread with butter and toast.

HUMUS

1 16-oz. can garbanzo beans (chickpeas), drained
2 T. tahini (sesame seed paste) or peanut butter
Juice of ½ lemon (about 2 T.)
2 garlic cloves, minced
2 T. olive oil

In food processor or blender, combine beans, tahini, lemon juice and garlic and process until smooth. Transfer to a serving bowl, drizzle with olive oil; cover and chill. Makes 2 cups.

Pronounced ree-yets, this spread is made by cooking pork and spices until the meat is very tender. It is then puréed to make it spreadable. Rillettes will keep up to 3 weeks in the refrigerator.

PORK RILLETTES

1 lb. boneless pork, cut into ½-inch cubes
½ lb. bacon, cut into ½-inch pieces
2 c. water
1 bay leaf
1 garlic clove, crushed
1 tsp. dried thyme leaves
¾ tsp. freshly ground black pepper
½ tsp. salt

In medium saucepan, combine pork and remaining ingredients. Over high heat, heat to boiling. Reduce heat to low; cover and simmer 1 to 1 ¼ hours, or until only ½ cup liquid remains. In food processor or blender, process until mixture is finely chopped. Pack into crock; cover and refrigerate. Serve with thin slices of toasted French bread. Makes 2 cups.

Pita toasts are a natural here. See suggestions for Humus (page 155). Or, serve sesame breadsticks and sweet red pepper strips for dipping.

MIDDLE EASTERN EGGPLANT DIP

1 lb. eggplant, halved lengthwise
2 T. tahini (sesame seed paste)
  or peanut butter
1 garlic clove, minced
1 T. chopped fresh parsley
¼ tsp. salt

Heat broiler. Broil eggplant, 30 minutes, turning once; cool. Squeeze liquid from eggplant; scoop flesh into a bowl. Beat in tahini, garlic, parsley and salt. Makes 1½ cups.

This dip is a natural with tortilla chips. Adjust the spiciness by adding more or less jalapeño pepper. Canned whole green chilies are a bit hotter than the canned chopped ones.

JALAPEÑO DIP

1 c. mayonnaise
1 c. plain yogurt
1 4-oz. can green chilies,
  drained and chopped
1 6 to 7 ½-oz. jar roasted red
  peppers, drained and chopped

In small bowl, combine all ingredients. Cover and refrigerate at least 1 hour before serving to blend flavors. Makes 2 cups.

Fresh coriander, or cilantro, the herb that flavors these shrimp, is pungent, assertive and distinctive. If this fresh herb is not sold at your market, substitute the same amount of parsley and a dash of dried ground cumin.

CORIANDER SHRIMP

⅓ c. fresh lime juice
⅔ c. vegetable oil
2 garlic cloves, minced
2 T. minced fresh coriander
  (cilantro)
1 fresh jalapeño pepper,
  seeded and minced
1 ½ lbs. cooked shelled and
  deveined shrimp

Combine lime juice, vegetable oil, garlic, coriander and jalapeño in a screw-top jar. Shake well to combine. In a bowl, toss with shrimp. Makes about 10 appetizer servings.

When you're asked to "bring something," try these. Transport them in the pan and cut when you arrive.

SPINACH CHEESE SQUARES

1 T. butter or margarine
1 medium onion, chopped
2 10-oz. pkgs. frozen chopped
  spinach, thawed and well-
  drained
3 eggs, lightly beaten
½ lb. feta cheese, crumbled
¼ c. chopped parsley
¼ tsp. grated nutmeg
⅛ tsp. freshly ground black pepper
¾ c. butter or margarine, melted
½ lb. phyllo dough (strudel leaves)

Heat oven to 350°F. In medium frying pan over medium heat, melt butter or margarine. Sauté onion until tender. Add spinach and cook until dry. Meanwhile, combine eggs, cheese, parsley, nutmeg and pepper. Add the spinach. Brush 10- by 16-inch jelly-roll pan with melted butter. Lay one piece of phyllo in the pan, folding the edges where necessary; brush with butter. (When working with phyllo keep it covered with a damp towel to prevent it from drying out.) Repeat, layering with phyllo and brushing with butter six more times. Spread the spinach mixture over the phyllo and cover with remaining leaves of phyllo (about 5 more) brushing each leaf with butter. Using a sharp knife, score top layers into 1-inch squares or diamond shapes. Bake 50 minutes or until puffy and slightly browned. Makes 60.

Use a variety of nuts and seeds for this appetizer. Peanuts, walnuts, sunflower seeds may be substituted for the ones listed here.

CUMIN-SPICED MIX

2 c. unblanched almonds
2 c. pecans
2 c. shelled pumpkin seeds
1 tsp. ground red pepper
2 tsp. ground cumin
1 tsp. salt

In a large skillet, over medium heat, toast the nuts and seeds, stirring often. When the nuts begin to brown, add the pepper and cumin. Continue to toast until lightly golden. Pour into a bag and toss with the salt. Makes 6 cups.

Make lots of non-stop nibbles for before, during and after dinner. Stored in airtight tins or jars they'll keep about a month.

SUGARED ALMONDS

3 T. butter or margarine
1 c. whole unblanched almonds
1 c. whole blanched almonds
1 egg white, lightly beaten
½ c. sugar
½ tsp. ground cinnamon
¼ tsp. grated nutmeg

Heat oven to 325°F. In large, heavy skillet, melt butter; add nuts and sauté them, stirring frequently. When nuts are toasted, remove from pan and drain well on paper towels. Toss nuts with beaten egg white. In large bowl combine sugar, cinnamon and nutmeg. Stir in the nuts, coating them well. Line a jelly-roll pan with waxed paper and spread the nuts in one layer. Bake 25 minutes, turning nuts occasionally. Cool. Makes 2 cups.

This recipe is similar to Sugared Almonds. The quality of your curry powder will affect the pungency of the results. Buy the best.

CURRIED WALNUTS

3 T. butter or margarine
1 ½ c. walnut pieces or halves
1 egg white, lightly beaten
1 T. curry powder
¼ c. sugar

Heat oven to 325°F. In large heavy skillet, melt butter; add nuts and sauté for about 5 minutes, stirring frequently. Remove from pan and drain on paper towels. Toss nuts with beaten egg white. In medium bowl combine curry powder and sugar. Stir in nuts and coat them well. Line a jelly-roll pan or cookie sheet with waxed paper and spread nuts in one layer. Bake 25 minutes, turning nuts occasionally. Makes 1½ cups.

Although this pizza will serve six nicely for lunch, don't let that limit you. It is also terrific cut in small wedges, as cocktail-party food. If making crusts is not your thing, skip it and top lightly toasted flour tortillas or split pita breads with the tomatoes and herbs and bake as directed.

PIZZA WITH FRESH HERBS AND PLUM TOMATOES

CRUST:
3 c. all-purpose flour
1 tsp. salt
⅓ c. unsalted butter, cut into bits
½ c. ice water
TOPPING:
About 9 plum tomatoes,
**   sliced lengthwise**
3 T. chopped fresh basil
1 T. chopped fresh rosemary
Salt
Freshly ground black pepper
3 T. olive or salad oil
¾ c. grated provolone cheese

In medium bowl, combine flour and salt. With fingertips, rub in butter until mixture resembles cornmeal. Stir in water. Knead in bowl until dough forms a ball. Knead dough on a floured surface for 2 minutes. Wrap in waxed paper and let stand at room temperature 30 minutes. Cut dough into 3 pieces and on a lightly floured surface, with lightly floured rolling pin, roll each into 8-inch rounds. Place rounds on cookie sheets and prick with a fork in 1-inch intervals. Let stand 30 minutes so dough will settle otherwise it will shrink while cooking. Heat oven to 450°F. Bake for 12 to 15 minutes or until brown. Remove crusts from oven. Arrange some tomato slices over each crust in concentric circles, slightly overlapping. Sprinkle each pizza with some basil, rosemary, a little salt and pepper. Drizzle 1 T. oil over each. Return to oven and bake 10 to 15 minutes more. Sprinkle ¼ c. grated cheese over each. To serve, garnish each with fresh sprigs of rosemary and basil and cut each into quarters. Makes 6 luncheon servings.

When crudités leave you flat, marinate them—no need for an extra dish for a dip.

MARINATED VEGETABLE PLATTER

1 bunch broccoli, cut into florets
1 head cauliflower, cut into florets
2 lbs. mushrooms,
    quartered if large
3 medium zucchini,
    cut into 2- by ¼-inch pieces
1 16-oz. bag baby carrots
2 large turnips,
    peeled and thinly sliced
3 6-oz. jars miniature
    corn on the cob
4 to 5 c. olive oil
4 large garlic cloves, crushed
2 bay leaves, crumbled
2 tsp. salt
⅓ c. red wine vinegar

Fill a large saucepan with water; heat to boiling. Using a blanching basket or sieve, blanch vegetables (except corn) separately. As a guide: Blanch broccoli 3 minutes; cauliflower 4 to 5 minutes; mushrooms 2 minutes; zucchini 3 minutes; carrots 3 minutes; and turnips 4 minutes. Rinse each under cold water to stop cooking. Vegetables should be tender-crisp. Drain corn. In large bowl, combine oil with remaining ingredients except vinegar. Add vegetables and toss to coat well. Cover and refrigerate overnight. To serve, drain vegetables (save marinade for a salad dressing), arrange on platter and sprinkle with wine vinegar. Serve with toothpicks. Makes 25 appetizer servings.

These hot bites take some time to assemble. You fold them up as you would a flag. But, because they freeze so well, you can prepare them ahead and bake as many as you want.

SAVORY HAM TRIANGLES

¼ lb. ham, minced
4 oz. Gruyère or Swiss cheese,
    shredded
½ c. chutney, chopped
1 T. dry mustard
½ lb. phyllo dough
½ c. unsalted butter, melted

Combine ham with cheese, chutney and mustard; set aside. Cut phyllo dough lengthwise into 2-inch strips. (When working with phyllo, keep it covered with damp towel to prevent it from drying out.) Brush one strip of phyllo lightly with butter. Place about 1 teaspoonful of filling at end of strip. Fold corner of strip diagonally over filling so that short end meets long edge of strip, forming a right-angle triangle. Continue folding over at right angles until you reach end of strip. Place triangle, seam-side down, on jelly-roll pan; brush with butter. Repeat, using remaining filling and dough. Do not crowd pan. (Can be made ahead to this point. Wrap well and freeze.*) Heat oven to 425°F. Bake 5 to 10 minutes or until golden. Serve hot. Makes 60.
*To bake frozen: Bake in heated 425°F oven 10 to 15 minutes.

These nachos have heaps of refried beans on them. If you like, leave them off to save calories.

NACHOS

36 large tostada chips
    or plain tortilla chips
1 c. canned refried beans
1 c. shredded Monterey Jack
    or sharp Cheddar cheese
½ 4-oz. can (¼ c.) chopped green
    chilies
4 scallions, chopped, including
    green part

Heat broiler. Place tostada chips on cookie sheet. Spread each chip with some refried beans, then sprinkle with some cheese, chilies and scallions. Broil 3 to 5 minutes or until cheese is hot and bubbly. Makes 3 dozen.

Salmon spread is more sophisticated than tuna and a nice change. Serve it on "crackers" of thinly sliced raw zucchini and turnip.

SALMON SPREAD

½ small onion, minced
1 7 ¾-oz. can salmon, drained
2 T. lemon juice
1 8-oz. package cream cheese,
    softened
1 T. prepared horseradish
¼ tsp. Worcestershire sauce

¼ tsp. Tabasco

In medium bowl with fork, combine all ingredients until blended and smooth. Makes 2 cups.

———

This is an easy pâté to make. However, you'll need to plan ahead. Make it at least one day before serving for best flavor and texture.

COUNTRY PÂTÉ

**8 oz. bacon
2 T. butter or margarine
1 bunch scallions, chopped
1 lb. lean ground pork
1 lb. ground veal
2 eggs
½ lb. chicken livers, chopped
½ c. Calvados or apple brandy
¾ c. fresh bread crumbs (made
    from 2 slices bread)
⅓ c. milk
1 ½ tsp. salt
½ tsp. grated nutmeg
¼ tsp. freshly ground black pepper**

Heat oven to 350°F. Line bottom and sides of 9- by 5- by 3-inch loaf pan with bacon strips. Reserve 3 strips for top. In small skillet over medium-high heat, melt butter or margarine. Add scallions and sauté until tender. Transfer to large bowl. Add ground pork and remaining ingredients, mix well. Pack firmly into lined loaf pan. Place reserved bacon strips on top. Cover tightly with aluminum foil. Bake 1 hour. Remove foil and bake 45 minutes longer or until meat thermometer inserted in center reads 170°F. Remove from oven. Pour off fat. When cool, remove from pan; wrap tightly in foil and refrigerate overnight. Makes 18 ½-inch slices.

———

This is a great sandwich to make for a light lunch or supper. Serve it as a sandwich for one, or cut it into 2-inch pieces for hors d'oeuvres. The key to the success here is a good dark-green, fruity olive oil.

BAGUETTE AU FROMAGE ST. ANDRE

**½ loaf French bread
2 to 3 oz. St. André (or any favorite
    cheese)
2 plum tomatoes, or 1 medium
    tomato, sliced
Fresh or dried rosemary
Fresh or dried thyme leaves**

**Freshly ground black pepper
Olive oil**

Heat oven to 375°F. With serrated knife, split French bread lengthwise in half. Heat in oven 3 to 5 minutes, or until dry but not toasted. Remove from oven and arrange alternating slices of tomato and cheese on each half. Sprinkle with herbs and pepper; drizzle with olive oil. Bake 7 to 10 minutes, or until the cheese is melted and bubbly. Cut the bread into 2-inch pieces. Makes 1 serving.

———

A very special sandwich—super for spring and summer. It is a version of a French Pan Bagna, packed with tuna, pungent olives and fresh herbs.

BAGUETTE NIÇOISE

**1 small French baguette
    or hero roll
2 curly lettuce leaves
1 3 ½-oz. can tuna, drained
½ tomato, sliced
¼ red onion, thinly sliced
6 to 8 black olives, pitted
Fresh thyme, oregano
    or basil leaves
2 T. olive oil**

Slice bread horizontally in half. Arrange lettuce tuna, tomato, onion and olives in the baguette. Sprinkle with fresh herbs and olive oil. Wrap up in foil or plastic wrap and let stand before eating to let the flavors mingle. Makes 1 sandwich.

———

Sheer indulgence! Top an artichoke with a good dollop of crème fraîche or sour cream and, even better, a spoonful of caviar.

CAVIAR-FILLED ARTICHOKES

**6 artichokes, trimmed
6 T. minced fresh parsley
¾ cup crème fraîche, or sour cream
1 2-oz. jar red lumpfish caviar
Lemon wedges**

Cook artichokes, covered, in boiling water, 30 minutes, until a leaf pulls away easily. Drain; cool. Gently spread leaves apart to open center. Reach down into center; pull out cone of center leaves. Scrape out fuzzy choke. Dip cone rim into parsley. Invert; place in choke to form cup. Fill with crème fraîche and caviar. Serve with lemon wedges. Makes 6 servings.

When you're in the mood for... the simple comforts of bread and soup

Homemade soup and bread are soothing foods. That doesn't mean they are wimpy or for convalescents only. There are plenty of gutsy ones among these recipes: Beef-Barley, right, Old-Fashioned Chicken and sensational Lentil, below. For the times when you're looking for something not quite so hearty try the sophisticated starters for classy dinners. Two excellent choices, depending on the season, are Tomato-Basil Soup and Sherried Pumpkin Soup, both on page 164. There are quick soups too to help solve a time-crunch. Check out the New England Clam Chowder, page 163 when time is short. All the bread accompaniments are quick breads. Whether you crave freshly baked biscuits drizzled with honey, a wonderful partner for a warming soup, a bread to serve with tea or a not-too-sweet-dessert, you'll find it here. Extra plus: Even if you feel all thumbs when it comes to baking, the recipes in this section will help you turn out breads like a pro.

There is nothing more comforting than a potful of chicken soup simmering on the stove on a raw winter day.

OLD-FASHIONED CHICKEN SOUP

1 4 to 4 ½ lb. chicken
3 qt. water
2 onions, peeled
6 whole cloves
6 stalks celery
6 carrots
3 leeks, cleaned (page 39)
½ c. parsley sprigs
2 sprigs dill or ½ tsp. dried dill weed

Clean chicken, removing excess fat. Place chicken in a large pot and add water. Pierce onions with cloves; add to pot. Over high heat, heat to boiling. Cover; reduce heat to low and simmer 1 ½ hours. Cut 3 stalks of celery and 3 carrots into 2-inch pieces. Add to pot with leeks, parsley and dill. Cook 1 hour longer. Remove chicken and strain stock. When chicken is cool enough to handle, remove meat from bones and skin. Skim off and discard fat from stock. Return chicken meat to pot; return to stove and heat to boiling. Meanwhile, slice remaining celery and carrots. Add to pot and simmer, covered, 20 to 25 minutes, or until vegetables are tender. Makes about 4 quarts.
SERVE WITH:
● *Oatmeal-Chocolate Chip Muffins, page 97*
● *Vegetable Tart, page 138, to make a more substantial meal*
● *Chocolate Heart Cookies page 206*

Hearty and warming, this soup is scented with cumin for an extra punch of flavor. Try it as an energy restorer after a long day of skiing or a football game.

LENTIL SOUP

2 T. vegetable oil
2 garlic cloves, chopped
1 tsp. cumin seeds
2 parsnips, peeled and cut in 2- by ¼-inch strips
2 carrots, sliced diagonally
1 16-oz. can whole tomatoes, undrained
3 c. chicken broth
½ c. lentils
1 c. chopped kale or spinach
Freshly ground black pepper

In a large saucepan, over medium-high heat, heat oil. Add garlic, cumin seeds, parsnips and carrots and sauté until garlic is brown. Add tomatoes, chicken broth and lentils. Heat to boiling. Reduce heat to low, cover and simmer 20 minutes. Stir in kale and pepper. Simmer 3 to 5 minutes more. Makes 6 cups.

SERVE WITH:
● *Cheese Herb Bread, page 166, with apple butter*
● *Crudités such as carrots and cucumber sticks*
● *Whole-Wheat Peanut Butter Cookies, page 207*

The secret to getting a hearty stock and rich, full flavor for beef soup is to have the oil very hot and to brown the meat well.

BEEF-BARLEY SOUP

1 lb. stewing beef, cut into ½-inch cubes
2 T. vegetable oil
6 c. water
1 large onion, coarsely chopped
½ c. medium barley, rinsed
1 tsp. salt
¼ tsp. freshly ground black pepper
2 carrots, sliced
1 celery stalk, sliced
1 sm. turnip, peeled and cubed (about 1 c.)
1 c. frozen peas, thawed

In a large heavy saucepan over medium-high heat, cook beef in hot oil, a few pieces at a time, until well browned. Remove pieces as they brown, if crowded. Return beef to saucepan and add water, onion, barley, salt and pepper. Over high heat, heat to boiling. Reduce heat to low; cover and simmer 1 hour, stirring occasionally. Skim off fat. Add carrots, celery and turnip. Simmer 40 minutes longer, or until vegetables are tender. Add peas. Heat through. Makes about 3 quarts.

SERVE WITH:
● *A sandwich, such as* Baguette au Fromage St. André, *page 161*
● *Iced Tea*

This is the superstar at Sunday brunch. Make it a day ahead; leave the garnishing until the last minute.

BLACK BEAN SOUP

1 lb. black beans
¼ lb. bacon, chopped
1 medium onion, chopped
1 medium carrot, chopped
1 celery stalk, chopped
4 garlic cloves, minced

1 8-oz. can tomatoes, chopped, with juice
½ tsp. freshly ground black pepper
½ tsp. dried oregano
6 c. beef broth
2 T. sherry
GARNISH:
1 lemon, thinly sliced
4 scallions, minced

Wash beans; discard any stones or shriveled beans. Place beans in large saucepan and add enough water to cover. Over high heat, heat to boiling. Cook 2 minutes. Remove from heat, cover and let stand 1 hour. In stockpot, cook bacon until browned. Add onion, carrot, celery and garlic. Add beans and soaking liquid; add remaining soup ingredients. Heat to boiling. Reduce heat to low; cover and simmer 2 hours. Skim off fat. If you like, purée half of soup in blender and add to remaining soup. Garnish each serving with a slice of lemon and minced scallion. Makes 3 quarts.

SERVE WITH:
● *Bloody Marys, page 196*
● *Sausage and Pepper Frittata, page 136*
● *A basketful of steaming whole-wheat toast*

This is the creamy New England version of clam chowder. Manhattan style is made with tomatoes instead of cream or milk.

NEW ENGLAND CLAM CHOWDER

2 T. butter or margarine
1 medium onion, diced
1 10-oz. can whole baby clams, with juice
½ c. water
1 large potato, peeled and diced
½ tsp. salt
¼ tsp. freshly ground black pepper
1 c. half-and-half
1 c. milk
Chopped parsley

In medium saucepan over medium heat, melt butter or margarine and sauté onion until tender but not brown. Add clams with their liquid, water, potato, salt and pepper. Simmer chowder 15 minutes. Stir in half-and-half and milk; heat through. Sprinkle soup with parsley. Makes 6 servings.

SERVE WITH:
● *Corn Madeleines, page 25*
● *Golden Tossed Salad, page 151*
● *Rich-Rich Brownies, page 206*

When two summer classics—vine-ripened tomatoes and fresh basil— are combined, the result is extraordinary. Make this recipe with buttermilk, it's very refreshing.

TOMATO-BASIL SOUP

1 T. butter or margarine
¼ c. finely chopped onion
1 garlic clove, minced
1 large tomato, peeled and
    chopped (1 c.)
1 c. chicken broth
2 T. chopped fresh basil
    or 1 tsp. dried
¼ tsp. salt
⅛ tsp. freshly ground black pepper
½ c. buttermilk or plain yogurt

In a medium saucepan, over medium heat, melt butter or margarine. Add onion and garlic. Cover and cook 5 to 10 minutes, until soft, but not brown, stirring occasionally. Add tomato, chicken broth, basil, salt and pepper. Cover and simmer 10 minutes. Remove from heat. Stir in buttermilk or plain yogurt. Serve immediately. Makes 2 servings.
SERVE WITH:
● *A cold and juicy sandwich such as,* Baguette Niçoise, *page 161*
● *Fresh peaches*
● *Chocolate Heart Cookies, page 206*
● *Old-Fashioned Lemonade, page 194*

To impress guests, ladle this soup from a hollowed-out pumpkin. It can be made a day ahead; just before serving, lace with sherry and pour into pumpkin.

SHERRIED PUMPKIN SOUP

2 T. butter or margarine
½ c. finely chopped onion
¼-inch piece fresh ginger, peeled
    and minced
¼ tsp. grated nutmeg
2 13¾-oz. cans chicken broth
2¾ c. canned pumpkin
1 c. half-and-half
3 T. dry sherry
¼ tsp. salt
⅛ tsp. freshly ground black pepper
Minced chives, for garnish

In saucepan over medium heat, melt butter or margarine. Add onion and sauté until tender. Add ginger, nutmeg, and broth. Stir in pumpkin and half-and-half. Heat to boiling. Reduce heat and cook until heated through. Add sherry, salt and pepper. Top with chives. Makes 8 servings.
SERVE WITH:
● *Stuffed and roasted turkey*
● *Steamed Brussels sprouts*
● *Mashed Potatoes with Scallions, page 178*
● *Winter Compote, page 144*

Make this version of the chunky Italian vegetable classic. It's even better the second day. Pour it into individual plastic storage containers and freeze so you'll have a homemade soup for one whenever you want.

MINESTRONE

2 T. olive or vegetable oil
1 medium onion, chopped
6 c. beef broth
2 potatoes, peeled and diced (2 c.)
2 med. carrots, sliced
1½ lbs. green beans,
    cut into 1-inch pieces
2 med. zucchini, sliced
½ small head cabbage, chopped
    (about 4 c.)
1 28-oz.can whole tomatoes,
    coarsely chopped, with their
    juices
½ tsp. dried basil
1 tsp. salt
¼ tsp. freshly ground black pepper
1 15 ¼-oz. can kidney beans,
    drained
½ c. grated Parmesan cheese

In a large saucepan, over medium-high heat, heat oil; add onion and sauté 5 minutes. Add broth, potatoes and carrots. Over high heat, heat to boiling. Reduce heat to low; cover and simmer 15 minutes. Add green beans, and remaining ingredients except kidney beans and cheese. Simmer 40 minutes. Add kidney beans during last 5 minutes. Serve with cheese. Makes about 3 ½ quarts.
SERVE WITH:
● *Tortellini Salad, page 150*
● *Cheese Straws, page 157*
● *Cassata, page 205*

Pick up fresh corn at the market and make a mouth-tingling soup.

JUST-OFF-THE-COB SOUP

6 T. butter or margarine
4 c. corn kernels, about 6 ears
3 c. chicken broth
2 jalapeño chilies,
seeded and minced
1 sweet red pepper, diced
1 sweet green pepper, diced
¼ c. half-and-half
¼ c. fresh tarragon leaves
or 4 tsp. dried
1 large tomato, cored and diced

In a large saucepan over medium-high heat, melt 3 tablespoons butter or margarine. Add corn; sauté about 3 minutes. Add broth. Heat to boiling. Reduce heat to low; cover and cook 15 minutes. With a slotted spoon, remove and reserve 3 cups corn kernels. In blender purée remaining corn and broth and return to saucepan. In skillet, heat remaining butter. Sauté jalapeños and peppers 5 to 7 minutes, or until tender. Add peppers and reserved corn to purée. Stir in half-and-half. Heat to boiling. Remove from heat and stir in 3 tablespoons fresh tarragon or 3 teaspoons dried. Combine diced tomato and remaining tarragon. Top soup with tomato-tarragon garnish. Serve hot or at room temperature. Makes about 2 quarts.
SERVE WITH:
* *Mexican Chicken, page 190*
* *Warm flour tortillas*
* *Your favorite tossed green salad*

These biscuits are a treat smeared with butter and drizzled with honey.

GOLDEN BUTTERMILK BISCUITS

2 c. all-purpose flour
2 ½ tsp. baking powder
½ tsp. baking soda
½ tsp. salt
⅓ c. cold butter, cut into bits
1 ¼ c. buttermilk

Heat oven to 450°F. Grease a cookie sheet; set aside. Combine dry ingredients. With fingertips, rub in butter until it resembles coarse crumbs. Stir in buttermilk and blend until just mixed. Drop by spoonfuls onto cookie sheet. Bake 12 to 15 minutes, until golden. Makes 12 biscuits.

Just-off-the-Cob soup with fresh corn and zippy chilies

Enjoy this authentic Irish soda bread as they do in Ireland, with fresh, creamy butter, strawberry jam and an ice-cold glass of buttermilk.

MAE CONDRY'S SODA BREAD

3 c. all-purpose flour
½ c. sugar
1 T. baking powder
1 tsp. salt
½ tsp. baking soda
1 c. dark or golden raisins
1 T. caraway seeds
1 ½ c. buttermilk
4 T. butter or margarine, melted

Heat oven to 350°F. Grease a 2-quart, round casserole. In medium bowl combine flour, sugar, baking powder, salt and baking soda. Stir in raisins and caraway seeds. With fork, blend in buttermilk and melted butter until mixture is evenly moist. Turn into casserole and cut an "X" on top ½ inch deep. Bake 1 hour and 10 minutes, or until toothpick inserted in center comes out clean. Remove from casserole. Cool completely on wire rack. Makes 1 loaf.

This bread tastes fabulous with any and all soups. During the summer months, substitute twice the amount of fresh herbs for dried.

CHEESE HERB BREAD

2 c. all-purpose flour
½ tsp. salt
2 tsp. baking powder
½ tsp. baking soda
½ tsp. dried basil
¼ tsp. dried oregano
Pinch dried thyme leaves
4 T. cold butter or margarine
2 eggs
¼ c. honey
¾ c. milk
1 c. grated Cheddar cheese

Heat oven to 350°F. Grease 8-inch round cake pan. Combine flour, salt, baking powder and baking soda. Add herbs and stir until well blended. With pastry blender or with fingertips, cut or rub in butter or margarine until it resembles coarse crumbs. In small bowl with a fork, beat eggs, honey, milk and cheese until blended. Stir

liquid into dry ingredients, just until mixed. Pour into pan. Bake 45 to 55 minutes, or until top springs back when touched lightly. Cool in pan; cut into wedges. Makes 1 loaf, 12 servings.

Slice this bread thinly and spread it with cream cheese to make finger sandwiches for an afternoon pick up.

DATE-NUT BREAD

1 ½ c. all-purpose flour
1 c. light brown sugar, firmly packed
2 tsp. baking powder
½ tsp. salt
1 c. chopped pitted dates
¾ c. chopped walnuts
¾ c. milk
2 eggs
2 T. vegetable oil
½ tsp. vanilla

Heat oven to 350°F. Grease a 9- by 5-inch loaf pan. In bowl, combine flour, sugar, baking powder, salt, dates and walnuts. In small bowl, with fork, combine milk, eggs, oil and vanilla. Stir liquid into flour mixture; mix just until evenly moist; turn into pan. Bake 1 hour, or until toothpick inserted in center comes out clean. Cool in pan on wire rack 10 minutes. Remove from pan and cool on rack completely. Makes 1 loaf.

This sweet and aromatic bread is perfect for tea time. Or pack it up and tote it along to a picnic. Any leftovers make great toast.

ORANGE BREAD

2 ¼ c. all-purpose flour
1 c. sugar
2 tsp. baking powder
½ tsp. salt
12 T. cold butter or margarine
2 T. grated orange peel
3 eggs
½ c. milk
¼ c. fresh orange juice
Orange Glaze (recipe follows)

Heat oven to 350°F. Grease a 9- by 5-inch loaf pan. In bowl combine flour, sugar, baking powder and salt. With pastry blender or fingertips, cut or rub butter or margarine into flour until it resembles coarse crumbs. Stir in orange peel. In small bowl, with fork, combine eggs, milk and orange juice. Stir liquid into dry ingredients just until evenly moist. Turn into pan. Bake 1 hour and 15 minutes or until toothpick inserted in center comes out clean. Make Orange Glaze. Cool bread in pan on rack, 10 minutes. Spoon glaze evenly over top. Remove from pan; Cool completely. Makes 1 loaf, about 18 slices.

ORANGE GLAZE

⅓ c. fresh orange juice
3 T. sugar

In small saucepan over medium heat, combine juice and sugar; heat to boiling. Cook, stirring often, until slightly thickened, about 5 minutes.

A fiber-rich bread, gently sweetened with dates and maple syrup, this makes a great nighttime nibble.

APPLESAUCE MAPLE BREAD

2 c. all-purpose flour
2 tsp. baking powder
½ tsp. baking soda
½ tsp. salt
1 tsp. ground cinnamon
½ tsp. grated nutmeg
¼ c. wheat germ
¾ c. chopped walnuts
½ c. chopped pitted dates
2 eggs
⅓ c. maple or maple-flavored syrup
¼ c. vegetable oil
1 ½ c. applesauce

Heat oven to 350°F. Grease 9- by 5-inch loaf pan. In large bowl combine flour, baking powder, baking soda, salt, cinnamon and nutmeg. Blend in wheat germ, walnuts and dates; set aside. In small bowl, beat eggs. Add syrup, oil and applesauce; stir liquid into dry ingredients until just mixed. Pour into pan. Bake 50 to 55 minutes, or until toothpick inserted in center comes out clean. Cool in pan on rack, 10 minutes; remove from pan and cool. Makes one loaf.

Serve this bread with fruit salad for dessert or with Honey Butter (page 26) at brunch.

PUMPKIN CORNBREAD

1 ½ c. whole-wheat flour
1 c. yellow cornmeal
2 tsp. baking powder
1 tsp. baking soda
1 tsp. ground cinnamon
1 tsp. grated nutmeg
¼ tsp. ground cloves
½ tsp. salt
½ c. butter or margarine, softened
⅔ c. brown sugar, firmly packed
4 eggs, lightly beaten
1 c. fresh or canned pumpkin purée
1 c. milk

Heat oven to 350°F. Grease a 9- by 5- by 3-inch loaf pan. Combine flour, cornmeal, baking powder, baking soda, cinnamon, nutmeg, cloves and salt in a bowl. In a bowl, cream butter until smooth. Add brown sugar and beat until fluffy. Stir in eggs and pumpkin; beat until smooth. Add milk and dry ingredients alternately, stirring just until blended. Turn into pan. Bake 65 minutes, or until toothpick inserted in center comes out clean. Remove bread from pan and cool on rack. Slice thinly. Makes 1 loaf.

This walnut-studded bread tastes marvelous spread with butter, cream cheese or honey.

WALNUT BREAD

3 c. all-purpose flour
1 c. granulated sugar
4 tsp. baking powder
1 ½ tsp. salt
4 T. cold butter or margarine
2 tsp. grated orange rind
1 ½ c. coarsely chopped walnuts
1 egg, beaten
1 ½ c. milk
1 tsp. vanilla

Heat oven to 350°F. Grease and flour 9- by 5- by 3-inch loaf pan. In bowl, combine flour, sugar, baking powder and salt. With pastry blender or with fingertips, cut or rub in butter or margarine until it resembles coarse crumbs. Add orange rind and 1 ¼ cup of the walnuts. In small bowl, combine egg, milk and vanilla. Add liquid to dry ingredients just until blended. Turn into loaf pan. Sprinkle remaining ¼ cup walnuts over top. Bake 60 to 70 minutes, or until toothpick inserted in center comes out clean. Cool on wire rack in pan 10 minutes. Turn out and cool completely on wire rack before slicing. Cut into 18 ½-inch slices. Makes 1 loaf, 18 slices.

When you're in the mood for... food favorites with a new twist

Turn to this section when you'd like to cook something familiar but still special. There is a super Macaroni and Cheese (the perfect Sunday supper) on page 176; a special version of Chicken Pot Pie sweetened with cider and topped with a cornmeal crust (a great party dish); and a marvelous tomato-based spaghetti sauce (with surprising secret ingredients). You'll also find a few things you might not expect, such as Braised Shallots, page 176, terrific with any roast meat, and a heavenly rich Tortellini with Gorgonzola Sauce, page 174. Menu suggestions are given and, of course, all of these recipes make great party food. Look for several bonus charts: 30-minute Chicken Dinners and Seven 30-minute Pastas. They're lifesavers when time is short. You'll also find a chart, page 179, to guide you through an array of vegetable preparations.

This homey dish is perfect for Sunday supper. It is a one-dish meal—a plus in a time crunch.

ROASTED CHICKEN WITH APPLE-RAISIN STUFFING

3 to 4 lb. roasting chicken
1 c. chopped apple (cored)
½ c. raisins
5 c. French bread cubes
1 c. apple juice or cider
½ c. chopped onion
1 T. poultry seasoning
½ c. chopped celery
1 egg
1 T. chopped parsley
4 carrots, cut into 3-inch pieces or
   1 10-oz. pkg. baby carrots
6 to 8 small red potatoes, halved

The simple pleasures of a roast chicken dinner

Heat oven to 350°F. Rinse chicken under cold running water; pat dry with paper towels. Combine remaining ingredients except carrots and potatoes. Spoon stuffing into neck and chest cavities. Secure with skewers. Place bird, breast-side up, on a rack in a roasting pan. Arrange carrots and potatoes in pan around chicken. Roast 1 hour or until juices run clear when thigh joint is pierced with a fork and vegetables are fork-tender. Makes 4 servings.
SERVE WITH:
● *Mulled Wine, page 198*
● *Golden Buttermilk Biscuits, page 165*
● *Fudge Sauce, page 200, over ice cream*

One of the all-time great party dishes, this version of chicken pot pie is slightly sweet (the sauce is made with cider) and crunchy (the crust is made with cornmeal).

CHICKEN PIE WITH CIDER AND CORNMEAL CRUST

CRUST:
2 c. all-purpose flour
¼ c. cornmeal
⅔ c. solid vegetable shortening
6 to 8 T. cold water
FILLING:
6 T. butter or margarine
6 T. all-purpose flour
½ c. cider or apple juice
1 ½ c. heavy cream
¼ c. chopped fresh parsley
1 T. Dijon mustard
1 T. ground coriander
½ tsp. salt
¼ tsp. freshly ground black pepper
1 ½ lb. cooked chicken or turkey,
**   cut into 1-inch chunks**
18 small white onions,
**   peeled and steamed 5 minutes**
2 large carrots, thickly sliced and
**   steamed 4 minutes**
½ lb. mushrooms,
**   quartered and sautéed**
¾ c. frozen peas, thawed
1 egg beaten with 2 T. heavy cream
**   or milk**

Make crust by combining flour and cornmeal in a medium-sized bowl. With pastry blender or with fingertips, cut or rub in shortening until it resembles coarse crumbs. Stir in enough water to make the dough hold together. Wrap dough in waxed paper and refrigerate at least 1 to 2

hours, or until well chilled and firm. In medium saucepan over medium heat, melt the butter. With wire whisk, blend in flour making a thin paste. Cook until it begins to bubble. Mixture should be yellow; don't let it brown. Blend in cider and cream. Over medium heat, cook, stirring constantly, until very thick, 5 to 7 minutes. Stir in parsley, mustard, coriander, salt and pepper. Combine sauce with chicken and vegetables. Place in a 2- to 2 ½-quart baking dish. Heat oven to 450°F. Roll out the dough about ¼-inch thick, to fit over baking dish with about 1 ¼ inches of overhang. Fit dough over rim of dish. Crimp the edges to seal crust to casserole. Cut slits in the top of pie for steam to escape. Use leftover dough to decorate top of pie if desired. Brush pastry with egg-cream wash to glaze. Bake pie for 15 minutes. Reduce heat to 350°F and bake about 30 minutes more, until the crust is nicely browned and the sauce is bubbling. Let pie sit about 15 minutes before serving. Makes 6 to 8 servings.
SERVE WITH:
● *Marinated Vegetable Platter, page 160*
● *Tossed salad with avocado slices added*
● *Chocolate Rum Roll with Rum Cream, page 200*

If you make a little more than you need of this chicken save leftovers for a super chicken salad with a lemony dressing instead of vinegar.

LEMON CHICKEN

2½ to 3 lb. chicken,
**   cut into serving pieces**
2 lemons, sliced
2 T. dried oregano
Salt and freshly ground black
**   pepper to taste**

Heat oven to 425°F. Rinse chicken under cold running water and pat dry with paper towels. Arrange lemon slices in the bottom of a baking dish. Combine oregano and salt and pepper and rub thoroughly over chicken pieces. Place chicken pieces, skin side down, over lemon. Bake 20 minutes. Turn chicken skin side up; reduce heat to 350°F and continue cooking 35 minutes longer, or until chicken is very tender. Makes 4 to 6 servings.
SERVE WITH:
● *Parmesan Bread Sticks, page 158*
● *Garlicky Greens, page 90*
● *Strawberry Nut Tart, page 202*

Even people who look at curry with a wary eye will love this subtly seasoned entrée. Carrots and raisins give a nice sweetness to the pungency of the curry and red pepper.

COUNTRY CAPTAIN CHICKEN

2 ½ to 3 lb. broiler-fryer chicken,
   cut into serving pieces
3 T. vegetable oil
½ c. chopped onion
½ c. diced carrots
1 sweet green pepper, cut into
   strips
10 mushrooms, quartered
1 garlic clove, minced
½ tsp. crushed red pepper flakes
¼ tsp. salt
1 T. curry powder
1 16-oz. can whole tomatoes,
   drained and chopped
½ c. raisins

In large skillet over medium-high heat, cook chicken in hot oil until well browned on all sides. Remove pieces as they brown. Add onion, carrots, green pepper, mushrooms, garlic, red pepper flakes and salt to drippings remaining in skillet. Cook over medium heat until onion is tender, about 10 minutes. Blend in curry. Return chicken to skillet. Add tomatoes and raisins. Over high heat, heat to boiling. Reduce heat to low; cover and simmer 30 to 35 minutes, or until chicken is fork-tender. Skim off and discard fat. Makes 4 servings.
SERVE WITH:
● *Chutney Cheese Spread, page 155*
● *Mashed Potatoes with Scallions, page 178*
● *Sautéed Bananas, page 144*

For best flavor make this the day before serving. Reheat over medium heat for 20 minutes or until warmed through.

FRENCH COUNTRY CHICKEN

2½ to 3 lb. chicken,
   cut into serving pieces
¼ c. all-purpose flour
2 T. olive or vegetable oil
12 small white onions, peeled
1 lb. small mushrooms
4 carrots, cut into 3-inch pieces

or 1 10-oz. pkg. baby carrots
1 c. red wine
½ c. water
1 T. chopped fresh parsley
1 garlic clove, minced
½ tsp. salt
¼ tsp. freshly ground black pepper

Dredge chicken in flour until well coated. In large saucepan, over medium-high heat, cook chicken in hot oil until well browned on all sides. Remove chicken; set aside. Add onions, mushrooms and carrots to drippings in pan; cook 5 minutes. Return chicken; add remaining ingredients. Over high heat, heat to boiling. Reduce heat to low; cover and simmer 30 to 35 minutes or until chicken is fork-tender. Skim and discard fat. Makes 4 servings.
SERVE WITH:
● *Herbed Goat Cheese Spread, page 155*
● *Rice with Peas and Parsley, page 87*
● *Apple-Raisin Clafouti, page 202*
● *Espresso*

This chicken is cooked and then marinated. It is a terrific picnic food—just pack it up along with the marinade. Bring lots of napkins!

SESAME CHICKEN

¼ c. sesame seeds
2 ½ to 3 lb. chicken,
   cut into serving pieces
1 c. all-purpose flour
¼ c. vegetable oil
¼ c. cider vinegar
¼ tsp. ground ginger
½ tsp. garlic powder
2 T. soy sauce

Toast sesame seeds in small skillet, over medium-low heat, until lightly golden; set aside. Dredge chicken in flour until well coated. In large skillet over medium-low heat, fry chicken in hot oil until well-browned on all sides and fork-tender, about 20 to 25 minutes. In baking dish combine remaining ingredients; add chicken. Stir gently until well-coated. Serve warm or cold. Makes 4 servings.
SERVE WITH:
● *Asparagus-Carrot Salad, page 151*
● *Chicory Bacon Salad, page 53*
● *Sugar cookies*
● *Grapes*

Chicken salad can be simple—a quick blend with mayo and freshly ground pepper. Or, dressed up—with exotic fruits. It's a super sandwich fixing and can make a great summer supper with rolls and a carafe of wine. There are infinite variations. Try these proven winners.

SENSATIONAL CHICKEN SALAD

1 bunch watercress
1 head radicchio
1 head Boston lettuce
1 bunch arugula
3 c. cubed cooked chicken
6 shiitake mushrooms, sautéed
½ pkg. enoki mushrooms
8 each baby zucchini, yellow
    squash, (or 1 large zucchini and 1
    yellow squash, cut into 2-inch
    pieces), steamed
DRESSING:
⅔ c. olive oil
¼ c. red wine vinegar
2 tsp. Dijon mustard
1 T. chopped fresh tarragon leaves
    or ½ tsp. dried
½ tsp. salt
¼ tsp. freshly ground black pepper

Remove and discard watercress stems. Tear lettuce into bite-sized pieces. Combine watercress and lettuce leaves with remaining ingredients in a large bowl. Combine dressing ingredients in a jar with tight-fitting lid; shake well to combine. Toss salad with dressing. Makes 6 to 8 servings.

WINTER CHICKEN SALAD

About 6 c. cooked cubed chicken
    (duck, turkey or goose may be
    substituted)
10 c. bibb, romaine, Boston
    or iceberg lettuce leaves,
    torn into bite-sized pieces
¾ c. crumbled Roquefort
    or blue cheese
½ c. coarsely chopped walnuts
    or pecans
SHALLOT VINAIGRETTE:
¾ c. olive or vegetable oil
⅓ c. red wine vinegar
1 garlic clove, mashed
¼ c. minced shallots or scallions
½ tsp. salt
¼ tsp. freshly ground black pepper
GARNISH:
4 avocados, peeled and cubed
1 large red onion, sliced into rings

4 oranges, peeled and sectioned

Combine chicken, lettuce, cheese, and walnuts. Blend dressing ingredients; toss with chicken. Arrange on serving platter or individual plates and garnish with avocado, onion and orange sections. Makes 8 servings.

CHICKEN-APRICOT SALAD

3 c. diced cooked chicken
1 c. diced dried apricots
½ c. walnut halves
2 scallions, sliced
¼ c. raisins
Lettuce leaves
DRESSING:
½ c. mayonnaise
1 c. plain yogurt
⅓ c. milk
2 T. fresh lemon juice
1 T. curry powder
2 tsp. Dijon mustard
¾ tsp. salt

In large bowl, combine chicken, apricots, walnuts, scallions and raisins. Blend dressing ingredients and toss to coat. Serve on lettuce leaf-lined plates. Makes 4 servings.

WARM SESAME CHICKEN SALAD

DRESSING:
1 T. sesame seeds
¼ c. honey
¼ c. white vinegar
2 T. soy sauce
2 T. Oriental sesame oil
1 scallion, minced
1 garlic clove, minced
1-inch piece fresh ginger, peeled
    and minced
½ tsp. crushed red pepper flakes
SALAD:
2 c. mixed salad greens
2 c. steamed cut-up vegetables,
    such as beans, broccoli, carrots
3 to 4 c. cooked sliced chicken
Sesame seeds for garnish

Toast 1 T. sesame seeds in a small, dry saucepan over low heat until lightly golden. Add honey and remaining dressing ingredients and heat through; keep warm. Arrange greens and vegetables on each of 4 plates. Arrange chicken on greens. Pour warm dressing over salad just before serving. Garnish with sesame seeds. Makes 4 servings.

NINE 30-MINUTE CHICKEN DINNERS

So that you can prepare meals in a hurry, keep a bag of individually wrapped chicken breast halves in your freezer. Thaw them in the refrigerator during the day or overnight. Before cooking, pound each between sheets of waxed paper with the flat side of a French knife or a rolling pin until ¼ inch thick. Each recipe serves two.
THE TECHNIQUE:
Dredge one whole chicken breast, skinned, boned, split in half and pounded, in 2 T. flour.* In medium skillet over medium-high heat, cook 1 T. oil and 1 T. butter or margarine until hot and foamy. Add chicken and sauté until golden brown on both sides. Add the flavor makers. Cover and simmer until fork-tender, about 10 minutes. Remove chicken to plate and keep warm. Over medium-high heat, boil sauce in skillet rapidly until slightly thickened. Add finishing touches and heat through. Spoon sauce over chicken and add garnishes.

THE DISH	FLAVOR MAKERS	FINISHING TOUCH	GARNISH
Marsala	¾ c. sliced mushrooms; ¾ c. Marsala wine	2 T. chopped parsley	Additional parsley
California	1 c. sliced mushrooms; ¾ c. dry white wine	½ avocado, sliced	Chopped parsley
Milanese *Instead of flour, dredge in seasoned bread crumbs.	1 garlic clove, minced; ½ c. chicken broth; ¼ c. white wine	2 T. chopped parsley	Additional parsley
Picatta	1 garlic clove, minced; ½ c. white wine; 2 T. lemon juice	2 T. chopped parsley	Lemon slices
Yucatán	½ c. lemon juice; 3 T. raisins; 2 T. canned chopped hot chilies	1 T. chopped cilantro (fresh coriander)	Toasted pine nuts
Santa Fé	½ c. red wine; ¼ c. tomato purée; ¾ tsp. dried oregano; ½ tsp. chili powder		Lime wedges; sour cream
Provencal	⅓ c. chopped onion; 1 tsp. dried basil; ¾ c. white wine	½ c. chopped, canned tomatoes; ¼ c. black olives, chopped	Chopped parsley or fresh basil
Sesame Mix 1 egg with 2 T. milk. After dredging in flour, dip chicken into egg mixture, then coat with 3 T. sesame seeds.	¾ c. chicken broth; ½ tsp. soy sauce; ½ tsp. grated fresh ginger; 1 garlic clove, minced; ¼ tsp. sesame oil; ⅛ tsp. crushed red pepper flakes		Chopped parsley or cilantro (fresh coriander)
With peppers	¼ c. diced, cooked ham; ¼ c. chopped onion; ½ c. white wine; ¼ red pepper, cut into slivers; ¼ green pepper, cut into slivers; ¼ tsp. dried thyme leaves		Chopped parsley

Use spring vegetables to make this savory stew. But you don't have to wait for the spring produce . . . carrots, cut into chunks are fine instead of baby ones.

SPRING LAMB STEW

¼ c. **vegetable oil**
4 lbs. **boneless lamb stew meat, cut into 1 ½-inch cubes**
1 T. **sugar**

¼ c. **all-purpose flour**
3 **garlic cloves, crushed**
¼ c. **tomato paste**
3 c. **beef broth**
½ tsp. **dried thyme leaves**
½ tsp. **dried rosemary**
1 lb. **turnips, peeled and cut into 1 ¼-inch cubes**
1 12-oz. **bag baby carrots, trimmed**
24 **small pearl onions**
¾ lb. **green beans, trimmed**

In large Dutch oven or large heavy saucepan, heat the oil until almost smoking. Cook the meat in batches, turning to brown them on all sides, removing pieces with slotted spoon as they brown. When all the meat is browned, pour off any fat from Dutch oven. Return pan to high heat and add the sugar; cook, stirring constantly, about 2 minutes or until brown and caramelized. Add meat and flour and toss to coat. Stir in the garlic, tomato paste, beef broth, thyme and rosemary. Heat to boiling. Reduce heat to low; cover and simmer 1 hour. Skim off and remove fat. Add the turnips and carrots and simmer, covered, 1 hour more. Meanwhile, peel the onions. Cut an "X" in the stem end so they won't burst when cooked. Place onions in a saucepan and cover with cold water. Heat to boiling. Reduce heat to low, cover and simmer 10 minutes; drain and set aside. About 10 minutes before stew is finished, add the onions and green beans. Cover and simmer until beans are tender-crisp. Makes about 10 servings.
SERVE WITH:
● *Herbed Olives, page 157*
● *Parsleyed boiled new potatoes*
● *Almond Lace Cookies, page 207*
● *Pears in Raspberry Sauce, page 146*

When you'd like to impress (your in-laws perhaps?) this is the entrée to serve. It looks stupendous, but is very easy to prepare.

RACK OF LAMB WITH ROSEMARY-MUSTARD CRUMBS

2 racks of lamb*
 about 6 to 7 ribs each
Salt
Freshly ground black pepper
2 T. Dijon mustard
2 T. dried rosemary
2 T. finely chopped fresh parsley
2 garlic cloves, minced
2 T. olive oil
½ c. chicken broth
½ c. dry vermouth
2 T. unsalted butter,
 cut into small pieces

*Have butcher trim racks, scrape ribs and crack bone between ribs

Heat oven to 475°F. Stand the 2 racks, with bone sides facing, and press together so that bone ends are interlaced. Tie securely in 3 places with butcher's twine. Sprinkle lightly with salt and pepper, then rub with mustard. Combine rosemary, parsley and garlic in small bowl. Press the herbs firmly onto lamb. Place double rack in an open roasting pan; drizzle with olive oil. Cover bones with aluminum foil. Cook roast 10 minutes, then lower heat to 350°F. Roast 30 minutes longer, or until internal temperature reaches 145°F, or to desired degree of doneness. Transfer racks to a carving board and keep warm. Pour off excess fat in roasting pan. Pour in broth and wine and boil on top of stove until reduced to ¾ cup. Strain into bowl, then whisk in butter. Remove strings from lamb and carve racks into chops; serve with sauce. Makes 4 servings.
SERVE WITH:
● *White Beans with Thyme, page 177*
● *Braised Shallots, page 176*
● *Walnut Green Beans, page 61*
● *Chocolate Mousse Cake with Crème Anglaise, page 204*

This cold roast pork is jazzy enough for an outdoor dinner party on a sultry summer night or a picnic before a classical concert under the stars. Make it a day ahead so it's ready when you are.

COLD ROAST PORK

⅔ c. soy sauce
⅓ c. dry sherry
2-inch piece fresh ginger,
 peeled and minced
1 T. sugar
1 tsp. dry mustard
3 garlic cloves, minced
5 lbs. boneless pork loin roast
Mango or peach chutney

In measuring cup or bowl, combine soy sauce, sherry, ginger, sugar, mustard and garlic. Place roast in large, heavy-duty plastic bag and pour in marinade. Tie bag and marinate in refrigerator 8 hours or overnight, turning frequently. Heat oven to 375°F. Remove roast from bag. Place roast, fat-side up, in roasting pan and cook 25 to 30 minutes per pound, or until meat thermometer reads 160°F. Remove from pan. Cool and refrigerate until cold, about 2 hours. Serve with mango or peach chutney. Makes 10 servings.
SERVE WITH:
● *Middle Eastern Eggplant Dip, page 156*
● *Tomatoes with Fresh Dill, page 105*
● *Broccoli-Walnut Salad, page 34*
● *Plum Pie, page 203*

For a hearty lunch serve this pie hot from the oven or at room temperature. Pack it up, uncut, for picnic food. If you prefer a more piquant flavor use hot sausage instead of sweet.

DEEP-DISH SPINACH PIE

CRUST:
2 c. all-purpose flour
2 T. sugar
½ c. butter or margarine, chilled
1 egg
5 to 6 T. ice water
FILLING:
½ lb. sweet Italian sausage,
** casings removed**
6 eggs
2 10-oz. packages frozen chopped
** spinach, thawed and well**
** drained**
1 lb. mozzarella cheese,
** shredded**
⅔ c. ricotta cheese
½ tsp. salt
¼ tsp. grated nutmeg
⅛ tsp. freshly ground black pepper
½ lb. prosciutto or salami, diced
1 egg yolk, beaten

In large bowl combine flour and sugar. With pastry blender or with fingertips, cut or rub butter into flour until it resembles coarse crumbs. Add egg and water, mixing until dough forms a ball. Wrap and chill while making filling. In small skillet, cook sausage; remove from pan and drain. In large bowl, beat eggs and remaining ingredients, except prosciutto or salami and egg yolk, until well blended. Stir in sausage. Heat oven to 350°F. On lightly floured surface with lightly floured rolling pin, roll half the dough into an 11-inch circle. Use to line bottom of a 9-inch pie plate. Spoon in half the filling. Arrange prosciutto or salami on top; spoon on remaining filling. Roll remaining dough into an 11-inch circle and place on top of pie. Seal edges and pinch to make a border. Brush with beaten egg yolk. Cut a hole in top of pie for steam to escape. Bake 1 hour and 15 minutes, or until crust is brown and the filling bubbles. Makes 8 servings.
SERVE WITH:
● *Tomato-Basil Soup, page 164*
● *Tossed green salad*
● *Moroccan Mint Tea, page 21*

This is a spaghetti sauce with rich, old-world flavor. The lemon rind and red wine are the secret. It takes some time to make, but your kitchen will never smell better.

THICK RICH SPAGHETTI SAUCE

2 T. olive or vegetable oil
1 medium onion, chopped
1 medium carrot, chopped
1 stalk celery, chopped
1 garlic clove, minced
¼ c. chopped fresh parsley
¾ lb. lean ground beef
½ c. dry red wine
2 14-oz. cans Italian plum
** tomatoes, chopped with juice**
1 6-oz. can tomato paste
1 tsp. dried oregano
1 tsp. salt
1 tsp. sugar
1 tsp. grated lemon rind
½ tsp. freshly ground pepper
½ tsp. dried basil

In large saucepan over medium-high heat, heat oil. Add onion, carrot, celery, garlic, parsley; sauté until tender, about 5 minutes. Add ground beef; cook until brown, breaking it up with wooden spoon. Stir in wine and cook until evaporated. Add remaining ingredients; heat to boiling. Reduce heat to low; cover and simmer, over low heat for 2 ½ hours, stirring occasionally. Makes 1 ½ quarts, enough for 2 pounds spaghetti.
SERVE WITH:
● *Bacon Sticks, page 157*
● *Garlic Bread, page 54*
● *Green salad*
● *Fresh Fruit Marsala, page 143*

This is a very rich pasta dish. It's a perfect first course for a meal of simply roasted meats such as chicken or lamb. With a salad, it makes a filling lunch or light supper.

TORTELLINI WITH GORGONZOLA SAUCE

1 ½ c. dry white wine
1 8-oz. pkg. cream cheese,
** softened**
Freshly ground black pepper
Large pinch grated nutmeg

1½ lbs. green tortellini, frozen or dried
1 ½ T. freshly grated Parmesan cheese
¾ lb. Gorgonzola cheese, crumbled (or other blue-veined cheese)

In small heavy saucepan, heat white wine to boiling. Cook over high heat until reduced by half. With wire whisk, blend in cream cheese until smooth. Heat to boiling. Reduce heat to low and simmer, uncovered, 15 minutes, or until reduced and thickened. Stir in pepper and nutmeg. Cook tortellini according to package directions until *al dente*. Drain. Blend Parmesan and half of Gorgonzola cheese into cream sauce. Pour cream sauce over tortellini. Sprinkle reserved Gorgonzola cheese over pasta. Makes 10 first course or 6 to 8 luncheon servings.

This spicy green pasta is a great first course to a rich and creamy main dish.

PASTA WITH SPICY BROCCOLI

1 lb. corkscrew pasta
1½ lbs. broccoli
⅓ c. olive oil
3 garlic cloves, crushed
1 2-oz. can anchovies, drained
1 tsp. crushed red pepper flakes

Cook pasta according to label directions. Chop broccoli and steam for 5 minutes. Heat oil in large skillet. Sauté garlic, anchovies and pepper until golden. Add broccoli and cook 1 minute more. Drain pasta reserving ⅓ cup cooking water. Add pasta and water and toss to coat. Makes 8 first course or 4 main-dish servings.

SEVEN 30-MINUTE PASTAS

Pasta has come a long way from spaghetti and meatballs. Here, seven pasta recipes to satisfy any taste. Three are tomato based, and four are made with creamy sauces. The sauces make enough to coat one pound of dry pasta, cooked—four main course servings. Use fettuccine, or if you prefer penne, corkscrews or another sturdy pasta.

TOMATO-BASED TECHNIQUE: Heat 2 T. olive oil in a large skillet. Add flavor makers except tomatoes; sauté 1 minute. Add tomatoes; simmer 15 minutes more. Add finishing touches; simmer 5 minutes. Toss with cooked pasta; garnish.
CREAM-BASED TECHNIQUE: In a large skillet cook the flavor makers for 5 minutes. Add finishing touches; heat through. Toss pasta and garnishes.

TOMATO-BASED	FLAVOR MAKERS	FINISHING TOUCHES	GARNISHES
Amatriciana	1 garlic clove, crushed; ¼ tsp. red pepper flakes; 4 c. chopped, peeled tomatoes	4 oz. bacon or pancetta, cooked and diced	Chopped parsley
Puttanesca	2 garlic cloves, crushed; ¼ tsp. red pepper flakes; 1 can anchovies, drained; 4 c. chopped peeled tomatoes	¼ c. oil-cured olives, pitted	Chopped parsley; 2 T. capers
Zucchini-Eggplant	2 garlic cloves, crushed; 1 lb. eggplant, cut into ½-inch cubes; 4 c. chopped peeled tomatoes	2 c. sliced zucchini; 1 roasted red pepper, chopped	Chopped basil
CREAM-BASED	**FLAVOR MAKERS**	**FINISHING TOUCHES**	**GARNISHES**
Carbonara	8 oz. bacon, diced	⅓ c. half-and-half; ¼ tsp. freshly ground black pepper	¾ c. grated Parmesan cheese; 4 eggs, beaten; chopped parsley
Crab-Artichoke	1 T. butter; 1 garlic clove, minced; 1 c. chopped fennel or celery	1 c. half-and-half; 8 oz. cooked crab meat; 1 c. sliced, cooked artichoke hearts	½ c. shredded Gruyère cheese; chopped parsley
Romana	1 T. butter; ½ c. chopped ham or prosciutto; 3 c. sliced mushrooms	1¼ c. half-and-half; 1½ c. cooked green peas	½ c. grated Parmesan cheese
Walnut-Basil	1 T. butter; 2 garlic cloves, minced; 1 c. chopped fresh basil	1¼ c. half-and-half; 1 c. chopped, toasted walnuts	½ c. grated Parmesan cheese

Need a little comfort? This may do the trick. Use a sharp Cheddar for more pronounced flavor.

MACARONI AND CHEESE

**1 8-oz. pkg. elbow macaroni
2 T. butter or margarine
2 finely chopped scallions
1 T. all-purpose flour
1 ½ c. milk
2 c. shredded Cheddar cheese
2 tsp. Dijon mustard
1 tsp. Worcestershire sauce
1 tsp. salt
½ tsp. freshly ground black pepper**

Heat oven to 350°F. Grease a 2-quart casserole; set aside. Cook macaroni according to label directions for baked dishes; drain. In large saucepan over medium heat, melt butter. Add scallions and sauté until tender, but not brown, about 5 minutes. With wire whisk, blend in flour. Gradually add milk. Cook, stirring constantly, until sauce is thick and has boiled 1 minute. Remove from heat and stir in cheese, mustard, Worcestershire, salt and pepper. Stir until cheese melts. Add macaroni; toss well. Spoon into casserole. Bake 20 minutes. Makes 4 servings.
SERVE WITH:
● *Herbed Carrots, right*
● *Gingerbread Muffins, page 140*
● *Baked Apple Dumplings, page 204*

Serve these apples as a vegetable with pork chops or a roast. They make an accompaniment to the Thanksgiving dinner, too.

SAUTÉED APPLES

**2 T. butter or margarine
2 apples, each cut into eight
    wedges and seeded
½ tsp. salt
2 T. brown sugar
1 c. apple juice
1 T. cornstarch**

In skillet over medium heat, in hot butter, sauté apples until tender. Stir in salt and brown sugar. In cup combine juice and cornstarch. Stir into apples and cook, stirring constantly, until sauce boils. Makes 6 servings.

While the carrots are still warm, toss them with the dressing. This way they will soak up lots of the lemon-herb flavor.

HERBED CARROTS

**½ lb. carrots, peeled and sliced
1 T. olive oil
1 T. lemon juice
½ tsp. dry mustard
1 tsp. dried dill
¼ tsp. salt
⅛ tsp. freshly ground black pepper**

In steamer or in 1 inch boiling lightly salted water, steam carrots 7 minutes. In small bowl with wire whisk, combine oil and remaining ingredients; add carrots and toss until well coated with dressing. Makes 2 servings.

Peeling shallots takes a little time (see page 45) but is worth it for this recipe. If no shallots are on the market, substitute small white onions. The flavor may be stronger though.

BRAISED SHALLOTS

**3 T. butter or margarine
1 T. vegetable oil
1 ½ lbs. shallots or pearl onions,
    peeled
1 tsp. sugar
½ c. dry red wine**

In large heavy skillet over medium heat, heat butter and oil. Add shallots and sugar; cook 10 to 15 minutes, uncovered, or until browned and tender, stirring frequently but gently. Add wine and cook 5 to 10 minutes longer, uncovered, until most of the wine has evaporated and the shallots are glazed. Makes 8 servings.

In spring to celebrate asparagus season, serve this as a main course for two at lunch or dinner with soup and some crunchy bread.

ASPARAGUS MIMOSA

**1 lb. asparagus
¼ tsp. salt
Boston lettuce leaves
Vinaigrette Dressing (page 152)
1 hard-cooked egg, chopped**

Trim tough ends from asparagus. Arrange spears in a skillet no more than 2 inches deep. Add salt and cold water to cover. Over high heat, heat to boiling. Reduce heat to low, cover and cook 5 to 7 minutes, or until tender-crisp. Drain; refrigerate until cold. To serve, arrange on lettuce leaves. Sprinkle with dressing, then with egg. Makes 4 servings.

Try this variation of classic mashed potatoes substituting sweet potatoes. It's particularly good with turkey or duck. Serve with other root vegetables alongside.

MASHED SWEET POTATOES

**2 lbs. sweet potatoes,
    peeled and cut into chunks
5 T. butter or margarine
About 1 c. pineapple juice**

Steam potatoes over boiling water until tender, 15 to 20 minutes. Mash with a potato masher or electric hand mixer. Beat in the butter. Beat in enough pineapple juice to make potatoes creamy and smooth. Makes 8 servings.

Extra-special slaw is a good bet with grilled fish or chicken. Or, serve it whenever you need a little taste of sunshine. It's an updated version of it's mayonnaised cousin.

SUMMER SLAW

**4 c. thinly sliced green cabbage
1 ½ c. coarsely chopped watercress
    leaves
1 large carrot, shredded
1 cucumber, peeled, seeded and
    shredded
6 radishes, trimmed and shredded
2 scallions, sliced
2 T. chopped fresh mint leaves
1 c. shredded coconut
¼ c. vegetable oil
¼ c. water
3 T. fresh lime juice
1 garlic clove
1 T. soy sauce
¼ tsp. ground red pepper**

Combine cabbage, watercress, carrot, cucumber, radishes, scallions and mint, in large bowl; cover and refrigerate. In blender container or in food processor, purée coconut, oil, water, lime juice, garlic, soy sauce and pepper. Toss with vegetables. Makes 6 servings.

Serve this room-temperature recipe for fresh asparagus with simply roasted meats like lamb or grilled chicken or fish. Remember this recipe too, for an interesting alternative to the usual crudité.

ASPARAGUS WITH ORANGE SAUCE

**3 lbs. fresh asparagus spears
SAUCE:
3 egg yolks, at room temperature
1 T. lemon juice
2 T. orange juice
Pinch of Salt
1 c. safflower oil or other mild-
    flavored oil
Grated peel of 1 orange**

Using a sharp knife, trim asparagus spears just where white end becomes green. Remove small leaves along stalks. If stalks are large, remove tough peel with vegetable peeler. Heat lightly salted water in large skillet. Cook asparagus in batches, laying stalks in single layer in skillet. Cover and simmer 8 to 12 minutes until tender-crisp. Remove spears, drain and cool. For sauce, combine the yolks, lemon and orange juices and salt in food processor or blender. Run the machine until well combined. Add oil by droplets with machine running. Stir in grated peel. Arrange asparagus on serving platter. Pour sauce over asparagus. Makes 6 servings.

Until you try them you won't know how mouthwatering white beans are paired with a roast leg of lamb, lamb chops or any kind of pork. Use canned beans to save time instead of starting with dry.

WHITE BEANS WITH THYME

**4 T. butter or margarine
4 c. cooked or canned white beans
    (Great Northern or cannellini)
½ tsp. dried thyme leaves
¼ tsp. coarsely ground black
    pepper
Generous pinch grated nutmeg**

In a heavy saucepan over medium-low heat, melt butter. Add beans, thyme, pepper and nutmeg and cook gently until warmed through, 3 to 5 minutes. Stir occasionally with a rubber spatula, but take care not to "overwork" beans or they will be mushy. Makes 8 servings.

Like squash? Try it dressed up for Sunday dinners and special occasions by blending it with carrots. For a more pronounced flavor, substitute turnip or rutabaga for the carrots.

CARROT AND SQUASH PURÉE

**½ lb. carrots, peeled and cut into
  2-inch pieces
½ lb. butternut squash, peeled
  and cut into 2-inch pieces
2 T. heavy cream
2 T. butter or margarine
½ tsp. salt
¼ tsp. freshly ground black pepper
Dash grated nutmeg**

In saucepan over high heat, heat carrots and 1 inch lightly salted water to boiling. Reduce heat to low; cover and simmer 12 to 15 minutes, until tender. Cook squash in a separate pan in 1 inch boiling water 10 to 12 minutes, until tender. Drain vegetables; place in food processor with knife blade attached or use hand electric mixer. Purée and add cream, butter, salt, pepper and nutmeg. Makes 2 servings.

This is heavy-duty comfort food. Rich and delicious. Serve with turkey or slices of Mom's meatloaf.

MASHED POTATOES WITH SCALLIONS, PARSLEY AND HEAVY CREAM

**4 all-purpose potatoes, peeled
2 T. butter or margarine
½ c. heavy cream
2 scallions, sliced
1 T. chopped fresh parsley
¼ tsp. salt
Freshly ground black pepper
  to taste**

In saucepan over high heat, heat potatoes and 1 inch lightly salted water to boiling. Reduce heat to low; cover and cook 20 minutes or until fork-tender; drain. With electric mixer on medium speed, beat potatoes and butter until smooth. Gradually add heavy cream, beating until smooth, about 3 minutes. Add more cream if desired. Fold in scallions and parsley. Add salt and pepper. Makes 4 servings.

Savoring an ear of corn is a rite of summer. Here's an update of that simple pleasure. The corn can be prepared outdoors or in—instructions below.

SOUTH-OF-THE-BORDER CORN ON THE COB

**4 T. softened butter or margarine
1 T. paprika
½ tsp. ground red pepper
½ tsp. ground cumin
1 garlic clove, crushed
6 ears fresh corn**

Combine all ingredients except corn in a small bowl; beat until smooth. Peel back corn husks, leaving them attached at base; remove all the corn silks. Spread butter over corn. Pull husks back up and tie with string. Grill on hot coals for 10 minutes, or until tender. Or, if you prefer, steam the corn on a rack over boiling water for 10 minutes. Makes 6 servings.

A versatile vegetable stew, ratatouille is good served hot or cold. It stars always-available vegetables, so you can make it year round.

RATATOUILLE

**¼ c. olive or vegetable oil
1 large onion, coarsely chopped
1 garlic clove, minced
1 eggplant, peeled and cut
  into 1-inch cubes
2 small zucchini,
  cut into ½-inch slices
1 sweet green pepper, cored,
  seeded and cut into strips
1 4-oz. can tomatoes,
  drained and chopped
1 tsp. dried thyme leaves
½ tsp. dried oregano
¼ tsp. ground coriander
½ tsp. salt
¼ tsp. freshly ground black pepper**

In large skillet over medium heat, heat oil. Add onion and garlic; sauté 5 minutes. Add eggplant, zucchini and pepper; sauté 5 minutes more. Add remaining ingredients; stir 2 minutes. Reduce heat to low; cover and simmer 15 minutes, or until tender, stirring occasionally. Serve hot or cold. Makes 6 servings.

GET THE MOST FROM YOUR VEGETABLES

Armed with this chart you'll never have to wonder about the how-to's of vegetables. A quick look will tell you that there are lots of great tasting ones besides celery and carrots. Here, a chart on what to look for, how to store and some special ideas for serving.

VEGETABLE	LOOK FOR...	STORE...	GREAT BITES
Beans, snap	crisp beans and bright color.	in refrigerator in plastic bags, up to 1 week.	Stir-fry with walnuts, garlic and ginger; season with soy sauce.
Beets	firm, round beets with slender roots and a rich red color.	in refrigerator up to 2 weeks.	Simmer 2 grated beets in ¾ c. orange juice and 1 tsp. Worcestershire sauce until tender.
Bok Choy	white stems and dark shiny leaves. Often topped with yellow flower.	in refrigerator up to 2 weeks.	Chop coarsely and stir-fry with chopped onion and ginger. Season with honey and soy sauce.
Corn	fresh green husks and milky kernels.	unhusked in refrigerator 1–2 days. Best used immediately.	Simmer ears of corn in 1 inch vermouth and ½ tsp. tarragon until tender.
Fennel	crisp, pale green bulbs.	in crisper 1–2 weeks.	Quarter bulbs. Steam 5 minutes. Bake at 400°F, 10 minutes with butter and Parmesan.
Leeks	very pale, tightly rolled leaves with green tops. Look for the small, tender ones.	in refrigerator up to 1 week.	Trim and split lengthwise. Rinse; drain. Cook in 1 inch boiling water, 8–10 minutes. Chill. Serve with oil/vinegar dressing.
Peppers: hot, green	shiny firm flesh, free of blemishes.	in refrigerator in plastic bags, up to 2 weeks.	Combine chopped pepper with grated Cheddar cheese. Spread on whole-wheat bread; broil.
Peppers: sweet, red, green and yellow	firm, thick, brightly colored flesh.	in crisper 1 week.	Chop; toss with pecans, candied ginger and grapefruit. Sprinkle with sherry.
Peas, sweet	fairly large, well-filled, crisp pods.	unshelled 3–5 days in crisper. Best if eaten immediately.	Cook; toss with yogurt and mayonnaise; top with dill and scallions.
Spaghetti Squash	light yellow, creamy-colored firm squash; egg-shaped between 8–12 inches long.	in cool dry place.	Pierce with fork. Bake at 350°F 1½ hours. Remove seeds; rake out strands. Toss with butter and Parmesan.
Snow and Sugar Snap Peas	firm, crisp pods with bright green color.	in crisper in plastic bags, 3–5 days.	Stir-fry and combine with thin strips of cooked roast beef. Toss with blue cheese dressing.
Tomatoes	firm, well-shaped tomatoes.	at room temperature, out of direct sunlight.	Fill hollowed halves with sautéed spinach and onions. Bake at 350°F for 15 minutes.
Yellow or Zucchini Squash	smooth, glossy skin. Should be heavy for its size.	in refrigerator in plastic bags 3–5 days.	Marinate chunks of squash, white onions and mushrooms in vinaigrette; thread alternately on skewers and grill.

When you're in the mood for... the taste of the sea

Fish, in all its varieties, is a low calorie nutritious food. Both fish and shellfish are a snap to cook as long as you follow a few simple rules. The fish cookery know-how on page 185 takes you step by step from buying to serving. There is great entertaining food in this section; the Paella, page 184 and Cioppino, page 183 are tried and true party recipes. They are stars at any gathering. Or for a simple meal, try a seafood salad, a poached fish, or pasta tossed with seafood. In summer, the taste of salmon barbecued on the grill is hard to beat. You'll find that recipe on the next page. You'll also find lots of encouragement to try new food combinations: Mackerel with Anchovy-Onion Relish, page 181, Pasta with Caviar and Cream, page 182 and Oysters with Curried Leeks, right, are all deliciously different. All these recipes include complete menu suggestions for hassle-free planning.

A perfect summer dish, the poached salmon can be served at room temperature or chilled either as an entrée or a first course followed by a simply prepared dish such as roast chicken.

POACHED SALMON

1 onion, coarsely chopped
¼ c. coarsely chopped celery
1 c. dry white wine
2 c. water
5 6-oz. salmon fillets
MUSTARD SAUCE:
½ c. sour cream
½ c. yogurt
1 T. Dijon mustard
3 dashes Tabasco
2 tsp. chopped fresh dill
½ tsp. salt
Salmon caviar for garnish
Dill sprigs for garnish

In a skillet, combine vegetables, wine and water. Over high heat, heat to boiling. Add salmon and reduce heat to low; cover and simmer 4 minutes, covered, until salmon feels firm yet springy. Remove salmon from sauce and cool. In a bowl, combine sauce ingredients. Arrange salmon on plates. Spoon on sauce; garnish with caviar and dill. Makes 4 servings.
SERVE WITH:
● *Tomato-Basil Soup, page 164*
● *Cheese Straws, page 157*
● *Blueberry-Peach Compote with Raspberry Sauce, page 142*

If you prefer, you can substitute clams or mussels for the oysters in this recipe. If you do, also substitute about one 8-oz. bottle clam juice for the oyster liquid.

OYSTERS WITH CURRIED LEEKS

1 pt. oysters, with their liquid
2 T. plus 1 tsp. butter
1 T. olive oil
2 c. thinly sliced whites of leeks
1 tsp. curry powder
½ tsp. salt
1 large zucchini, shredded
   (about 3 c.)

In a large skillet, combine oysters and their liquid. Over high heat, heat to boiling. Reduce heat to low. Cover and simmer 2 minutes. With slotted spoon remove oysters and keep warm. Reserve liquid. Melt 2 tablespoons butter and the oil in the skillet. Add leeks. Cover and cook over medium heat for 5 to 6 minutes. Uncover and cook 10 to 12 minutes more, stirring occasionally. Add curry powder and salt; cook 3 minutes. Stir in the reserved oyster liquid. Increase heat to high and cook, stirring occasionally, until the liquid is syrupy. Heat 2 inches of water in a medium saucepan to boiling. Add zucchini and cook 2 to 3 minutes. Drain and toss with remaining butter. Arrange zucchini on the bottom of a serving platter. Arrange the leeks down the center; place the oysters on top. Spoon sauce over and serve immediately. Makes 4 servings.
SERVE WITH:
● *Rice with Peas and Parsley, page 87*
● *Bread with Brie Butter, page 74*
● *Tangerines or oranges*

This salmon recipe can also be made with halibut, swordfish, tuna or your favorite fish steak. If the weather keeps you inside, heat up the broiler and enjoy.

GRILLED SALMON STEAKS WITH LIME BUTTER

½ c. butter
Juice of 3 limes
1 T. fresh thyme leaves
    or 1 tsp. dried
8 1-inch-thick salmon
    steaks
Lime slices
Thyme sprigs

On stove top or barbecue grill melt butter in small saucepan. Stir in lime juice and thyme leaves; mix well. Heat barbecue until coals are very hot. Grill salmon over hot coals for 5 minutes on first side. Baste occasionally with lime butter; turn salmon and brush again. Grill for another 5 minutes. Serve fish garnished with lime slices and thyme sprigs. Makes 8 servings.
SERVE WITH:
● *Corn on the cob*
● *Skillet-Grilled Vegetables, page 117*
● *Orange Ice with Tequila-Soaked Strawberries, page 105*

Any fish that is oily or fatty will work well with this recipe, especially bluefish or fresh sardines.

MACKEREL WITH ANCHOVY-ONION RELISH

3 T. olive oil
8 onions, sliced
6 anchovy fillets
4 6-oz. mackerel fillets
⅓ c. chopped fresh parsley

In a large skillet over medium-low heat, heat olive oil. Add onions and cook until very soft and golden, about 25 minutes. Add anchovies and cook 10 minutes more. Heat broiler. Broil mackerel on a well-oiled broiler pan for about 4 minutes. Turn fillets and broil 4 minutes on other side. Stir parsley into anchovy-onion relish and spoon over mackerel fillets. Makes 4 servings.
SERVE WITH:
● *Steamed potatoes*
● *Asparagus Mimosa, page 176*
● *Pineapple with Kirsch*

For an interesting brunch entrée make this trout dish. It's also wonderful served with simply prepared vegetables for a light dinner.

TROUT BROILED WITH DILL

12 large dill sprigs
2 T. finely chopped shallots
4 whole trout (6 to 8 oz. each, or
    2 1-lb. trout), gutted
    and rinsed
¼ c. chopped fresh dill
2 T. olive oil
⅓ c. fresh lemon juice
¼ tsp. salt
Freshly ground black pepper

Heat broiler. Divide dill sprigs and shallots evenly among the cavities of the trout. Combine chopped dill, oil, lemon juice, salt and pepper. Brush over trout on both sides. Broil 2 to 3 inches from heat for 4 minutes. Turn trout and broil 3 to 4 minutes on other side. Makes 4 servings.
SERVE WITH:
● *Carrot and Squash Purée, page 178*
● *Red Pepper and Snap Bean Salad, page 150*
● *Wild rice*
● *Fudge Sauce, page 200 on coffee ice cream*

This is roll-up-your-sleeves-and-dig-in food. Here they're served hot, but they are also great chilled as hors d'oeuvres.

SHRIMP STEAMED IN BEER

1 lb. cleaned fresh or frozen shelled
    and deveined medium shrimp
1 bay leaf
6 sprigs dill or 1 tsp. dill weed
1 garlic clove, minced
Juice of ½ lemon
¼ tsp. whole peppercorns
⅛ tsp. dried red pepper flakes
1 c. beer

Combine all ingredients in a saucepan. Over high heat, bring to a full rolling boil. Cover; remove from heat. Let stand 4 minutes or until shrimp are pink and curl. Drain. Serve hot with melted butter if you like. Makes 4 servings.
SERVE WITH:
● *Corn on the cob*
● *Golden Buttermilk Biscuits, page 165*
● *Beer*
● *Rich-Rich Brownies, page 206*

Lobster is the classic for Seafood Normandy, but shrimp is just as good. If you can find them, try Langoustines (frozen lobster tails).

SEAFOOD NORMANDY

**3 lbs. large raw shrimp or 1 ½ lbs.
  frozen, shelled and deveined
  shrimp, partially thawed
6 T. butter or margarine
¾ tsp. salt
⅛ tsp. ground red pepper
2 scallions, minced
¾ c. Calvados or apple brandy
1 c. heavy or whipping cream
Juice of ½ lemon
3 T. chopped fresh parsley**

Remove shells and devein shrimp or lobster tails. Melt 4 T. butter or margarine in large skillet over medium heat. Add shrimp and cook, turning frequently until they become uniformly pink and curl. Season with salt and pepper. With slotted spoon remove to plate and keep warm. Add scallions to fat in skillet. Remove skillet from heat; add Calvados. Carefully ignite Calvados with match. When flame dies out, scrape any bits from bottom of skillet. Return skillet to heat and boil liquid rapidly until almost completely evaporated. Add the rest of the butter and, stirring constantly, add the cream. Continue cooking until sauce is thickened. Stir in lemon juice. Pour sauce over shrimp. Sprinkle with parsley. Makes 6 servings.
SERVE WITH:
● *Plain rice or boiled potatoes*
● *Walnut Green Beans, page 61*
● *Raspberry Sorbet, page 146*

Here's a party dish that saves time. It can be done a day ahead and reheated.

SHRIMP-STUFFED PEPPERS

**10 sweet yellow or red peppers
2 T. olive oil
2 garlic cloves, crushed
1 large onion, chopped
½ lb. peeled and deveined
  medium shrimp
½ c. golden raisins**

**⅓ c. chopped sun-dried tomatoes
½ c. chopped fresh basil
  or ½ c. chopped fresh parsley
  plus 1 T. dried basil
½ tsp. dried thyme leaves
6 c. cooked brown rice
½ tsp. salt
1 28-oz. can tomato purée
3 c. water**

Cut tops from peppers; discard seeds and white membrane. Set aside peppers and tops. In a large skillet, heat the oil until hot. Add the garlic and onion and cook until the onion is wilted, about 10 minutes. Cut each shrimp in half lengthwise and add to skillet along with raisins, sun-dried tomatoes and herbs. Cook until shrimp turn pink, about 3 to 4 minutes. Stir in rice and salt, mixing until combined. Heat oven to 375°F. Combine tomato purée and water in bottom of a large casserole dish. Spoon shrimp and rice stuffing into peppers. Do not pack down the rice. Replace tops on peppers and arrange in casserole. Cover casserole tightly and bake 50 minutes. Serve each pepper on a bed of sauce. Makes 10 servings.
SERVE WITH:
● *Spicy Chicken Wings and Blue Cheese Dip, page 120*
● *Sausage and Pepper Biscuits, page 109*
● *Chocolate-Dipped Pecan Shortbread, page 109*

A rich pasta like this is an elegant way to start a meal. As an appetizer it will serve eight.

PASTA WITH CAVIAR AND CREAM

**2 c. heavy cream
Juice of ½ lemon
1 lb. thin spaghetti
1 3½-oz. jar black lumpfish caviar**

In a medium saucepan over medium-high heat, simmer cream until reduced to 1 ½ cups. Stir in lemon juice. Cook pasta according to package directions. When done, drain and toss with sauce. Gently fold in caviar. Makes 8 servings.
SERVE WITH:
● *Rack of Lamb, page 173*
● *Walnut Green Beans, page 61*
● *Braised Shallots, page 176*
● *Lemon sorbet, splashed with iced Vodka*

This is called "Christmas" pasta because of its red and green color. Enjoy it all year long.

CHRISTMAS PASTA

1 lb. vermicelli
1 garlic clove
1 T. olive oil
1 8-oz. can tomato sauce
1 c. heavy cream
½ tsp. dried oregano
¼ tsp. dried mint
¾ lb. smoked salmon,
**   cut into thin strips**
¼ c. chopped fresh parsley

Cook pasta according to label directions. Meanwhile, in medium saucepan over medium heat, cook garlic in oil until golden. Discard garlic. Stir next four ingredients into flavored oil; cook 5 minutes. Add salmon and parsley. Drain pasta; toss with sauce. Makes 4 servings.
SERVE WITH:
● *Caviar-Filled Artichokes, page 161*
● *Sparkling wine*
● *Chocolate-Dipped Strawberries, page 200*

If you don't have the time to poach the salmon, substitute two 7-oz. cans of salmon.

SALMON AND PASTA PRIMAVERA

1 8-oz. bottle clam juice
½ c. white wine
1 lb. salmon fillet
½ lb. vermicelli noodles
2 T. butter or margarine
2 garlic cloves, minced
2 c. shredded carrots
½ summer squash, shredded
1 large zucchini, shredded
¼ lb. snow peas
½ c. fresh or frozen peas
8 radishes, thinly sliced
½ c. heavy or whipping cream
½ c. chopped fresh basil
½ tsp. salt
Freshly ground black pepper

In a medium skillet, heat clam juice and wine to boiling. Add salmon; reduce heat to low, cover and simmer 10 minutes. Remove salmon from liquid. Cool salmon and flake into bite-sized pieces, discarding skin; cover and keep warm. Cook pasta as label directs. Melt butter or margarine in a large skillet. Add garlic and carrots and sauté 3 minutes. Add summer squash and zucchini and sauté 2 minutes. Stir in the snow peas, peas, radishes and cream, and cook, 2 minutes. Drain pasta. Toss gently with salmon, basil and vegetable sauce. Season with salt and pepper. Makes 4 servings.
SERVE WITH:
● *Asparagus Mimosa, page 176*
● *Whole-Wheat Italian bread*
● *Green salad*
● *Lime sherbet with raspberries*

This is a peasant-style fish stew which is one of the best party foods around.

CIOPPINO

3 T. olive oil
2 large onions, chopped
2 sweet green peppers, chopped
3 large garlic cloves, minced
½ c. minced fresh parsley
1 6-oz. can tomato paste
2 28-oz. cans tomatoes
1 8-oz. bottle clam juice
1 ½ c. dry white wine
1½ tsp. salt
1 T. dry dry basil
2 bay leaves
½ tsp. crushed red pepper flakes
1 lb. fresh or frozen cod fillets*,
**   cut into 2-inch cubes**
1 lb. fresh or frozen sea scallops*
1 lb. fresh or frozen cleaned
**   medium shrimp**
24 littleneck clams in shells
2 lbs. fresh or frozen Alaska King
**   crab legs* in shell, cut into**
**   2-inch pieces**
*If using frozen fish, partially thaw before using.

In 8 quart stockpot or Dutch oven, heat oil. Add onions, green pepper and garlic and sauté 10 minutes until tender. Add parsley and remaining ingredients except fish and shellfish. Heat to boiling. Reduce heat to low; cover and simmer 30 minutes, stirring occasionally. Add cod and scallops and simmer 5 minutes. Add shrimp and simmer 3 minutes more, or until shrimp curl. Add clams and crab and cook until clams open, about 2 minutes. Makes about 12 servings.
SERVE WITH:
● *Focaccia, page 125*
● *Green Bean and Onion Salad, page 105*
● *Chocolate-Walnut Pie, page 125*

Make this wonderful party dish the evening's entertainment. It's the kind of recipe that everyone will want, and the kind of preparation that everyone will want to help with.

PAELLA

3 T. olive oil
1 2-lb. chicken, cut into pieces
6 garlic cloves, minced
1 medium onion, sliced
½ lb. pepperoni, sliced
1 sweet green pepper,
    seeded and cut into strips
½ c. dry vermouth
2 8-oz. bottles clam juice
1 13-oz. can chicken broth
½ tsp. saffron
1 tsp. paprika
1 tsp. salt
2 bay leaves
1 ½ tsp. dried oregano
1 tsp. dried thyme leaves
2 c. long-grain rice
12 clams, scrubbed
1 lb. shelled and deveined fresh
    or frozen shrimp
2 tomatoes, diced
1 9-oz. pkg. frozen artichoke hearts
1 10-oz. pkg. frozen peas
½ 10-oz. pkg. frozen green beans

In large saucepan over medium heat, heat oil. Add chicken and brown on all sides. Add garlic and onion. Cook 5 to 7 minutes until onion is translucent. Add pepperoni and green pepper. Cook until tender, about 6 to 8 minutes. Pour in vermouth, clam juice and chicken broth. Heat to boiling. Add saffron, paprika, salt, bay leaves, oregano and thyme. Heat to boiling. Reduce heat to low. Cover and simmer 15 to 20 minutes. Stir in rice. Boil rapidly, uncovered, 15 minutes until rice begins to swell and absorbs liquid. Stir occasionally to keep rice from sticking. Add clams and shrimp. Cover and reduce heat to low. Simmer 3 to 4 minutes. Add tomatoes, artichokes, peas and green beans. Cover and simmer 7 to 8 minutes, or until clams open up. Makes 6 to 8 servings
SERVE WITH:
● *Walnut Bread, page 167*
● *Crudités*
● *White wine or beer*
● *Raspberry Tart, page 101*

This is a wonderful salad for a summer lunch or late summer supper. Make it early in the day and it will be ready when you are.

SHRIMP AND FETA SALAD

1 ½ lbs. large shrimp
    or ½ lb. shelled and deveined
    frozen shrimp
1 bunch scallions, minced
½ lb. feta cheese,
    cut into ½-inch pieces
2 tomatoes, cut into ½-inch pieces
DRESSING:
2 hard-cooked egg yolks
¼ c. olive oil
¼ c. safflower or vegetable oil
¼ tsp. salt
Dash of freshly ground black
    pepper
1½ tsp. white wine vinegar
Juice of ½ lemon
1 T. minced fresh dill or 1 tsp. dried
½ head romaine or other lettuce

Cover shrimp with water in saucepan. Heat to boiling. Cover and remove from heat; let stand 4 minutes. Drain; rinse. Shell and devein shrimp. If using frozen shrimp follow label directions. Toss shrimp with scallions, feta and tomatoes. Mash yolks. Put in jar with remaining dressing ingredients. Shake well. Toss with salad. Serve on lettuce leaves. Makes 6 servings.
SERVE WITH:
● *Fresh Fruit Marsala, page 143*
● *Crusty French bread*
● *Sparkling wine*

Here is a nice change from the usual. If fresh tuna is not available, substitute two 7-oz. cans tuna, drained and skip poaching.

FRESH TUNA SALAD WITH GINGER VINAIGRETTE

1 8-oz. bottle clam juice
1 lb. fresh tuna fillet
8 oz. string beans, trimmed
1 medium zucchini, sliced
Ginger Vinaigrette (recipe follows)
¼ lb. mushrooms, thinly sliced
1 bunch radish sprouts or
    watercress, rinsed and trimmed

In a medium skillet, combine clam juice and enough water to cover tuna by 1 inch. Cover and heat to boiling. Add tuna, reduce heat to low, cover and simmer gently for 8 to 10 minutes. Remove fish from cooking liquid and cool completely. Steam the beans over boiling water for 2 to 3 minutes, until tender-crisp. Steam zucchini for 1 to 2 minutes. Cool; Break the tuna into chunks and combine with the vegetables, mushrooms and sprouts in a large bowl. Toss with the vinaigrette. Makes 4 servings.

GINGER VINAIGRETTE

4 T. red wine vinegar
1 T. Dijon mustard
½ tsp. minced fresh ginger
½ tsp. fresh ground pepper
½ c. olive oil

In a small bowl with whisk, combine the vinegar, mustard, ginger and pepper. Gradually whisk in the olive oil, beating constantly.
SERVE WITH:
● *Prosciutto-Wrapped Asparagus, page 154*
● *Gingerbread Muffins, page 140*
● *Frozen Fruit on Skewers, page 142*

TIPS ON BUYING AND COOKING SEAFOOD

● *Fish should smell "oceany," not fishy.*
● *Fish should look moist and glossy, have a slightly translucent color. Cuts of fish—steaks or fillets—that look dry and/or brownish at the edges are past their freshness prime.*
● *Fish should feel firm and the flesh should spring back when pressed. Scales should be firmly attached. On a whole fresh fish, eyes will be bright and bulging, not brown, milky or sunken.*
● *Shrimps and scallops should be firm and have a subtle sea-breeze scent—not fishy.*
● *Oysters, mussels and clams should be tightly closed.*
● *Lobsters and crabs should be moving if live; or, if cooked, should have white meat with a reddish tinge.*
● *Fish such as bluefish, mackerel, swordfish or salmon, that are high in fat, have a stronger, more distinctly fish-like taste than those that are leaner, milder and more delicate, such as sole, flounder or halibut. Counterbalance these with more assertive flavor with equally strong ingredients such as lemons, tomatoes, peppers, capers, wine, mustard, wine vinegar, dill, and ginger.*

QUICK GUIDE TO TIMING

Measure fish at its thickest point and cook it 10 minutes per inch of thickness (plus or minus any fraction) regardless of the cooking method (see photo). For example, a salmon steak that is 1 ½ inches thick will take 15 minutes. A ¼ inch thick fillet will take only 2 to 3 minutes.

THE RIGHT METHOD FOR YOUR FISH

For some kinds of fish one cooking method may be preferred over others. Here's a rundown.
Sautéing
or pan frying, is best for small whole fish and fillets. Heat a small amount of fat (equal amounts of butter and oil) in a skillet. Add fish; fry 3 to 5 minutes on each side. Season with salt, pepper and fresh lemon juice.
BEST BETS: perch, smelt, flounder and sole.
Broiling
is good for any type of fish, best for fillets and steaks. Baste fish with melted butter or oil. To broil with butter sauce, mix 2 T. melted butter or margarine, 1 tsp. each fresh lemon juice and white wine, dash paprika, salt and pepper to taste. Broil on broiling pan without a rack 3 to 4 inches away from heat source for 10 minutes per inch thickness of the fish. Don't turn. The heat of the broiling pan cooks the underside.
BEST BETS: swordfish, snapper, mackerel and pompano.
Baking
is best for lean, dry fish. Place fish in greased baking pan in preheated 350°F oven. Baste frequently with melted butter or oil 10 minutes per inch of thickness of the fish. For Oreganata: Blend 1 c. flavored bread crumbs with 2 T. oil. Coat fish. Sprinkle with salt and pepper, 1 tsp. each lemon juice and white wine and 2 tsp. melted butter; bake 10 minutes per inch thickness of fish.
BEST BETS: cod, haddock, hake, flounder, sole, scrod (a young cod, less than 3 lbs.).

When you're in the mood for... hot and spicy sizzlers

ot for the taste-timid, these mouth-watering recipes will set palates tingling. These are foods with exotic flair, great for sharing with friends; Chicken Curry, page 188, Moroccan Couscous with Hot Pepper Sauce, page 190, and Indonesian Chicken Saté, right. Look here too for recipes with lots of down-home flavor—Barbecued Ribs, right, and a spicy chili, page 191. To ensure that you get more piquantly flavored meat, poultry or fish, try marinating them several hours before cooking. The chart on page 189 will let you in on all the secrets of marinating. Plus, if you check out the grilling how-tos on page 193, you'll be barbecuing more than franks and burgers during the summer. Leg of lamb, shrimp, even vegetables and fruits taste extraordinary when grilled outdoors. Try them!

This spicy chicken is prepared on bamboo skewers. So that skewers do not catch fire while broiling, soak them in water before using.

INDONESIAN CHICKEN SATÉ

2 whole large chicken breasts, skinned, boned and split
MARINADE:
¼ c. soy sauce
2 T. dark brown sugar
2 T. fresh lime juice
1 T. vegetable oil
1-inch piece fresh ginger, peeled and minced
1 large garlic clove, minced
1 tsp. cumin seed
½ tsp. crushed red pepper flakes
Peanut Sauce (recipe follows)

Dried chilies and garlic give this lamb its zest

Cut chicken breasts into ½-inch strips. In medium bowl, combine remaining ingredients except Peanut Sauce; add chicken strips and toss to coat well. Cover and refrigerate. Let marinate at least 2 hours, stirring occasionally. Heat broiler. Thread chicken on 12-inch-long bamboo skewers; reserve marinade. Broil 10 to 12 minutes, turning often and basting with marinade. Serve with Peanut Sauce. Makes 6 servings.

PEANUT SAUCE

½ c. hot water
½ c. smooth peanut butter
2 T. fresh lime juice
1 T. brown sugar

In medium bowl with wire whisk, blend hot water with peanut butter. Whisk in lime juice and brown sugar until well blended. Makes 1 cup.
SERVE WITH:
● *Yellow rice: Make white rice as package label directs, but add 2 tsp. turmeric to water*
● *Tossed green salad*
● *Banana Sorbet, page 146*

Plan to do Chili-marinated Lamb in stages, two minutes here, ten minutes there—then all you have to do is light the coals and grill.

GRILLED CHILI-MARINATED LAMB

½ oz. small, hot dried chilies
6 garlic cloves, peeled
¾ c. olive oil
1 5-lb. butterflied leg of lamb, trimmed
Salt
Freshly ground black pepper
Assorted steamed vegetables such as zucchini, red potatoes, leeks, baby eggplant and sweet red peppers
Tomato Salsa*

Available in the Mexican food section of your supermarket or in specialty food stores.

Place chilies on cookie sheet and toast a few minutes on each side (be careful not to burn them). Place toasted chilies in bowl and cover with boiling water to soften. Set aside for 1 hour. In food processor with knife blade attached, process garlic until finely chopped. Remove chilies from soaking water and process them with garlic until chopped. With motor running, add oil in a

slow, steady stream. Continue to process until peppers are finely chopped and mixture is emulsified. Season lamb with salt and pepper, then rub chili sauce into the meat on all sides. Cover and marinate 4 hours or overnight. Heat broiler or prepare outdoor grill. Grill lamb over medium-hot coals 8 to 10 minutes per side or until medium rare. (Coals are medium hot when you can hold your hand a few inches above the coals at the level of the grill for four seconds.) Grill steamed vegetables 2 to 4 minutes per side. Slice lamb thinly and serve with Salsa and grilled vegetables. Makes 6 servings.
SERVE WITH:
● *Curried Citrus Dressing, page 152 on sliced tomato and sliced red onion*
● *Tabouli Salad, page 151*
● *Frozen Fruit on Skewers, page 142*

Short ribs, baby back or pork ribs are equally good for this recipe. The secret is to first boil the ribs before grilling them with the sauce.

BARBECUED RIBS

5 lbs. short ribs
Barbecue Sauce (recipe follows)

In 8-quart Dutch oven or saucepan, place short ribs. Cover with water. Over high heat, heat to boiling. Reduce heat to low; cover and simmer 1½ hours or until fork-tender. Meanwhile make Barbecue Sauce. Place ribs in shallow pan; cover with sauce and marinate at least 1 hour. Heat grill or broiler as manufacturer directs. Place ribs on grill (or in broiler pan), reserving sauce. Cook over medium coals 20 to 25 minutes, turning often and brushing with Barbecue Sauce. Makes 12 servings.

BARBECUE SAUCE

1 T. vegetable oil
1 small onion, chopped
1 c. ketchup
½ c. water
¼ c. white vinegar
2 T. brown sugar
2 T. Worcestershire sauce
2 tsp. Tabasco
1 tsp. freshly ground black pepper
½ tsp. salt

In medium saucepan over medium heat in hot oil, sauté onion until tender, about 10 minutes. Add ketchup and remaining ingredients. Over high heat, heat to boiling. Reduce heat to low;

cover and simmer 20 minutes, stirring occasionally. Makes 2 cups.
SERVE WITH:
- *Summer Slaw, page 177*
- *Cheddar-Beer Biscuits, page 125*
- *Pecan Shortbread, page 207*

———

The crunchy cornmeal batter is full of fire. Make the cooling sauce early in the day so it mellows.

FIERY SHRIMP WITH EXTINGUISHER SAUCE

EXTINGUISHER SAUCE:
6 T. plain yogurt
1 medium cucumber, peeled, seeded and diced
1 T. finely chopped fresh mint or 1 tsp. dried
1 tsp. fresh lemon juice
½ tsp. sugar
Freshly ground black pepper
SHRIMP:
1 ½ lbs. large raw shrimp
Oil for frying
1 c. cornmeal
¼ c. all-purpose flour
1 tsp. ground red pepper
¾ tsp. salt
1 egg beaten with ¼ c. water

Prepare sauce: In medium bowl mix yogurt, cucumber, mint, lemon juice, sugar and pepper. Cover and refrigerate at least 2 hours to release flavors. Shell shrimp, leaving tails on. With a small sharp knife, cut along backs of shrimp almost, but not all the way, through. Remove and discard veins. Fill a medium-deep saucepan or deep-fat fryer with 4 inches oil. Over medium-high heat, heat oil to 365°F on deep-frying thermometer. While oil is heating, in medium bowl, mix cornmeal, flour, red pepper and salt. Working with one shrimp at at time, dip shrimp into egg mixture and then coat well with cornmeal. Fry in small batches, about 6 at a time. Let oil return to 365°F between batches. Drain on paper towels and serve with Extinguisher Sauce. Makes 6 servings.
SERVE WITH:
- *Tomato-Basil Soup, page 164*
- *Assorted raw vegetables such as celery and carrot sticks, radishes and scallions*
- *Cheese Herb Bread, page 166*

———

For a spicy, festive, super party, try this recipe. The Sambals, or condiments, bowlfuls of raisins, chutney, peanuts and coconut, are sprinkled over the curry—making it as sweet, crunchy or nutty as desired.

CHICKEN CURRY

3 T. vegetable oil
1 T. cumin seed
2 large onions, chopped
3 large garlic cloves, minced
1-inch piece fresh ginger, peeled and minced
2 medium potatoes, peeled and cubed
2 4-oz. cans green chilies, drained and chopped
1 16-oz. can tomatoes, drained and chopped
1 T. ground coriander
2 tsp. salt
1 tsp. turmeric
2 bay leaves
¼ tsp. ground red pepper or to taste
2 ½ c. chicken broth
2 2 ½ to 3 lb. chickens, cooked, boned and skinned and cut into cubes, or 5 c. leftover chicken or turkey, cubed
1 10-oz. package frozen peas, thawed
SAMBALS:
Chopped peanuts
Grated coconut
Chutney
Raisins

In 5-quart saucepan or Dutch oven, over medium heat, heat oil. Add cumin seed and cook 30 seconds. Add onions, garlic and ginger. Sauté 10 minutes or until tender. Add potatoes, chilies, tomatoes, coriander, salt, turmeric, bay leaves, red pepper and chicken broth. Over high heat, heat to boiling. Reduce heat to low; cover and simmer 30 minutes. Add chicken and peas and cook to heat through. Serve with rice and Sambals. Makes 12 servings.
SERVE WITH:
- *Hot cooked rice, see page 70 for how to*
- *Tomatoes with Fresh Dill, page 105*
- *Chocolate Rum Roll with Rum Cream, page 200.*

BENEFITS OF MARINATING

Here are popular cuts of meat and fish paired with a variety of zingy marinades. First, a few things to keep in mind:

● *Marinating times vary greatly depending on the cut of meat and whether you want a hint of flavor or something that is strongly seasoned.*

● *Marinades that are high in acid, such as vinegar, citrus juice, soy sauce or wine, will tenderize a tough cut of meat such as chuck steak, flank steak or brisket. For these cuts of meat, marinate at least overnight or up to two days in the refrigerator.*

● *To flavor fish, only an hour or two is necessary. For just a hint of flavor or to seal in juices, a blend of dry herbs can be rubbed on the food a half hour before cooking.*

● *Don't marinate in an aluminum pan. Aluminum reacts with the acid in the marinade and gives the food a metallic taste. Instead, use a glass or enamel-coated dish or, better still, a leak proof plastic bag. A plastic bag works well with pieces of meat, poultry or fish or small roasts. There's no need to turn the food or take up precious refrigerator space with large baking dishes.*

● *Don't use leftover marinades on cooked food for sauces since the juices picked up from the previous uncooked raw meat, poultry or fish are fertile ground for bacteria.*

TRY THIS	WITH THIS
Chicken Pieces	Place chicken in plastic bag. Combine 1 c. chopped fresh basil leaves, ½ c. oil, ¼ c. fresh lemon juice, 1 tsp. salt, ½ tsp. pepper. Pour over chicken; seal bag. Toss to coat. Marinate in refrigerator several hours. Cook over hot coals or in 350°F oven 35–45 minutes; turn once.
Cornish Hens	Place split hens in plastic bag. In a blender, purée 1 c. yogurt, 1 c. diced onion, 2 T. curry powder, 1 T. ground cumin, 1 T. ground coriander, 1 tsp. salt. Pour over hens; seal bag. Toss to coat. Refrigerate several hours or overnight. Cook over hot coals or in 350°F oven for 30–35 minutes; turn once.
Whole Fish	Combine 1 T. paprika, 1 tsp. salt, 1 tsp. garlic powder, ½ tsp. thyme leaves, ½ tsp. dried oregano, ¼ tsp. ground red pepper, ¼ tsp. pepper. Rub in cavity and all over outside of fish. Cover; refrigerate 30 minutes. Cook over hot coals or in 400°F oven, 10 minutes per inch of thickness.
Butterflied Leg of Lamb	In a shallow baking dish, combine 1 c. dry white wine, ¼ c. oil, ¼ c. lemon juice, 2 crushed garlic cloves, 1 tsp. rosemary, 1 tsp. thyme. Add meat; turn until coated. Cover; refrigerate 4 hours or overnight. Cook over hot coals or in broiler for 35–40 minutes.
Boneless Pork Loin	In a blender purée 1 c. parsley leaves, ¼ c. oil, 1 tsp. thyme leaves, 1 tsp. salt, ½ tsp. pepper. Cut 4 garlic cloves into slivers. Make random slits in the meat; insert the garlic. Rub paste over meat. Cover; refrigerate 2–3 hours. Cook over hot coals for 15–17 minutes per inch or in 350°F oven, 15 minutes per pound.
Pork Cutlets	Place pork in a plastic bag. Combine 1 c. coconut cream, 2 T. soy sauce, 2 T. fresh lime juice, 1 T. grated fresh ginger, ¼ tsp. ground red pepper, 1 crushed garlic clove. Pour over cutlets; seal bag. Refrigerate several hours. Cook over hot coals or in broiler for 15–17 minutes per inch.
London Broil or Chuck Steak	In shallow baking dish, combine 1 c. beer, ¼ c. oil, 2 T. Dijon mustard, 1 tsp. salt, ¼ tsp. pepper, 1 crushed garlic clove. Add the beef; turn to coat. Cover; refrigerate 4 hours or overnight. Turn occasionally. Sear over very hot coals, then cook over medium hot coals or in broiler 8–10 minutes per inch for rare; 10–12 minutes per inch for medium.
Baby Beef Ribs	Place ribs in plastic bag. Combine ¼ c. orange juice, ¼ c. oil, ¼ c. soy sauce, ¼ c. sherry, 1 T. grated orange peel, 1 T. grated fresh ginger, 2 crushed garlic cloves. Pour over ribs; seal bag. Refrigerate overnight. Cook, wrapped in foil, over hot coals or in 350°F oven 30 minutes; unwrap and cook 15 minutes more.

Here's an elegant alternative to tacos and burritos when you're in the mood for the taste of south-of-the-border food. The sauce is rich and spicy yet mellow.

MEXICAN CHICKEN

3 T. olive or vegetable oil
½ c. cornmeal
2 2 ½ to 3 lb. chickens, cut up
1 large onion, finely chopped
3 garlic cloves, minced
2 T. chili powder
1 tsp. ground coriander
1 tsp. cumin seed
1 tsp. salt
1 tsp. sugar
½ tsp. ground cinnamon
1 c. white wine
½ c. water
GARNISH:
1 medium tomato, chopped
3 tsp. minced fresh parsley
1 T. sesame seeds

Over medium-high heat, in large skillet heat oil. Meanwhile, spread cornmeal on sheet of waxed paper. Dredge chicken in cornmeal. Brown chicken, a few pieces at a time, in hot oil, removing pieces as they brown. In oil remaining in skillet cook onion and garlic until tender, about 5 minutes. Add chili powder and next 5 ingredients and cook 3 minutes more. Pour in wine and water. Stir to blend; pour into oven-proof casserole. Arrange chicken, skin-side up on sauce in casserole. Heat oven to 325°F. Cover casserole and cook in oven for 1½ hours or until chicken is tender. With tongs or slotted spoon remove chicken to serving platter. Cover with foil; set aside and keep warm. Skim fat from sauce remaining in casserole. Pour sauce into saucepan. Over high heat, heat to boiling. Cook rapidly until reduced and thickened. Spoon sauce over and around chicken on platter. Garnish with chopped tomato, parsley and sesame seeds. Makes 8 servings.

SERVE WITH:
● *Flour tortillas*
● *Beer*
● *Boiled potatoes*
● *Avocado, Orange, Red Onion Salad, page 69*

You'll find the sauce is what's hot in this recipe. Lamb is used, but it can be made without meat if you like. See Vegetable Couscous, page 21.

MOROCCAN COUSCOUS WITH LAMB AND HOT PEPPER SAUCE

½ c. butter or margarine
4 lbs. boneless lamb,
    cut into 2-inch cubes
2 tsp. salt
½-inch piece fresh ginger, peeled
    and minced
½ tsp. freshly ground black pepper
½ tsp. grated nutmeg
¼ tsp. turmeric
¼ tsp. ground cinnamon
3 whole cloves
5 c. water
1 ½ lbs. onions, peeled and
    quartered
4 carrots, peeled and cut into
    2-inch pieces
4 tomatoes peeled, seeded
    and chopped
3 medium zucchini, halved and
    cut into 2-inch pieces
½ c. raisins
1 c. canned garbanzo beans
    (chickpeas), drained
1 16-oz. box presteamed couscous
Hot Pepper Sauce (recipe follows)

In large stockpot over medium-high heat, melt butter or margarine. Add lamb, salt and next six ingredients. Stir until meat is well coated with spices. Add 5 cups water. Over high heat, heat to boiling. Reduce heat to low; cover and simmer 1 hour. Add remaining ingredients except couscous and Hot Pepper Sauce; cover and cook ½ hour more. Make couscous according to package directions. To serve, spoon couscous and lamb into warm serving dish. Serve with Hot Pepper Sauce on the side. Makes 8 servings.

HOT PEPPER SAUCE

2 T. crushed red pepper flakes
3 T. water
1 T. vegetable oil
½ tsp. ground cumin

In saucepan, over medium heat, combine pepper flakes and water. Heat to boiling. Remove from heat; add oil and cumin. Makes ⅓ cup.

SERVE WITH:
● *Moroccan Mint Tea, page 21*
● *Whole-wheat pita bread*
● *Oranges or tangerines*

This is a basic chili recipe. . .a good starter to adapt to your own taste. Vary the "heat" with the amount of green chilies and the quality of the chili powder you use.

THE WILDEST CHILI

2 lbs. ground beef
3 medium onions, chopped
1 small sweet green pepper,
 chopped
2 garlic cloves, sliced
1 28-oz. can tomatoes, undrained
1 6-oz. can tomato paste
1 4-oz. can green chilies, chopped
3 T. chili powder
2 tsp. ground cumin
2 tsp. salt
2 15-oz. cans red kidney beans,
 drained

In large saucepan over medium heat, cook ground beef with onions, green pepper and garlic until beef is browned and meat juices evaporate. Add tomatoes and their liquid, tomato paste and remaining ingredients except beans. Heat to boiling. Reduce heat to low; cover and simmer 1½ hours, stirring occasionally. Add beans; heat through. Makes 10 cups.
SERVE WITH:
● *Bean Dip or Guacamole Dip, page 157*
● *Corn bread*
● *Margaritas, page 197*

To accompany any plain grilled or roasted meat this is a good choice. Or, it can be served as a vegetarian main dish.

INDIAN PEA CURRY

2 ½ tsp. dry mustard
2 T. water
2 T. vegetable oil
1 medium onion, chopped
2 jalapeño peppers, seeded
 and chopped
½-inch fresh ginger, peeled
 and minced
½ tsp. salt
¾ tsp. cumin seed
¼ tsp. turmeric

1 10-oz. pkg. frozen peas, thawed
2 medium potatoes, cooked,
 peeled and cut into 1-inch cubes
3 tomatoes, each cut into 8 wedges
2 T. chopped fresh coriander leaves
 (cilantro) or parsley, chopped for
 garnish

In small cup, blend dry mustard and water to make paste; set aside. In large skillet over medium heat, heat oil. Add onion, chilies and ginger and sauté until onion is tender, about 5 minutes. Add salt, cumin and turmeric and cook 3 minutes more. Add peas and cook 5 minutes, stirring frequently. Gently stir in potatoes and tomatoes; cook until heated through. Blend in mustard paste. Spoon into serving dish; sprinkle with coriander. Makes 6 servings.
SERVE WITH:
● *Pecan-Orange Rice, page 45*
● *Watercress and cucumber salad*
● *Beer*

Serve these spicy beans for the perfect accompaniment for a barbecued brisket, ribs— even burgers. Add cole slaw, a bucket of ice-cold beer, a smoking grill, and an orange-red sunset. . .it doesn't get much better than that!

FRIJOLES SUPREMO

1 lb. dry pinto beans
Water
¼ c. minced onion
2 garlic cloves, minced
2 T. vegetable oil
1 4-oz. can whole green chilies,
 coarsely chopped
 or 2 fresh jalapeño peppers,
 seeded and minced
1 8-oz. can tomato sauce
1 tsp. salt
½ tsp. ground coriander

Wash beans; discard any stones or shriveled beans. Drain and place in large saucepan. Cover with water and soak overnight. (For quick method, combine beans and 6 cups water. Heat to boiling; boil 2 minutes. Remove from heat; cover and let stand 1 hour.) Drain beans. Return beans to pot and add 3 cups water. In small skillet over medium-high heat, sauté onion and garlic in hot oil until tender, about 5 minutes. Add to beans. Over high heat, heat to boiling. Reduce heat to low; cover and simmer 1 hour. Stir in chilies and remaining ingredients and cook 1 hour longer, until beans are very tender. Makes 10 servings.

Try the two great and spicy condiments here for a before dinner dip or to brighten up burgers or dollop on omelets.

SPICED YOGURT

**½-inch piece fresh ginger
2 garlic cloves, minced
1 fresh jalapeño, minced
½ tsp. ground turmeric
2 tsp. ground coriander
¼ tsp. ground red pepper
1 T. water
4 T. vegetable oil
½ tsp. cumin seed
2 medium onions, minced
1 tsp. salt
⅛ tsp. freshly ground black pepper
3 c. plain yogurt**

In bowl combine first seven ingredients. Heat oil in medium skillet over medium heat. Add cumin seeds and cook until they just begin to pop. Add onions. Cook for 3 minutes, stirring constantly until onions are golden but not browned. Add spices and salt and pepper. Sauté 1 minute. Blend in yogurt and remove from heat. Cool. Makes 3¼ cups.

CHILI MAYONNAISE

In small bowl combine ½ c. mayonnaise and ¼ to ½ tsp. ground red pepper.
Makes ½ cup.

Use this fiery blend of dry spices to rub it into chicken, pork, beef or fish. Let stand 15 minutes, then bake, broil or grill as usual.

BUENA MESA BLEND

**3 T. dried oregano
3 T. paprika
2 T. onion powder
1 T. garlic powder
2 ½ tsp. ground cumin
2 ¼ tsp. ground red pepper**

With a mortar and pestle, or between the palms of your hands, crush oregano until powdered. In a small bowl, combine oregano with paprika, onion and garlic powders, cumin and red pepper. Store at room temperature in tightly sealed jar. Makes about ⅔ cup.

Here's a great dipping sauce. Wonderful when served with chilled shrimp, roasted pork or fried chicken.

CALYPSO SAUCE

**½ c. light brown sugar,
   firmly packed
¼ c. fresh lime juice
2 T. light rum
1-inch piece fresh ginger,
   peeled and minced
2 garlic cloves, minced
¼ tsp. salt
¼ tsp. Tabasco
⅛ tsp. ground cloves**

In small saucepan, combine brown sugar with remaining ingredients. Cook over medium heat, stirring, until the sugar is completely dissolved. Makes ¾ cup.

START WITH THE RIGHT TEMPERATURE

For best results, barbecue your food at the right temperature. Unfortunately, your grill doesn't come with a thermometer, so use this simple test to tell just how hot the coals are: Hold your hand, palm down, at cooking height, the level where the grill will sit (see photo). Using the seconds hand of a clock, time how long you can keep your hand there, being very careful not to burn yourself. Two seconds—the coals are very hot, a bit too hot for most foods. Three seconds—the coals are medium-high or hot. Four seconds—the coals are medium and five seconds for low coals. If the coals are too hot, spread them out or raise the grill level. If the coals are too cool, tap the ash from them and move them closer together with a barbecue tool or, if you can, lower the grill level.

THE EASIEST GRILLING EVER!

With this chart and a little imagination, you'll soon find there's more to barbecuing than just burgers and franks.

FOOD	COAL TEMP.	COOKING TIME APPROX. MINS.	HOW TO
Hamburgers	Hot	1st side: 3 2nd side: 4 rare; 5 med. rare; 6 med.	Cook quickly, turning with spatula. Try serving with grated horseradish instead of pickles.
Tender steaks sirloin, tenderloin, porterhouse	Hot	1st side: 5 2nd side: 8 rare; 10 med. rare; 12 med.	Press cracked pepper into steaks on both sides. Let stand 30 minutes, then grill.
Less tender steaks chuck, cube, flank	Med.	1st side: 8 2nd side: 10 rare; 12 med. rare; 15 med.	Marinate in oil and wine vinegar several hours or overnight. Baste with marinade while grilling.
Fish salmon, trout, swordfish, flounder	Hot	10, per inch of thickness	If using frozen, partially defrost, then cook. Oil both the grill and the fish. Baste with lemon juice and butter. Turn once.
Shrimp, scallops	Hot	5	Marinate in soy sauce, sherry and chopped ginger. Thread on skewers. Oil grill and fish. Turn once.
Leg of lamb	Med. to Low	pink (140° F): 20-25 per lb. well-done (165° F): 25-30 per lb.	Have leg boned and butterflied by butcher. Insert slivers of garlic in several places and rub with rosemary. Check internal temperature with meat thermometer.
Pork chops	Hot	1st side: 12-15 2nd side: 12-15	Slash fat at ¾-inch intervals to keep chops from curling. Marinate in tomato juice and fresh chopped basil. Grill, basting with sauce.
Spareribs	Med.	precook: 30 grill: 45	Simmer in water 30 minutes, drain and cool. Then grill, turning ribs frequently. Brush with 1 c. fruit jelly combined with 1 T. each dry mustard, Worcestershire sauce and lemon juice.
Chicken parts	Med. to Low	45-60	Baste with a mixture of olive oil, vermouth, chopped onion and parsley. Cook slowly so interior is cooked through.
Precooked sausages franks, knockwurst, kielbasa, bratwurst	Med. to Low	5-15, depending on size	Precooked sausages only need to be heated through. Serve with sauerkraut and crock of mustard.
Uncooked sausages Italian, hot and sweet	Med. to Low	precook: 10 grill: 10	Simmer in water for 10 minutes. Drain, and grill until well done. Serve with skewers of red and green peppers cooked on the grill.
Mushrooms	Hot	10	Thread on skewers. Grill, turning frequently, and brush with butter and tarragon.
Tomatoes	Hot	small: 5 large: 10	Thread large wedges or whole cherry tomatoes on skewers. Brush with garlic-flavored olive oil.
Summer squash	Hot	20-30	Grill on skewers, whole or sliced. Baste with dill butter.
Corn on the cob	Hot	in husk: 20-25 without husk: 10-20	In husk: Pull husk back; remove silk and replace husk. Soak in water 30 minutes. Grill, turning several times. Without husk: Remove husk and silk. Wrap in foil. Grill, turning frequently.
Bananas	Med.	10	Make slit (for steam to escape) in one side of unpeeled banana; grill until charred and soft. Peel, sprinkle with rum and serve.
Peaches	Med.	8	Peel; split in half (removing pit). Grill, turning until done. Sprinkle with brown sugar.

When you're in the mood for...
long and cool,
short and sweet drinks

A special drink can add just the right fillip to a meal or make an evening memorable. This is a collection of great beverages. Many are alcohol-free, perfect for quenching summer thirst. Don't miss the Old-Fashioned Lemonade, right, to store in a pitcher in your refrigerator for something different and refreshing anytime. Turn to this section for the absolutely best recipes for favorite standbys—brunch time Bloody Marys, page 196, cool and satisfying Frozen Cappuccinos, below, and nostalgic Egg Creams, right. When romance is in the air, serve sultry French Kisses, or a Sparkling Raspberry Cocktail, both on page 198, to stir things along. Ladle out Mulled Wine, page 198, at a winter time open-house or White Wine Sangría, page 198, while on a picnic. Look for helpful hints here on bar basics, page 199: How much of everything from limes to scotch to keep on hand, blender techniques and how much liquor to buy for a party.

NONALCOHOLIC DRINKS

A frozen version of the traditionally steaming coffee, you'll be impressed by the frothy texture and intense flavor of this concoction.

FROZEN CAPPUCCINO

**⅓ c. espresso or very strong
   coffee, chilled
⅓ c. milk, chilled
⅓ c. crushed ice
1 tsp. sugar
Whipped cream
Ground cinnamon**

In blender at high speed, combine espresso, milk, ice and sugar. Blend until smooth. Pour into large goblet. Garnish with a dollop of whipped cream and a dusting of cinnamon. Makes 1 serving.

Probably the best thirst quencher ever. Try Ginger Water with Chinese food or whenever an exotic flavor is appropriate.

GINGER WATER

**4-inch piece fresh ginger,
   peeled and grated
¾ c. sugar
1 qt. water
1 orange, sliced**

Combine ginger, sugar and water in large pitcher. Refrigerate for 24 hours. Strain and discard pulp. Serve over crushed ice in sugar-frosted punch cups. Garnish each with an orange slice. Makes 6 servings.

Quench your thirst with an icy sipper: old-fashioned egg cream without eggs or cream! It's a New York City soda fountain invention. If made properly the seltzer forms an "egg white" foamy head on top.

OLD-FASHIONED EGG CREAM

**3 T. chocolate syrup
3 T. ice-cold milk
Seltzer or club soda**

Into a tall glass, pour chocolate syrup and milk. Fill glass with seltzer or club soda. Makes 1 serving.

If you've forgotton the taste of real lemonade, try this. There's nothing quite like it.

OLD-FASHIONED LEMONADE

**⅔ c. sugar
5 c. cold water
Lemon peels from 2 lemons
1 c. fresh lemon juice (sqeezed
   from approximately 10 lemons)**

Soul satisfying and thirst quenching lemonade

In a saucepan, combine sugar, one cup of water and lemon peels. Simmer gently over medium heat for 10 minutes; set aside. When cool, strain ingredients into a 2-quart serving pitcher. Add fresh lemon juice and remaining water. Stir in two trays of ice cubes. Makes 1½ quarts.

This is a nonalcoholic form of a Tom Collins with alcohol and syrup omitted, sugar added.

RASPBERRY-LIME RICKEY

3 T. raspberry syrup
1 ½ T. fresh lime juice
Ice cubes
Seltzer or club soda
Lime wedge, for garnish

Combine syrup and lime juice in a tall glass. Fill the glass with ice cubes. Add seltzer to the top. Garnish with lime. Makes 1 serving.

To excite your tastebuds, try a Strawberry Freeze for an afternoon refresher, with brunch or just to satsify your sweet tooth.

STRAWBERRY FREEZE

½ c. grapefruit juice
¼ c. fresh or frozen strawberries
1 T. honey
⅓ c. club soda

Combine grapefruit juice, strawberries and honey in blender and purée until smooth. Transfer to a tall glass filled with crushed ice and add club soda. Makes 1 serving.

There's no alcohol in this "cocktail," just lots of fresh fruity taste. A good variation for raspberry syrup is strawberry.

WATERMELON COOLER

4 c. cubed, seeded watermelon
¾ c. lemon sherbet
1 T. raspberry syrup
1 c. ice cubes

In blender container combine watermelon, lemon sherbet, raspberry syrup and ice cubes. Blend until smooth and thick. Makes 2 servings.

ALCOHOLIC DRINKS

This Bloody Mary is best made in a pitcher.

BLOODY MARY

1 24-oz. can tomato juice
1 ½ c. vodka
Juice of 2 limes (¼ c.)
2 to 3 T. Worcestershire sauce
1 T. prepared horseradish
¼ tsp. Tabasco
Freshly ground black pepper
Ice
Lime wedges for garnish

In a large pitcher, combine tomato juice with next 6 ingredients. Pour over ice; garnish with lime. Makes 8 servings.

Jalapeño pepper makes this version of the Martini firehouse tasty.

CAJUN MARTINIS

1 fresh jalapeño pepper
1 liter gin
2 T. dry vermouth
1 pint cherry tomatoes

Lengthwise, slice and thread jalapeño on a long skewer. Place in full gin bottle. Add enough vermouth to the bottle to fill the neck up entirely. Recap and refrigerate 2 hours or overnight. The longer the pepper remains in the bottle the spicier and hotter the martini will be. Pour the martinis into a pitcher to serve, straining out the pepper and seeds. Serve with cherry tomatoes as a garnish. Makes 8 servings.

This drink can be a sit-down "first course."

CAPE COD COBBLER

3 c. cranberry juice
1 c. vodka
Crushed ice
1 c. lime sherbet

In large pitcher combine cranberry juice and vodka. Serve in large wine goblets over crushed ice. Top each with a small scoop of lime sherbet. Makes 6 servings.

Instead of a selection of wines or a choice of cocktails, this is a good choice for an afternoon shower or a holiday party. This punch has lots of sparkle—warn your guests.

CHAMPAGNE PUNCH

1 750 ml bottle chilled champagne
2 liters chilled hard or regular cider
4 c. chilled brandy
1 c. chilled sparkling mineral water

For an elegant touch, make an ice block the night before: Freeze ½ inch water until slushy in a bowl that fits inside your punch bowl. Arrange orange slices in slushy ice. Freeze. Repeat procedure to add another layer of fruit. Make punch: In a large punch bowl, mix champagne, hard cider, brandy and sparkling mineral water. Float ice block in punch. Makes about 1 gallon or about twelve 5-ounce servings.

For frozen and fruited daiquiris use any fruit you like or a combination of fruits. Most berries will work—except blueberries (they freeze like beebees).

DAIQUIRI

3 c. ice
½ c. light rum
2 T. fresh lime juice
2 T. sugar
2 c. strawberries, 3 bananas or 1½ c. apricots

In blender container whirl ice and remaining ingredients until smooth. Makes 4 servings.

The name blends the fuzziness of peaches with navel oranges. Add sparkling wine to the orange juice and peach schnapps and serve it at brunch.

FUZZY NAVELS

6 c. fresh orange juice
1 c. peach schnapps, chilled
2 bottles sparkling white wine or champagne, chilled

In a large pitcher combine the orange juice and schnapps. Stir until blended. Pour about ½ cup into a tall champagne glass. Top with about ½ cup sparkling wine. Makes 12 servings.

Don't wait until March 17th to enjoy Irish coffee; make it whenever the temperature drops and the wind starts blowing. Irish coffee is best when made in individual servings.

IRISH COFFEE

1 tsp. sugar
1 ½ oz. Irish whiskey
Hot coffee
Sweetened whipped cream

Combine sugar and Irish whiskey in a mug. Fill with hot coffee. Top with dollop of whipped cream. Makes 1 serving.

You'll find that this drink tastes sweet and innocent and surprisingly like its namesake— but careful, it's stronger than you think!

LONG ISLAND ICED TEA

⅓ c. vodka
⅓ c. gin
⅓ c. tequila
¼ c. Triple Sec
3 T. fresh lemon juice
1 T. sugar
1 c. cola
4 lemon wedges

Combine liquors, lemon juice and sugar. Chill until ready to serve. Pour into pitcher and stir in cola. Serve in tall ice-filled glasses garnished with lemon wedges. Makes 4 servings.

Some prefer their margaritas straight up; others like them over crushed ice. For a frozen one, blend with a tray of ice in the blender. Careful—they pack a wallop.

MARGARITAS

2 c. tequila
2 c. fresh lime juice
1 c. Triple Sec
1 lime, cut into wedges
Salt
Crushed ice

In a large pitcher, combine tequila, lime juice and Triple Sec; refrigerate. To serve, rub the rim of chilled wine glasses with lime wedges. Invert glasses and dip rims ¼ inch into salt. Shake off excess. Fill glasses with crushed ice and Margaritas. Makes 10 servings.

French Kiss is a powerful drink to enjoy after a rich dinner. Vary the amounts of brandy and Grand Marnier to get the mix you like best.

FRENCH KISS

2½ oz. brandy or cognac
½ oz. Grand Marnier

Combine liqueurs in snifter. Makes 1 serving.

After a day of cross-country skiing, serve this warm up-cool down refresher.

MULLED WINE

1 liter dry red wine
6 to 10 whole cloves
1 cinnamon stick
Lemon twist
2 T. sugar
6 cinnamon sticks
6 orange slices, for garnish

In heavy saucepan, combine wine and next 4 ingredients and heat, but do not boil. Strain into glasses. Garnish each with cinnamon stick and orange slice. Makes 6 servings.

Nothing says summer like this classic. This recipe makes a pitcherful.

PIÑA COLADA

2 c. pineapple juice
⅔ c. coconut cream
⅔ c. light rum
2 c. crushed ice

In blender container, combine pineapple juice, coconut cream, rum and crushed ice. Blend at high speed until creamy and thick. Pour into stemmed wine glasses. Makes 4 servings.

Cranberry juice adds sweetness here. If you prefer yours a bit tarter, use less cranberry.

SEA BREEZE

3 c. grapefruit juice
¼ c. cranberry juice
4 oz. vodka

In tall pitcher, combine grapefruit juice, cranberry juice and vodka. Chill until ready to serve. Serve in ice-filled glasses. Makes 4 servings.

Watch the berries slowly go up and down with the bubbles from the champagne in this fun cocktail.

SPARKLING RASPBERRY COCKTAIL

1 glass champagne or sparkling wine
1 tsp. black raspberry liqueur or kirsch
2 to 3 blackberries or raspberries

Combine champagne and liqueur in champagne flute. Float berries for garnish. Makes 1 serving.

If you make this drink without the cream, you'll have a Black Russian. Both are often made with gin instead of vodka.

WHITE RUSSIAN

2 oz. vodka
1 oz. Kahlúa
Ice
¼ c. light cream

Blend vodka and Kahlúa and pour over ice; add cream. Makes 1 serving.

This is one of the prettiest—and most refreshing—wine punches you could hope to sip. Cut fruit peels into spirals for garnish.

WHITE WINE SANGRÍA

2 750-ml. bottles (or quarts) dry white wine
½ c. brandy
2 oranges, sliced
1 lemon, sliced
1 c. confectioners' sugar

In a large bowl combine wine, brandy, fruit and sugar. Cover and refrigerate 4 to 6 hours. To serve, pour over ice in old-fashioned or wine glasses, letting a little of the fruit fall into each glass. Makes about 2 quarts or 8 servings.

IMPORTANCE OF ICE

When you're having a party, your best ice bet is to buy packaged ice, which is made in an ice plant. Making enough in your refrigerator requires time and storage; the ice sometimes picks up odors from other things in the freezer.

● Drinks poured into pre-chilled glasses will stay colder longer.

● For an instant chill, fill the glass with ice and swirl around for a couple of minutes, then discard ice.

● Use ice cubes for long drinks and stirred cocktails; cracked ice for shaken cocktails.

NEVER-FAIL BLENDER TECHNIQUES:

● Use crushed ice. Buy it already crushed if available. Or, to make at home, put a few cubes at a time into your blender with a little water. This can be done ahead of time and stored in plastic bags in the freezer.

● For blender drinks with a sherbet-like consistency, figure about 1 cup crushed ice per drink. Pour all drink ingredients into blender, then add the crushed ice and blend. If drink gets too watery, switch off blender and add more ice. If a solid mass forms, switch off blender and break it up with a spatula.

HOW TO FLAME A DRINK

Flambéing is an easy way to make a big impression.

1. Fill a heavy glass or a mug three-fourths full with hot coffee, mulled cider or mulled wine. Remember that any drink or food to be flambéed must be warm.

2. Warm 2 T. cognac, brandy or other liqueur in a small saucepan or in a soup ladle over a flame. Heat just below simmering. If liqueur begins to boil, the alcohol will burn off and won't ignite.

3. With a match or a taper, ignite liqueur and pour it flaming into the drink. The flame will burn itself out.

Two ounces of warmed liqueur can be poured over desserts or entrées made in a chafing dish or skillet, then ignited by touching the edge of pan with a match or taper. Try this with crepes, omelets, sautéed meat, and poultry or fruit dishes.

BAR BASICS

What do you need on hand so you can feel reasonably sure of satisfying most requests?

● 1 bottle vodka
● 1 bottle rum
● 1 bottle whiskey
   (Canadian, Scotch or bourbon)
● 1 bottle dry vermouth
● club soda, tonic and cola
● beef broth
● 1 lemon
● 1 lime
● ice

Now you can serve the usual Vodka and Tonic, Rum and Coke, or get more specialized with a Vodka Martini, Bull Shot, Daiquiri, Bloody Mary, or Vermouth Spritzer.

BUYING FOR A CROWD

LIQUOR	10-20 PEOPLE	20-30 PEOPLE	30-40 PEOPLE	40-50 PEOPLE
Vodka	2 liters	2 liters	3 liters	4 liters
Gin	1 liter	1 liter	2 liters	2 liters
Scotch	1 liter	1 liter	2 liters	3 liters
Dry Vermouth	½ liter	½ liter	1 liter	1 liter
Tequila	1 liter	1 liter	1 liter	1 liter
Bourbon	1 liter	1 liter	1 liter	1 liter
Whiskey	1 liter	1 liter	1 liter	1 liter
Wine	½ case	1 case	1½ cases	2 cases
Beer	½ case	1 case	2 cases	3 cases
Brandy	1 liter	1 liter	1 liter	1 liter
Rum	1 liter	1 liter	2 liters	2 liters

When you're in the mood for...
sinfully rich desserts

When you are in the mood to splurge, try these recipes. They are perfect for entertaining or simply to pamper yourself. The desserts range from the fruity and elegant Strawberry Nut Tart, page 202, to a homey Apple-Raisin Clafouti, page 202. And for all those to whom sinful isn't sinful unless it includes chocolate, there are Chocolate-Dipped Strawberries, right, a Chocolate Soufflé, page 205, Rich-Rich Brownies, page 206 and a Chocolate Cheesecake, page 205. An idea to remember around the holidays: Many of these recipes make great gifts, particularly the Pecan Shortbread, page 207, and the Chocolate Heart Cookies, page 206. Pack into boxes or tins lined with several sheets of colorful tissue paper for pretty and delicious holiday treats.

You won't believe how light this roll is. It is truly an all-star dessert and can be made ahead.

CHOCOLATE RUM ROLL WITH RUM CREAM

6 eggs, separated
1 c. sugar
4 oz. German sweet chocolate, melted
1 pint heavy cream
½ tsp. rum extract
Cocoa
Fudge Sauce (recipe follows)
Strawberries for garnish

Heat oven to 350°F. Grease 15- by 10- by 1-inch jelly-roll pan then line bottom with waxed paper; grease waxed paper. In large bowl beat whites to a soft peak. Gradually add ½ cup sugar, 2 tablespoons at a time until stiff peaks form. Beat yolks to a pale yellow color (about 8 minutes). Add ½ cup sugar, 1 tablespoon at a time, beating until very thick. Blend melted chocolate into yolks. Fold into egg whites; spread in pan. Bake 15 to 20 minutes. Cake should spring back when lightly touched. Cool cake in pan on wire rack just until slightly warm (10 to 15 minutes). Meanwhile, whip cream with rum extract until stiff. Sift cocoa over top of cake in pan until evenly covered. Turn cake out onto sheet of waxed paper cocoa-side down. Peel paper from from bottom. Spread cream over cake. Roll up along long side. Don't worry if cake cracks a bit as you roll; it will not affect the look of the finished dessert. Place on platter; refrigerate. Serve with warm Fudge Sauce and strawberries. Makes 8 servings.

FUDGE SAUCE

1 c. sugar
½ c. heavy or whipping cream
4 oz. unsweetened chocolate
½ c. butter or margarine
2 egg yolks, beaten lightly
1 tsp. vanilla

In small saucepan over medium heat, combine sugar and cream. Cook, stirring constantly until sugar dissolves and mixture boils. Add chocolate and butter or margarine, stirring until melted and smooth. Remove from heat. Pour about ¼ cup chocolate into egg yolks, stirring quickly. Pour egg yolks back into chocolate, stirring quickly. Cook over low heat, stirring constantly, about 3 minutes, until sauce is shiny. Remove from heat; add vanilla. To reheat, heat in double boiler top. Makes 2 cups.

Some may consider this gilding the lily; others think it's fabulous. The sweeter the berries and the stronger the chocolate, the better they are.

CHOCOLATE-DIPPED STRAWBERRIES

2 pints strawberries, preferably with long stems
2 T. solid vegetable shortening
1 6-oz. pkg. semisweet chocolate pieces

Wash and dry strawberries, leaving stems intact. In double boiler top over hot, not boiling, water, melt shortening with chocolate. Dip in berries to cover about one-half of the fruit. Place on cookie sheet and refrigerate until set. Makes 2 pints.

Chocolate Rum Roll—decadent and rich yet lighter than air

Clafouti (rhymes with tofu-tea) is kind of a pancake and kind of a pie. Whichever it reminds you of—it is supereasy. To save time, prepare the batter and the apples and refrigerate them separately. When you're ready to enjoy the clafouti, assemble and bake.

APPLE-RAISIN CLAFOUTI

**4 apples, peeled, cored and sliced
   (about 4 c.)
3 T. butter or margarine
½ c. raisins
¼ tsp. grated nutmeg
½ c. granulated sugar
½ c. milk
3 eggs
1 T. vanilla
⅔ c. all-purpose flour
Confectioners' sugar**

Heat oven to 350°F. Grease an 8-cup shallow baking dish or 12-inch pie plate; set aside. Sauté apples in large skillet over medium heat in hot butter until lightly browned. Add raisins, nutmeg and ¼ cup granulated sugar; set aside. To make batter, place milk, eggs, vanilla, flour and remaining ¼ cup granulated sugar in blender. Blend on high 1 minute. Spread apples and raisins in prepared baking dish. Pour batter over apples. Bake 1 hour. Remove from oven and sprinkle with confectioners' sugar. Serve warm. Makes 8 servings.

This is a kind of upside-down apple tart. It's cooked in a skillet then turned out onto a plate. Use any apple that will hold its shape after cooking such as Golden Delicious, Rome Beauty, Cortland or Granny Smith.

TARTE TATIN

**6 large cooking apples
5 T. unsalted butter
6 T. sugar
1 sheet frozen puff pastry, thawed
   as label directs**

Heat oven to 400°F. Peel and core the apples. Cut each in half. In a 10-inch ovenproof cast-iron or other heavy skillet, cook 3 tablespoons of butter with 4 tablespoons sugar until the sugar caramelizes. Arrange the apple sections cut side up, in concentric circles in the skillet. Cook over medium heat for 4 to 5 minutes, shaking the pan occasionally to distribute juices. Remove from heat. Sprinkle with remaining 2 tablespoons sugar; dot with remaining butter. On lightly floured surface, with lightly floured rolling pin, roll out the pastry so that it is about 1 inch wider than the pan. Trim to make a circle. With a fork prick the pastry at 1-inch intervals. Fold in the edge of the pastry about ½ inch to make a thicker border. Place pastry over the apples with folded side down. Bake the tart for 30 to 35 minutes, until pastry is puffed and deep golden brown. Tilt the pan to see if there are any accumulated juices. If there are, cook over high heat for a minute or two. Invert tart onto serving dish. Use a metal spatula to transfer any apples that remain in the pan. Serve warm with whipped cream if desired. Makes 8 servings.

This is one of the prettiest tarts you can make. The strawberries are not cooked so you'll taste the "fresh-from-the-patch" flavor.

STRAWBERRY NUT TART

**CRUST:
1 c. ground almonds
½ c. butter or margarine, softened
3 T. sugar
1 ½ c. all-purpose flour
1 egg yolk, beaten
½ tsp. vanilla
FILLING:
1 pint strawberries
1 pkg. unflavored gelatin
1 T. orange liqueur
1 10-oz. jar red currant jelly**

Grease a 9-inch tart pan with removable bottom. In mixer at medium speed, combine all crust ingredients until blended. Press dough firmly into pan. Heat oven to 350°F. Bake crust 15 to 20 minutes, or until golden. Cool. Prepare filling: Wash and hull berries. Arrange whole berries, stem end down, on crust. In small saucepan combine gelatin and liqueur and allow gelatin to soften 1 minute. Add jelly and heat over medium heat until smooth and gelatin is completely dissolved. Cool sightly and spoon over berries. Allow glaze to stiffen 30 minutes before serving. Makes 8 servings.

This is the classic French apple tart. Take time and care slicing the apples and arranging them on the tart. The handsome results will be worth the extra effort.

TARTE AUX POMMES

**3 lbs. crisp apples
(such as Granny Smith)
1 tsp. fresh lemon juice
3 T. brandy
2 T. butter or margarine
½ tsp. ground cinnamon
¾ c. sugar
1 partially baked tart pastry shell
(recipe follows)
½ c. apple jelly
Whipped cream**

Peel apples, then quarter and core. Cut enough apples lengthwise into ⅛-inch even slices to make about 3 cups. Gently toss with lemon juice. Set aside for top of tart. Cut remaining apples into chunks. Place in heavy saucepan and cook over low heat, stirring occasionally, until soft, about 20 minutes. Stir in brandy, butter or margarine, cinnamon and ¾ c. sugar. Heat to boiling and cook, stirring constantly, until sauce is very thick and holds its shape on a spoon. Spread applesauce in partially baked shell. Heat oven to 375°F. Arrange reserved apple slices, overlapping, over applesauce. Bake 30 minutes. Remove from oven to wire rack. In small saucepan, over medium-low heat, heat apple jelly until melted, stirring occasionally. Heat to boiling. Cook 3 mintues; cool slightly. With pastry brush, brush over entire surface of tart to glaze. Serve warm or cold with whipped cream. Makes 8 servings.

TART PASTRY

**1 ½ c. all-purpose flour
2 T. sugar
¼ tsp. salt
6 T. butter or margarine, chilled
2 T. vegetable shortening, chilled
3 T. cold water**

Heat oven to 400°F. In medium bowl combine flour, sugar and salt. With fingertips rub butter or margarine and shortening into flour until it resembles coarse crumbs. Quickly mix in water. Form dough into a ball. Roll dough into 11-inch circle. Place into 9-inch tart pan with removable bottom (see page 22). Press dough lightly into bottom of pan. Then, lift the edges of dough and work it gently around the inside of pan forming a ½-inch border. Trim away excess pastry. Prick bottom and side of pastry with fork at 1-inch intervals. Bake 8 to 10 minutes, or until shell is just beginning to brown.

Four great pies from the same recipe? Sure! The procedure is the same, only the ingredients change. Start with your favorite pie crust or use the tart pastry at left and double the recipe for a two-crust pie. Wrap in waxed paper until ready to use.

PEACH PIE

**6 c. peeled, pitted, sliced peaches
1 c. sugar
2 T. cornstarch
1 T. butter, cut into bits**

PLUM PIE

**6 c. sliced plums
1 ⅓ c. sugar
3 T. cornstarch
1 T. butter, cut into bits**

ANY BERRY PIE

**6 c. berries (blueberries,
strawberries, raspberries
or blackberries)
1 to 1 ¼ c. sugar
3 T. cornstarch
1 T. butter, cut into bits**

APPLE PIE

**6 large, tart apples, peeled,
cored and sliced
¾ c. sugar
½ tsp. ground cinnamon
⅛ tsp. grated nutmeg
1 T. butter, cut into bits**

Make your favorite recipe for a double-crust pie pastry. Heat oven to 425°F. Combine fruit, sugar and cornstarch or spices in a bowl; let stand. Roll out half the pastry to fit a 9-inch pie plate. Ease pastry into plate, trying not to stretch it. Stir the fruit. (Note: for peach, plum and berry pies, if there is more than ¼ cup liquid in the bowl, add another tablespoon of cornstarch.) Scoop the fruit into the pastry; dot with butter. Roll out remaining half of pastry to fit top of pie. Cut several slits in pastry to vent steam. Ease pastry onto top of pie; crimp edges. Bake for 15 minutes; lower heat to 375°F and bake for another 30 to 35 minutes.

June is peak time for fresh fresh rhubarb. It makes a delicious cake, perfect for a weekend breakfast treat or mid-afternoon snack.

RHUBARB STREUSEL CAKE

1 ½ c. all-purpose flour
¼ c. sugar
1 ½ tsp. baking powder
¼ tsp. salt
5 T. butter or margarine,
**   cut in small pieces**
1 egg
½ c. milk
½ tsp. vanilla
3 c. thinly sliced fresh
**   or frozen rhubarb**
3 T. butter or margarine
¾ c. brown sugar, firmly packed
½ tsp. ground cinnamon

Heat oven to 400°F. Grease a 9-inch square baking pan. In a mixing bowl, combine flour, sugar, baking powder and salt. With fingertips, rub butter into dry ingredients until mixture resembles cornmeal. In a small bowl, beat egg with milk and vanilla. Stir into dry ingredients until just blended. Spread batter into pan. Scatter the rhubarb over top; press in gently. In small saucepan, over low heat, melt butter. Stir in brown sugar and cinnamon. Sprinkle over rhubarb. Bake for 25 minutes, or until toothpick inserted in center comes out clean. Cool on wire rack for 10 minutes. Makes 9 servings.

There's nothing like baked apples. These are special, filled with Calvados (the apple brandy from France) and covered in pastry.

BAKED APPLE DUMPLINGS

1 c. all-purpose flour
⅛ tsp. salt
½ c. butter
Water
4 apples
2 T. Calvados
4 T. apricot preserves
Beaten egg to glaze
Heavy cream (optional)

Prepare pastry: Mix flour and salt. Rub in butter with fingertips until mixture resembles cornmeal. Add enough water to form a ball (2 to 4 tablespoons). Roll pastry on lightly floured sur-face with lightly floured rolling pin to ¼-inch thickness. Cut into 4 squares. Heat oven to 375°F. Core the apples and peel halfway down. Fill each with a spoonful of preserves and a little Calvados. Place each in middle of a square. Lift the corners and press the pastry around the apple to cover completely. Seal firmly by moistening edges with a little water. Use scraps to make stems and leaves. Make a hole in top to allow steam to escape. Brush with egg wash. Bake 30 minutes, or until lightly browned. Serve with cream. Makes 4 servings.

Serve this dense, rich cake with Crème Anglaise, or vanilla ice cream.

CHOCOLATE MOUSSE CAKE

½ c. butter or margarine
8 oz. semisweet chocolate
2 tsp. instant coffee
2 T. all-purpose flour
2 T. rum
5 eggs
¾ c. sugar
Crème Anglaise (recipe follows)

Heat oven to 250°F. Butter, then lightly flour an 8- by 3-inch springform pan. In double boiler top over hot, not boiling, water, melt butter or margarine, chocolate and coffee. Stir in flour and rum until smooth. Set aside to cool. In medium bowl with mixer at medium speed, beat eggs. Gradually add sugar, beating until very thick and pale yellow, about 6 minutes. Blend in chocolate mixture. Pour into prepared pan. Bake 1 hour. Remove from oven and cool on wire rack. Refrigerate 6 hours or overnight before serving. Serve with Crème Anglaise. Makes 10 servings.

CRÈME ANGLAISE

4 egg yolks
⅓ c. sugar
1 c. light cream
1 c. milk
1 tsp. vanilla

In double boiler top over hot, not boiling, water, combine egg yolks and sugar. Beat with wire whisk until blended. Gradually add cream and milk and cook, stirring constantly until mixture is slightly thickened and coats a spoon lightly. Stir in vanilla. Remove from heat and cool, then refrigerate until cold. Makes about 2 ¼ cups.

Here's a good and easy dessert to make at the last minute. To save time, use store-bought pound cake.

CASSATA

1 15-oz. container ricotta cheese
½ c. semisweet chocolate pieces, chopped
½ c. sugar
1 tsp. grated orange peel
1 10 ¾ to 12 oz. pound cake
Chocolate Butter Cream Frosting (recipe follows)

In medium bowl combine ricotta cheese, chocolate, sugar and orange peel. With serrated knife, horizontally slice pound cake into 3 layers. Place one layer on serving plate. Spread half of cheese-chocolate filling on it. Top with middle layer and spread with remaining filling. Place top layer on top. Frost with Chocolate Butter Cream Frosting. Makes 8 servings.

CHOCOLATE BUTTER CREAM FROSTING

2 c. confectioners' sugar
4 T. butter or margarine, softened
2 T. milk
1 ½ square (1 ½ oz.) unsweetened chocolate, melted
1 egg yolk
1 tsp. vanilla

In medium bowl with mixer at medium speed, combine all ingredients until smooth and spreadable, adding more milk if necessary.

Don't be put off by the reputation soufflés have as being difficult. This one is a snap, and one of the most decadent desserts around.

CHOCOLATE SOUFFLÉ

TO LINE DISH:
1 T. butter or margarine
1 T. sugar
SOUFFLÉ:
2 T. butter or margarine
2 T. all-purpose flour
¾ c. milk
Dash salt
½ c. unsweetened cocoa
⅓ c. sugar

2 tsp. instant coffee
1 T. coffee-flavored liqueur
½ tsp. vanilla
3 egg yolks, lightly beaten
4 egg whites, at room temperature
Sweetened whipped cream
Strawberries for garnish

Heat oven to 375°F. Tear off a length of aluminum foil long enough to wrap around a 1-quart soufflé dish, overlapping slightly. Fold lengthwise in half. Wrap around dish; secure with tape. Grease dish and foil, using 1 T. butter; then sprinkle dish and foil with 1 T. sugar. In saucepan, melt 2 T. butter. Add flour and blend well. Remove from heat and gradually blend in milk. Add salt. Over medium heat, cook, stirring until thickened and smooth. Stir in cocoa, sugar, coffee, coffee liqueur and vanilla. Remove from heat and cool 5 minutes. Gradually beat in egg yolks. In large bowl with mixer at high speed, beat egg whites until stiff peaks form. Fold into chocolate mixture. Turn into soufflé dish. With back of spoon, make a 1-inch indentation all around soufflé, about 1 inch from edge of dish. Bake 35 minutes or until puffed and browned. Remove foil; serve immediately with whipped cream and strawberries. Makes 4 servings.

Two favorite flavors are combined in a single dessert, garnished with kiwi fruit. You can also try a dusting of cocoa or a sprinkle of cinnamon sugar instead of the kiwis.

CHOCOLATE CHEESECAKE

CRUST:
1 8 ½-oz. pkg. chocolate wafers
6 T. butter or margarine, melted
FILLING:
1 12-oz. pkg. semisweet chocolate pieces
3 8-oz. pkgs. cream cheese, at room temperature
1 c. sugar
1 T. brandy
3 eggs
1 8-oz. container sour cream
1 kiwi fruit, for garnish

In blender or food processor with knife blade in place, blend chocolate wafers to fine crumbs. Pour into 9- by 3-inch springform pan. With fork, blend in melted butter or margarine. Press about ⅔ of crumbs onto side of pan to within 1-inch of top. Press remaining crumbs onto bottom of the pan; set aside. Heat oven to 375°F. In double-boiler top over hot, not boiling, water, melt chocolate; set aside. In large bowl with mixer at medium speed, beat cream cheese, sugar and brandy until smooth. Beat in chocolate. Add eggs one at a time, beating well after each addition. Add sour cream; beat until smooth. Pour into crumb crust. Bake 1 hour. Remove to wire rack to cool completely. Cover with aluminum foil; refrigerate overnight before serving. To serve: Carefully remove side of pan. Peel and slice kiwi fruit; garnish top of cake with overlapping slices. Makes 16 servings.

If you like pumpkin pie, you'll love this light and creamy cheesecake. The crust is nutty and the filling spicy.

PUMPKIN CHEESECAKE

CRUST:
1 c. graham cracker crumbs
 (about 20 2-inch squares)
½ c. finely chopped pecans
 or walnuts
⅓ c. unsalted butter, melted
¼ c. sugar
FILLING:
4 8-oz pkgs. cream cheese,
 at room temperature
6 eggs, at room temperature
1 15- to 16-oz. can pumpkin purée
1 ¾ c. sugar
½ tsp. ground cinnamon
½ tsp. ground ginger
½ tsp. grated nutmeg
¼ tsp. ground cloves
⅛ tsp. salt

Heat oven to 325°F. In a bowl, mix crumbs and remaining crust ingredients with a fork until well blended. Pour into an 8- by 3-inch or a 9- by 2-inch springform pan. Using the back of a spoon, press crumbs onto bottom and up side of pan to within 1 inch of top of pan. Set aside. In a large mixing bowl, with mixer at medium speed, beat cream cheese until smooth. Add remaining ingredients and beat just until blended. Pour into crumb-lined pan. Bake 1 hour and 30 minutes (1 hour and 15 minutes for a 9-inch pan) or until lightly golden on top. Turn off oven and let cake stand in oven for 1 hour. Remove cake from oven; cool completely on wire rack. Cover with aluminum foil and chill overnight before serving. Makes 16 servings.

This recipe doesn't take much more work than a mix and you'll find the effort is worth it.

RICH-RICH BROWNIES

3 squares (3 oz.) unsweetened
 baking chocolate
½ c. butter or margarine
2 eggs
1 c. sugar
½ tsp. vanilla
½ c. all-purpose flour

Heat oven to 400°F. Grease an 8-inch square baking pan. In double boiler top over hot, not boiling, water, melt chocolate and butter or margarine. Cool. In bowl with mixer at medium speed, beat eggs. Gradually add sugar, beating until very thick and pale yellow, about 6 minutes. Add vanilla and chocolate. Fold in flour, blending gently but thoroughly. Spread in pan. Bake 15 to 20 minutes, or until toothpick inserted in center has moist crumbs clinging to it. Don't overbake. Brownies should be very moist. Cool on rack before cutting. Makes 9 2½-inch brownies.

These are the thinnest, most chocolatey cookies ever. Make extra and store in the freezer.

CHOCOLATE HEART COOKIES

2 c. all-purpose flour
2 tsp. baking powder
½ tsp. salt
½ c. butter or margarine, softened
1 c. sugar
2 eggs
1 tsp. vanilla
½ c. unsweetened cocoa
Granulated sugar

In large bowl, combine flour, baking powder, salt; set aside. In another bowl, with mixer at medium speed, beat butter or margarine and sugar until fluffy. Add eggs and vanilla, then cocoa. Add dry ingredients; blend well. Heat oven to 375°F. For the thinnest possible cookies, roll about ¼ of dough directly on a chilled cookie sheet, to about 1/16-inch thickness. Cut into hearts with 3-inch cutter. Remove dough around and between cookies. Sprinkle with sugar. Bake 8 to 10 minutes. Remove to wire rack to cool. Makes 4½ dozen.

These are delicate almost lighter-than-air cookies. Shape them over a rolling pin to form them into a gentle curve or cool flat.

ALMOND LACE COOKIES

1 c. butter or margarine
2 c. raw quick-cooking oats
1 c. sugar
⅔ c. all-purpose flour
¼ c. milk
½ c. blanched sliced almonds

Heat oven to 325°F. Grease a large cookie sheet. In medium saucepan, melt butter or margarine. Remove from heat. Stir in remaining ingredients except almonds. Drop batter by level teaspoonfuls 3 inches apart onto cookie sheet. With fingers, gently flatten; sprinkle each with almonds. Bake 10 to 15 minutes, or until golden. With spatula, quickly remove cookies and lay over rolling pin to curve. Cool completely. (If cookies get too hard to shape, return to oven for a few minutes to soften.) Repeat with remaining batter, greasing cookie sheet each time. Store in airtight container. Makes about 72 cookies.

Make these cookies when you're feeling like a kid. Same great flavor you remember, but they're made with whole-wheat flour.

WHOLE-WHEAT PEANUT BUTTER COOKIES

1 c. crunchy peanut butter
½ c. butter or margarine, softened
1 c. light brown sugar,
firmly packed
½ tsp. vanilla
1 egg
1 c. all-purpose flour
½ c. whole-wheat flour
1 tsp. baking powder
¼ tsp. salt

With mixer at medium speed, cream together peanut butter, butter or margarine and sugar until light and fluffy. Beat in vanilla and egg. In another bowl, combine flours, baking powder and salt. Gradually add to creamed mixture. Heat oven to 375°F. Form dough into 1-inch balls. Place on ungreased cookie sheets 2 inches apart. Flatten with tines of a fork in a criss-cross pattern. Bake 10 to 12 minutes. Allow to cool 1 minute before removing from sheet to wire rack. Makes 42 cookies.

A great—and easy do-ahead dessert, cut into squares and wrapped well, these cookies freeze beautifully. They also travel well.

PECAN SHORTBREAD

1 c. butter, softened
½ c. light brown sugar,
firmly packed
½ c. granulated sugar
1 egg, separated
2 c. all-purpose flour
1 T. ground cinnamon
1 tsp. grated orange peel
⅛ tsp. ground cloves
⅛ tsp. salt
1 ½ c. chopped pecans

Heat oven to 300°F. In medium bowl, with mixer at medium speed, cream butter, sugars and egg yolk until light and fluffy. In another bowl, combine flour, cinnamon, orange peel, clove and salt; mix well. Gradually add to creamed ingredients. Continue beating until well blended. (Dough will be stiff.) Spread into an ungreased 15- by 10- by 1-inch jelly-roll pan. Beat egg white until foamy. Spread over batter. Sprinkle with pecans. Press lightly into batter. Bake 35 to 40 minutes. Cut into 1½- by 2½-inch bars while still hot. Cool in pan on rack. Makes 36 bars.

Rumor has it that this fudge is the invention of Mamie Eisenhower. She may not have created it, but it truly never fails to come out perfectly.

NEVER-FAIL FUDGE

5 c. sugar
½ c. butter or margarine
1 ½ c. evaporated milk
1 16-oz. jar marshmallow creme
1 tsp. salt
1 ½ tsp. vanilla
2 12-oz pkgs. semisweet chocolate
pieces
1 c. chopped walnuts

Grease a 13- by 9-inch baking pan. In large saucepan, combine first five ingredients. Stir over low heat until blended. Increase heat to medium and heat to a full rolling boil, being careful not to mistake escaping air bubbles for boiling. Boil, stirring constantly, 5 minutes. Remove from heat. Stir in vanilla, then chocolate until melted. Blend in walnuts. Pour into pan and cool. Cut into 1-inch squares. Makes 5 pounds.

Index

If you are not already a subscriber to *Glamour* magazine and would be interested in subscribing, please call *Glamour's* toll-free number, 800-247-2160.